Instructing and Mentoring the African American College Student

Strategies for Success in Higher Education

Louis B. Gallien, Jr.
Regent University

Marshalita Sims Peterson
Spelman College

PEARSON

Boston   New York   San Francisco
Mexico City   Montreal   Toronto   London   Madrid   Munich   Paris
Hong Kong   Singapore   Tokyo   Cape Town   Sydney

Executive Editor: *Stephen D. Dragin*
Senior Editorial Assistant: *Barbara Strickland*
Senior Editorial-Production Administrator: *Beth Houston*
Editorial-Production Service: *Walsh & Associates, Inc.*
Marketing Manager: *Tara Whorf*
Composition and Prepress Buyer: *Linda Cox*
Manufacturing Buyer: *Andrew Turso*
Cover Administrator: *Joel Gendron*
Electronic Composition: *Cabot Computer Services*

Between the time Website information is gathered and then published, it is not unusual for some sites to have closed. Also, the transcription of URLs can result in typographical errors. The pubisher would appreciate notification where these errors occur so that they may be corrected in subsequent editions.

Library of Congress Cataloging-in-Publication Data

Gallien, Louis B.
    Instructing and mentoring the African American college student : strategies for success in higher education / Louis B. Gallien, Jr., Marshalita Sims Peterson.
      p. cm.
    Includes bibliographical references and index.
    ISBN 0-205-38917-1
    1. African Americans—Education (Higher). 2. Mentoring in education—United States. I. Peterson, Marshalita Sims. II. Title.

    LC2781.G33 2004
    378.1'9829'96073—dc22

                        2003068932

Printed in the United States of America

10 9 8 7 6 5 4 3 2 1   10 09 08 07 06 05 04

CONTENTS

3 Successful Mentoring Strategies within Historically Black Institutions   53

Cynthia Neal Spence

4 Strategies for Effective Oral Communication   69

Marshalita Sims Peterson

FOREWORD

My friend and mentor, Dr. Asa G. Hillard III (Nana Baffour Amankwatia II), says that, while teaching may be an art, "it is not rocket science." He often uses this statement to introduce his audience to the historical reality that from the time of our ancient African ancestors, we have known the way to teach students of African descent. Those students excelled in the civilization of Kemet (now known as Egypt)—the oldest in the world—under brilliant scholar/teachers, learning complex mathematical abstractions as well as astronomy, philosophy, literature, and other epistemologies. Many of their descendants, stolen from cultures that sprang from Kemet, taught themselves to read and write while enslaved, at great risk of physical torture and death. Later, the descendants of these African peoples, forced into segregated schools that were denied adequate resources, still became accomplished doctors, lawyers, teachers, spiritual leaders, and entrepreneurs. Given that rich 5,000-year-old educational legacy, we, obviously, do not need to do more research to learn how to assist those ancestors' children in reaching the academic "stars." And we certainly do not need more research that looks to discover the deficiencies of "those black students" that keep them from achieving at their highest levels.

What we do need, as the editors of this text suggest, is a commitment and a will to create learning environments that acknowledge, respect, and encourage the academic achievement of all our children of African descent from pre-K through Ph.D. The epistemologies and the strategies that produce such achievement are already known and practiced in some K–12 classrooms and most historically black colleges and universities (HBCUs) across the country. We need not wait for the strategies and the contexts to be invented.

While much has been written to document successful pedagogy in K–12 classrooms, little, until now, has been gathered together in one text to document the same for our college students of African descent. The professors from Morehouse and Spelman colleges who speak in this book have provided, by sharing their theoretical and practical experiences, a superior resource for those whose professional integrity leads them to explore more effective ways to teach descendants of the African diasporas, students with rich cultural and intellectual histories.

When living in Atlanta, Georgia, I often heard about the "Spelman and Morehouse Mystique." It was something I could almost feel when I walked onto those college campuses. The writers in this text make that feeling tangible. They ground the "mystique" in cultural and pedagogical insights, wisdom that can inform efforts to eliminate the failures of many institutions to successfully teach students of African descent. The amazing life stories of academic achievement, civic engagement, and world leadership of the graduates of these HBCUs warrant a serious look at just what it is these institutions offer students. What is it that propels their students into stellar accomplishment, while other prestigious institutions with considerably larger fortunes and resources fail miserably?

As Gallien and Peterson suggest, the research for decades has indicated that HBCUs outrank every other university in graduating African American scholars and leaders. I can only wonder, then, why educational foundations and governmental departments of education, knowing the success rates of these HBCUs, do not pour more of their money into programs that work, programs that have a proven track record in producing successful college graduates of African descent. Why does the bulk of the resources available for such efforts go to colleges and universities that have no record of success in producing large numbers of students of color who successfully graduate from their schools? What are the implications of racism, power, and class on such policies and practices that deliberately choose to fund failure over success? Why would corporations with large educational foundations advertise and loudly proclaim their commitment to diversity, yet donate hundreds of millions of dollars and stock to private, predominantly white universities while giving a minute fraction of that financial support to some of the oldest and most successful HBCUs, located where some of those corporate headquarters are based? With so much national rhetoric and research addressing the "academic achievement gap" between the mainstream students and "students of color," why would we not spend our dollars funding and replicating models of education like Morehouse, Spelman, and other great HBCUs that, for well over a hundred years, have proven they know how to teach students of African descent?

The writers of this text, through their stories of successful classroom strategies and their eloquent argument for culturally responsive college climates and classrooms, indicate that we know well how to close the "achievement gap." The challenge to society at large is to develop the will, the commitment, and the resources that put into educational practice the wisdom that unfolds in this book.

Lisa Delpit

Lisa Delpit is Executive Director of the Center for Urban Education and Innovation at Florida International University in Miami. An award-winning scholar, Lisa Delpit has written the following books: *Other People's Children: Cultural Conflict in the Classroom* (1995); *The Real Ebonics Debate* (1998); *The Skin We Speak: Thoughts on Language and Culture in the Classroom* (2002). A graduate of Harvard Graduate School of Education, she previously held the Benjamin Mays Chair of Urban Leadership at Georgia State in Atlanta.

PREFACE

This book focuses on the types of academic environments that are conducive to positive scholastic results for African American college students. Written from the dominant perspectives of professors and administrators who reside in historically black institutions (but who have also thrived in majority graduate institutions), this work assists administrators, professors, and graduate students who daily interact with black students in higher education with successful strategies to further their academic progress. It is, in many ways, also a primer for professors who have had little cultural contact with African American students because it highlights pedagogical, communication, and assessment strategies that have proven to be successful with this cohort. For administrators, the book offers both theoretical and practical applications for mentoring and retaining black college students.

The book is usefully divided into two parts: Part One presents the theoretical frameworks that undergird best practices, provided with relevant historical, cultural, social, and educational contexts for understanding the immediacy of the issue. Part Two, "Voices from the Field," presents practical and relevant strategies to use in effectively challenging and motivating black students in the classroom. The authors maintain that these strategies are also highly applicable to all students, regardless of color or ethnicity.

Finally, the book begins a critical conversation on college pedagogy—the topic of which has been neglected for far too long among researchers, instructors, and administrators. It offers a critical and nuanced understanding of optimal conditions, environments, and strategies for the academic success of African American college students.

Acknowledgments

I would like to thank my colleagues at Spelman College for their support of this project. I am indebted for their goodwill, support, and encouragement of my teaching, research, and service during my tenure there. Also, my research has been informed and inspired by the Warren Bonam, Sr., family members, especially their departed mother and brother, Sammie and Samuel Lorenzo, whose memory inspires me still.

Louis B. Gallien, Jr.

The ideas developed in this book have evolved as a result of working with colleagues and students, for whom I am sincerely grateful. I wish to acknowledge my husband Alan, children Alan and Alana, and parents Henry and Ruth Sims for their continued support and encouragement. Foremost, I acknowledge my Heavenly

Father as it is through Him that all things are possible. I dedicate this research in memory of my grandmother, the late Esther L. Butler, who said, "Say it and say it well."

Marshalita Sims Peterson

The editors would also like to thank the reviewers for their time and input: Daryl G. Smith, Claremont Graduate University; and Caroline S. Turner, Arizona State University.

PART ONE

Programmatic/Institutional Strategies

1

The Historical and Cultural Context of Educating African American College Students

Louis B. Gallien, Jr.
Regent University

The history of higher education for African Americans in the United States has been one of legal denial, uneven access, separate institutions, and recent quarrels over affirmative action. The first collegiate institutions to open their doors to African Americans were the midwestern radical reformatory colleges of the nineteenth century and a few liberal arts colleges in New England such as Middlebury, Bates, and Amherst College. The founders of these institutions were evangelical ministers and activists in the abolitionist movement: Charles Grandison Finney, Oberlin College (the college where the wealthy abolitionist's brothers, Arthur and Lewis Tappan, poured much of their fortune into its genesis), 1833; George Washington Gale, Knox College, 1845; Josiah Grinnell, Grinnell College, 1846; John Fee, Berea College, 1855; Jonathan Blanchard, Wheaton College, 1860 (Dayton, 1976). These institutions accepted both women and blacks in open defiance to societal norms and as an apocalyptic message to the plantation owners and religious leaders of the Deep South that their hegemonic stranglehold over the inalienable rights of blacks and women were at an end. However, these colleges educated only a fraction of the free African American population in the North (only 28 freed blacks received baccalaureate degrees before the Civil War). And enslaved blacks in the South (estimates range up to 5 percent of the slaves who were self-taught) were legally denied access to any formal education. Consequently, few blacks obtained college degrees of any kind in the early and middle nineteenth century. Those who did faced a questionable

Louis B. Gallien, Jr., is Professor of Urban Education at Regent University, VA.

vocational future in a country that doubted and debated their intellectual skills (Drewry & Doermann, 2001; Genovese, 1976).

Institutions of higher education for African Americans arose mostly in the South where their numbers exceeded some white populations. The assistance of northern missionary groups such as the American Baptist Home Missionary Society, the Congregational Church, the African Methodist Episcopal Church, the Methodist Episcopal Church, and scores of other religious and denominational groups helped to establish historically black institutions such as Howard University, 1866; Fisk University, 1866; Morehouse College, 1867; Hampton Institute, 1868; Clark College, 1869; Spelman College, 1881; and Morris Brown College, 1885; as well as earlier notable midwestern pioneer schools such as Cheney State (teacher's college), 1837; Lincoln University, 1854; and Wilberforce, 1855. Either philanthropic individuals like John D. Rockefeller, a generous benefactor to Spelman College, evangelical denominations from the North, or indigenous Black church denominations like the African Methodist Episcopal Church funded these institutions. Many of the black colleges and universities were founded in the basement of churches and none had the advantage of their majority counterparts of inhabiting new campuses with money from the Dukes, Vanderbilts, Reynolds, or Flaglers. These notable institutions were distinctly separate and unequal to their wealthier and more established white counterparts. And yet, they produced some of the more influential thinkers of the nineteenth and twentieth centuries. A notable example is Fisk University graduate W. E. B. Dubois (Drewry & Doermann, 2001).

It was well into the twentieth century before white collegiate institutions began considering the admission of blacks, and each admission was fraught with violence, political maneuvering, or outright denial. In the South, where Jim Crow laws and segregation were culturally and politically sacrosanct, state institutions like the Universities of Georgia, Alabama, and Mississippi actually made payments to send black scholars to attend northern institutions such as Columbia University in New York. Indeed, Spelman College has several distinguished faculty members—for example, Christine King Farris (the sister of Martin Luther King, Jr.)—who were paid to attend Ivy League institutions. Visual images remain of black pioneers such as James Meredith and Charlene Hunter Gault, who insisted upon attending their state institutions and dared cross the higher education color line in the South.

During the 1960s, most noticeably during the Kennedy and Johnson administrations, majority institutions all over the country began to admit students regardless of gender or race. The hard-fought battle over equal access was slowly won in the twentieth century; however, the issue of "chilly" campuses and segregated classroom environments for women and blacks is debated to this day. Numerous studies have shown that majority professors still favor white male students and are not as comfortable addressing questions or issues to students of color, especially when they are a distinct minority on campus. Thus, you have one of the more cogent rationales for the importance (and continued survival) of historically black colleges and women's colleges (Sandler, 1982).

Added to these debates over equity are the following discouraging statistics regarding the academic achievement "gap" between majority students and students of African descent. In his recent book entitled *Black American Students in an Affluent Suburb,* John Ogbu recounts some of these pathological figures:

1. Significant over- and underrepresentation of black students in special education and gifted programs.
2. A higher percentage of black students who withdraw from completion of their high school diploma.
3. A consistent gap between majority students and black students on standardized tests—the gatekeeper in admissions standards to many colleges, universities, and professional schools.
4. By twelfth grade, black students are about two or more years behind majority students in reading and mathematics.
5. Proficiency test scores are consistently lower than those of their white counterparts.
6. Grade point averages, graduation rates, and college attendance rates for blacks are much lower than their white peers.

And, if we disaggregate the data by race and gender (black men), these statistics become even more discouraging. Perhaps the most telling statistic is the fact that nearly 800,000 black men reside in prisons across the United States—this equates to the population of San Francisco. Clearly, black students who are both admitted to a higher educational institution and happen to graduate from one in four years climb over a statistical hurdle, and their degree completion is a significant achievement within the current social, political, racial, and economic conditions in the United States (Ogbu, 2003).

Currently, one of the most pressing contemporary issues for college administrators is the successful retention and graduation rate of African American students. As scholarships and affirmative action programs became nearly universal (although affirmative action is being challenged and curtailed in several states), the environments that black students find at these campuses are not as negotiable or successful as their admission or financial aid packages from these institutions. Many colleges and universities have stepped up their marketing and admissions efforts toward black students, but few have seriously considered how to transform their environments so that black students are equal participants with other students and valued as intellectual capital (ACT Corporate Report, 1999).

With regard to affirmative action, one of the most significant studies to be conducted on the subject within the context of elite higher educational institutions across the country found that the "prudent use of racial identity in the admissions process . . . is being achieved at a tolerable cost . . . (whose social benefits), graphic and quantifiable, are impressive" (Bowen & Bok, 1998, p. 1). While the Supreme Court has not ruled in the University of Michigan admissions case at the time of writing in 2003, administrators at top-ranked colleges already know and understand how diversity has benefited their students and academic environments. Despite this fact, persistent racial dilemmas exist on campus.

Campus Cultural Dissonance

Specifically, the problems that black students face at majority institutions can be categorized into several major areas:

1. Campus/cultural environment.
2. Classroom/pedagogical environment.
3. Curricular dissonance.
4. Patterns of miscommunication between black students and majority peers and professors.
5. Cultural differences and others' lack of familiarity with black history, tradition, and culture.
6. A lack of deliberate and systematic mentoring that affects overall retention rates and patterns.
7. The "double-edged" sword of affirmative action.

Campus Climate

Many colleges and universities successfully campaigned for more money and resource allocations for students of color in the last century. The overriding problem was that their campuses were not culturally responsive climates for African American students. African American students encountered people on campus who were ambivalent about their presence, and these students were offered few academic support services. Few campus-sponsored mentoring programs were available that could assist them in successfully negotiating a majority campus. In addition, existing faculty, students, and staff lacked the professional development and training to understand how the presence of African American students could fundamentally change the historical and cultural patterns of these institutions. As a result, few African American students were encouraged to claim their culture and comfortably reside with majority students. Many found themselves plagued by the moniker of "affirmative action babies" (Steele, 1989) and became the butt of hostile displays of some of these institutions' most cherished traditions (i.e., Old South Weekend, Confederate battle flags, all-white cheerleaders and homecoming attendants, and majority-oriented fraternities and sororities). Indeed, many majority students did not mind the presence of African American students as long as it did not change their campus environments and cherished traditions, no matter how racist or offensive these symbols were to black students (Thornton, 1988). Also, black athletes were living in sports ghettoes on campus and stereotyped as (in sociologist Harry Edward's words) "gladiators" for the alumni (Edwards, 1983). To complicate matters further, the lack of a significant cohort of black faculty members who could serve as mentors and visible role models compounded an already pejorative environment for black students who happened to remain for four years of study (Anderson, 1993).

Classroom Environment

As stated previously, many black students were perceived as "affirmative action cases" by majority students and in addition as lacking in rigorous college preparatory training. With the media portraying most black students as contained in persistently deficient and pathological public schools and neighborhoods, it is little wonder that majority students maintain this stereotype. As a result, the level of "stereotype threat" (in the words of Claude Steele) increased as black students came to realize that any classroom comment, in-class writing assignment, or research paper might be construed as a monolithic statement for all black collegians. For many black collegians, the classroom environment became one of increasing silence on their parts (Steele, 1999).

In addition, several in-depth studies on the racial climates experienced by black students on majority campuses has found that there are "hidden" and "passive" discrimination patterns that persist in relationship to black students' presence and behaviors that frustrate their abilities to achieve. There were pernicious forms of "doing business" on these campuses that black students did not culturally or socially understand that, gone un-mediated, left lasting negative impressions and, for some, led to withdrawals and eventually dropping out from higher education altogether. (Jackman & Crane, 1986; McClelland & Auster, 1990).

Added to a pejorative environment for black students is the lack of adequate pedagogical preparation of most college professors. Most professors taught as they had been instructed "back in the day" with lecture orientation or contrived Socratic questioning as dominant teaching strategies. Very few professors possess the cultural, historical, or pedagogical backgrounds that are congruent with the dominant learning styles and backgrounds of many African Americans, especially those black students who come from majority black schools and urban areas whose community has minimal culture contact with majority communities and educational environments. As a result, the classroom climate became as "foreign" to black students as the overall campus environment. This issue remains unaddressed on many college campuses because many professors believe that it is the students' role to accommodate to their teaching methods. While this position was largely unchallenged in an age when students were homogenous, it is an increasingly unacceptable stance in a demographically multicultural campus (Delpit, 1995; Palmer, 1999).

Curricular Dissonance

W. E. B. Dubois was one of the most successful black academicians to cross the color line in the nineteenth and twentieth centuries. The first African American to earn a doctorate in sociology at Harvard, he later noted:

. . . colored men trained in Northern institutions did not hear a word of any information concerning their disciplines, so far as Negroes are concerned, and has never been imparted to them. I speak from experience, because I came to Atlanta University to teach history in 1897, without the slightest idea from my Harvard tuition, that Negroes even had any history! (Sundquist, 1996)

One hundred years later, the college core curriculum has changed ever so slightly and not without a three-decade-old "canon war" on most college campuses. African American students rarely read or hear about their history, culture, or traditions (outside of the few African American studies programs across the United States) notwithstanding a few "progressive" educators who include the popular cinematic "standard" works of Alice Walker, Toni Morrison, Zora Neal Hurston, and Maya Angelou. If black students are very fortunate, they may have some courses that include the poetry of Langston Hughes and other black novelists such as James Baldwin and Ralph Ellison. What many multicultural scholars do not understand about this curious canon conflict is the monocultural approach taken by American cultural "purists," as if North America had solely arisen from Europe and contained no indigenous cultures. For most overseas scholars, the idea that a student has only enough time to master one culture is—on the face of it—incredulous, because most students abroad master several languages and study the history, traditions, and culture of many of their surrounding countries and peoples (Ehrenreich, 1991).

Patterns of Miscommunication

Several stereotypical patterns of miscommunication exist between majority students and professors and African American students. Among the most common are those patterns that mimic what one race believes about another based on popular culture, (or usually sensationalized representations in the media as emblematic of black folks' lives). Accordingly, when majority students encounter African American students in a campus residential setting, they commonly ask questions about topics such as sports, music, dress, and other subjects that are highlighted in the media. The result is that black students become defensive and wary over these anticipated conversations: Rather than confronting the issue "on the spot" (which could cause more discomfort and possible open conflict), they tend to ignore the stereotypical racial questions and avoid the person in the future. Majority students are then frustrated because they believe they reached out in good faith to African American students, unaware that they were replicating stereotypes and making assumptions about black students that were never previously tested. On the other hand, black students will also respond to stereotypes that they believe majority students have about them without testing those assumptions either. For instance, African American students will keep their rooms extremely neat, maintain strict study hours, and dress in a "mainstream" way in order to escape attention that would reinforce racist stereotypes.

In the classroom, majority professors will awkwardly "test the waters" by openly asking black students how they prefer to answer questions that center on their race. Or, implicitly, they will call on the usually few black students in their classes to unwittingly act as representatives of an entire race of people. Rather than developing personal relationships with African American students outside the class-room, many professors will use their students as "case studies" while experimenting with their cross-cultural pedagogical skills. The level of discomfort is very high for black students, and many fall into various patterns of silence or resentment for the rest of the semester (Morin, 2001; Steele, 1989; Tatum, 1997).

African American Culture

In a recent book entitled *We Can't Teach What We Don't Know,* Gary Howard echoes what black educators have stated for decades: It is nearly impossible for ma-jority teachers to be effective in educating black students if they do not have some background knowledge or significant experiences in the history, culture, and tradi-tions of African American students. The usual defensive retort to this thesis is "It is not my job to understand students' cultures; it is their responsibility to understand what I teach in my classroom." The problem with this posture is what it reveals about the teacher's ethnocentrism (Howard, 1999; King, 1991).

While many professors pride themselves on understanding a variety of Euro-pean cultures and languages, their knowledge rarely extends to African American culture. Because many believe that the onus is on another culture to master (or assimilate into) the majority culture, many instructors feel that they have no respon-sibility to contextualize their lessons or patterns of communication in a culturally responsive manner. Also, many do not want to take the time to examine or study the many strategies for transforming their classroom pedagogy to effectively educate a wider cultural audience (Gay, 2000).

Mentoring

Research suggests that the more successful African American college students had a mentor (or group of mentors) who encouraged and critiqued their work and fol-lowed them through their graduate school experience and beyond, to their profes-sional careers. The overwhelming majority of professors in this country are white, middle-aged men, who do not feel culturally adequate to take up the challenge of effective mentoring relationships with students of color. This dilemma, however, does not have to be insurmountable. In her recent book entitled *Lanterns,* Marian Wright Edelman fondly writes of two white male collegiate mentors (Spelman Col-lege board member and stock magnate Charles Merrill and Professor Howard Zinn of the Political Science Department) who left a lifetime impact upon her career as an international leader in the rights and protection of children. What made her story even more extraordinary was the fact that Ms. Edelman attended a historically black college that had scores of black professors on their academic rosters! This suggests that majority professors can successfully reach beyond the color line to effectively mentor students of color. African American students continuously maintain that they respond best to professors who care about them. This feeling of care and concern is a serious issue in the retention and eventual graduation rate of African American students across the country and has no distinct color advantage for professors (Edelman, 2001; Gallien, 1990).

Affirmative Action

For many black students, affirmative action has been a double-edged sword. In its infantile stages (1970s) affirmative action was viewed by many scholars as an historical corrective to the gross inequalities of the past and a leveling measure focused upon groups, especially African Americans, who were legally denied equal educational opportunities. Many students of color were encouraged to apply and gain admissions to universities and colleges across the country. This did not, however, guarantee scholarships, grants, or jobs to support four years of a higher education. As a result, affirmative actions programs merely "opened the gates" to African American students that had been closed to them for centuries. (Lack of finances coupled with isolation remains at the top of the list of reasons why black students drop out of college.)

With the Reagan administration and a more conservative Supreme Court (1980s), affirmative action policies began to be questioned and eventually rolled back in several states. The most famous "rollback" cases were in California and Texas (ironically, two of the country's most multicultural states). Also, the rise in popularity of black intellectual conservatives such as Thomas Sowell, Clarence Thomas, Alan Keyes, Glenn Loury, and John McWhorter (all of whom raised their voices against affirmative action) caused a reactionary pattern against this once "leveling" force in higher education (Garcia, 2002).

Some black students sided with this conservative tide, because they were tired of the racist assumptions that accompanied the term "affirmative action babies." However, when large numbers of black students are being turned down for admissions to institutions like UCLA, Michigan, and Texas (three of the most prestigious public universities in the nation), the issue of equitable admissions standards must be examined, especially in the context of a rising national racial and ethnic population base (Jones, 2002).

The Importance of This Book

There are, at least, three main reasons this book is important for higher education: (1) the paucity of research on the subject of pedagogy, mentoring, and retention of African American college students; (2) the need for a distinct perspective from historically black institutional experiences and/or viewpoints; and (3) the difference that enduring institutional cultures have on the advancement of African American students.

Years ago literary scholar Jane Tompkins (then at Duke University) wrote an essay entitled "The Pedagogy of the Distressed," where she cogently and persuasively outlined the reasons behind many professors' fear and ignorance of reflective pedagogical skills and methods of teaching: (a) pride, (b) insecurity, and (c) fear. She began her thesis with professors' typical journeys through their doctoral experiences, which inscribed in their hearts and heads—as it were—those attributes previously mentioned. When they land a tenure track position, those fears and insecurities only increase as a result of another journey through "measuring up" to more ambiguous and subjective standards for tenure. The problem is that we never do completely measure up, if we have been as traumatized as Tompkins and others such as Parker Palmer suggest. As a result, there is a lot of resistance to the idea that professors have "remedial" pedagogical work to do in the classroom. So, many fumble their way through the process, without mentoring, until they figure out how to receive consistent teaching evaluations (which do not guarantee that one is an outstanding teacher, they just suggest that he or she has found what the students care about: good grades!). Their pride gets in the way of receiving pedagogical knowledge that could jettison their learning curve. And, of course, one of the reasons for their slow progress in innovative college teaching (that Tompkins graciously does not mention) is the near-universal disrespect for existing pedagogical research and its position in the academy among arts and sciences professors (Palmer, 1999; Tompkins, 1990).

If we add to this thesis what we believe is essential—nuanced cross-cultural teaching skills—then African American students are really at a disadvantage at most majority institutions, especially those that are noted for their research production and not for their exemplary teaching. Therefore, it is not difficult to understand why many professors are not interested in research on pedagogical skills from a cross-cultural perspective. If it were not for the overwhelming statistical, demographic research on the future racial and ethnic composition of undergraduate students in this new century, then there would be a very small audience for this research.

Pedagogical research has always been either held in contempt or highly suspect with many professors. Therefore, very educational few scholars have attempted to break these historical barriers and prejudices in higher education. Also, some professors will confuse this work with that of other scholars who advocate a total African-centered approach to college students' curriculum and teaching methods. We do believe that Western culture can be "de-centered" without being diluted or abandoned. Students can begin their studies in Africa and end up in Europe and gain an excellent bicultural education. We also believe that not every African American learns the same way. What we are advocating are culturally sensitive or responsive models that respect, honor, and educate from most African American students' cultural, historical, and spiritual backgrounds (hooks, 1994).

The research is clear that historically black colleges and universities are able to retain, graduate, and mentor African American students in larger percentages than their white counterparts. There are positive affective, cognitive, and spiritual reasons behind this phenomenon. When black students are mentored and taught by people who, in the majority, look like them (or, who teach and interact with them in a culturally responsive pattern), then there is a greater emotional, cognitive, and spiritual commitment on the students' part to achieve. Also, many faculty members who work at historically black colleges and universities (HBCU) have an extraordinary personal and professional commitment to seeing to it that black students are successful in all realms of life. It is this holistic approach—mind, spirit, and emotions—that is missing on most majority campuses (Roebuck & Murty, 1993). Indeed, in her ground-breaking work on black colleges, Fleming found that the combination of a supportive community with high standards produced extraordinary results among HBCU graduates (Fleming, 1984).

We also find that a strong institutional saga and culture affects the learning outcomes of black students. As Burton Clark noted long ago, those sagas have powerful enduring qualities when accompanied by campus rituals such as chapel, homecoming, special event convocations, societies, clubs, and other cultural events that forever endear the institution to its students. Many will aspire to and/or send their children to the same HBCU they attended. We believe that such sturdy cultures have something to say on the subject of responsive pedagogy, retention, and mentoring of black students and, thus, this book is written by professors and administrators who have either graduated from an HBCU or are currently teaching and/or administrating at several of the academically strong HBCU institutions in the United States (Clark, 1999).

In Chapter 2, Zenobia Hikes, Spelman College alumna and Vice President for Student Affairs at Spelman College, draws from her years of research and administrative experiences at both majority and HBCU institutions to advance a coupled approach to student retention. Based on her dissertation at the University of Delaware, Dr. Hikes's work is one of the more comprehensive approaches to the retention of black students on both majority and HBCU campuses.

In Chapter 3, Cynthia Neal Spence, Spelman College alumna and Associate Professor of Sociology and former Academic Dean of Spelman College, presents mentoring strategies and relationships backed by twenty-one years of experience as both a successful administrator and professor of sociology. Spelman College's success with mentoring relationships has been well documented, as evidenced by distinguished alumnae such as Christine King Farris, Etta Falconer, Audrey Forbes Manley, Marian Wright Edelman, Beverly Guy-Sheftall, Gloria Wade-Gayles—all of whom have mentored a host of other prominent African American women in positions of leadership throughout the country. Dr. Spence offers several examples of successful programs and strategies from a distinguished career as an academic dean at one of the premier liberal arts colleges for women in America.

In Chapter 4, Marshalita Sims Peterson, Spelman College alumna and Assistant Professor of Education and Chair of the Department of Education at Spelman College, calls on her background in speech communication, curriculum design/implementation, and college teaching to forward new patterns of successful communication between professors and African American students. Dr. Peterson begins her chapter with a review of the theoretical framework relating to communication and also provides specific strategies/elements associated with effective communication skills including the contextualization approach, the interactive/participatory approach, the communal approach, paraphrasing and repetition, phrasing/pausing, pacing, listening skills, topic discourse variance, and nonverbal communication. Dr. Peterson highlights the impact of presentation and communication of content relating to culturally responsive pedagogy.

In Chapter 5, Louis Castenell, an HBCU alumnus and former administrator and presently Dean of the College of Education at the University of Georgia and President of the American Association of Colleges for Teacher Education, and his colleague Joya Carter, HBCU alumna and Assistant Professor of Education at Georgia State University, highlight assessment strategies used at historically black colleges and universities that examine and analyze personal accounts with faculty, students, and higher education administrators. Certain assessment strategies are found to exist in evaluating student performance at HBCUs that are markedly different than those most often used at majority institutions. Castenell and Carter identify the common themes that emerged from focus group investigations on how to effectively assess the learning performance of African American college students. In addition, these assessment strategies have implications for mentoring African American students for high academic achievement.

In Chapter 6, Joan Wynne, former Professor of English at Morehouse College for fourteen years, chronicles her teaching experiences within the context of her role as a majority female professor at an all-male African American college. Professor Wynne's chapter begins with a cogent and clear argument for culturally responsive teaching methods in the college classroom. Heavily influenced by her collegial relationships with black scholars such as Asa Hilliard and Lisa Delpit at Georgia State University, she suggests several pedagogical strategies that are culturally relevant and have led to academic success with this particular "endangered" cohort. The importance of this chapter lies not only in her suggested pedagogical strategies, but also in its grounding by her professional and personal experiences with one of the more precarious student collegiate populations. Despite a decade of so-called national educational reform, the percentages of black males who are remaining and/or graduating from college are falling each year and remain steadily behind those of their female peers (Associated Press, 2002). As a result, there must be more exacting efforts on the part of all educators to ensure the academic success of black males through to graduation. Undergirding all these strategies is a spiritual connection to learning. Since the last decade, several educational scholars have suggested that one of the missing links to a successful academic experience is the spiritual realm (Coles, 1990; Hilliard, 1997; hooks, 1994; Palmer, 1999). Wynne's chapter follows in a long and illustrative line of scholars who have dared entered spiritual realms and have met with successful academic outcomes.

In Chapter 7, Angela Farris Watkins, Spelman College alumna and Assistant Professor of Psychology at Spelman College, discusses the latest research (coupled with her teaching techniques) on learning styles. The importance of Professor Farris Watkin's chapter is the correlation between differential learning styles and the academic success of African American college students. Few scholars have demonstrated the impact that differential learning styles can have on black students' academic achievement from kindergarten to college. In addition, she echoes Wynne's call for a spiritual approach to the education of African American students by offering direct examples of her teaching strategies in the college classroom that connects with African American spirituality.

In Chapter 8, Duane Jackson, Associate Professor of Psychology at Morehouse College, demonstrates the success of cooperative learning techniques in his career as a successful teacher of African American males. Professor Jackson offers several pedagogical techniques from one of the "most feared" courses at Morehouse: statistics. Jackson explains how instructors can "demystify" this course for African American college students in any collegiate environment.

In Chapter 9, Fleda Mask Jackson, Spelman College alumna and visiting professor in the Rollins School of Health at Emory University, chronicles her years of directing the highly successful and ongoing Living-Learning Residential Program at Spelman College under the leadership of Dr. Johnetta Cole. Professor Jackson offers numerous examples of student academic and social programs that can be replicated in residential settings at other higher educational institutions.

Finally, in Chapter 10, the editors outline and highlight several strategies and implications for further investigation found in these collective studies.

REFERENCES

ACT Corporate Report, 1998–1999.

Anderson, J. (1993, Summer). Race, meritocracy, and the American Academy during the immediate post-war II era. *History of Education Quarterly, 33*(2), 151–175.

Associated Press. (2002, September 24). *Gap remains for college minorities.* CNN.com. Reprinted from the American Council on Education.

Bowen, W., & Bok, D. (1998). *The shape of the river: Long-term consequences of considering race in college and university admissions.* Princeton, NJ: Princeton University Press.

Clark, B. (1999). *The distinctive college.* New York: Transaction Publishers.

Coles, R. (1990). *The spiritual life of children.* Boston: Houghton-Mifflin.

Dayton, D. (1976). *Discovering an evangelical heritage.* New York: Harper and Row.

Delpit, L. (1995). *Other people's children: Cultural conflict in the classroom.* New York: The New Press.

Drewry, H., & Doermann, H. (2001). *Stand and prosper: Private black colleges and their students.* Princeton, NJ: Princeton University Press.

Edelman, M. W. (1999). *Lanterns: A memoir of mentors.* Boston: Beacon Press.

Edwards, H. (1983, August). Educating black athletes. *The Atlantic Monthly, 253*(2).

Ehrenreich, R. (1991, December). What campus radicals? The P.C. undergrad is a useful specter. *Cambridge Letter. Harper's Magazine,* 57–61.

Fleming, J. (1984). *Blacks in college: A comparative study of students' success in black and in white institutions.* San Francisco: Jossey-Bass Publishers.

Gallien, L. B. (1990, Fall). Lost voices: Reflections on education from an imperiled generation. *Eric Digest,* 1–64.

Garcia, J. L. (2002, May). Race and inequality: An exchange. *First Things, 123,* 22–40.

Gay, G. (2000). *Culturally responsive teaching: Theory, research, and practice.* New York: Teachers College Press.

Genovese, E. (1976). *Roll, Jordan, roll: The world the slaves made.* New York: Vintage House.

Hilliard, A. (1997). *The reawakening of the African mind.* Miami: Makare Publishing.

hooks, b. (1994). *Teaching to transgress: Education as the practice of freedom.* New York: Routledge Press.

Howard, G. (1999). *We can't teach what we don't know: White teachers, multicultural schools.* New York: Teachers College Press.

Jackman, M. R., & Crane, M. (1986). Some of my friends are black. . . : Interracial friendship and whites' racial attitudes. *Public Opinion Quarterly, 50,* 459–486.

Jones, R. (2002, October). Defining diversity in a post-affirmative action age: Forget about race. *American School Board Journal,* 18–23.

King, J. (1991). Dysconscious racism: Ideology, identity and mis-education of teachers. *Journal of Negro Education, 60*(2), 133–145.

McClelland, K., & Auster, C. (1990, November/December). Public platitudes and hidden tensions: Racial climates at predominately white liberal arts colleges. *Journal of Higher Education, 61*(6), 607–642.

Morin, R. (2001, July 11). Misperceptions cloud whites' view of blacks. *Washington Post,* A1–A4.

Ogbu, J. (2003). *Black American students in an affluent suburb.* Mahwah, NJ: Erlbaum Publishers.

Palmer, P. (1999). *To know as we are known: A spirituality of education.* San Francisco: Harper Press.

Roebuck, J. B., & Murty, E. (1993). *U.S. historically black colleges and universities: Their place in America's higher education.* Westport, CT: Praeger Press.

Sandler, B. (1982, February). The classroom climate: A chilly one for women? *Project on the Status and Education of Women.* Washington, DC: Association of American Colleges.

Steele, C. (1999, May/June). Stereotype threat and black college students. *About Campus,* 2–4.

Steele, S. (1989, February). The recoloring of campus life. *Harpers Magazine,* 47–55.

Sundquist, E. (1996). *The Oxford W.E.B. DuBois reader* (p. 430). New York: Oxford University Press.

Tatum, B. D. (1999). *Why are all the black kids sitting together in the cafeteria? And other conversations about race.* New York: Basic Books.

Thornton, K. (1988). Symbolism at Ole Miss and the crisis of Southern identity. *Southern Atlantic Quarterly,* 254–268.

Tompkins, J. (1990). The pedagogy of the distressed. *College English, 52,* 653–660.

2

Maximizing Student Success

A Coupled Approach to Student Retention

Zenobia Hikes
Spelman College

Blacks have attended American colleges since the 1800s. Since reconstruction, higher education has been sought after by African descendants—primarily in all-black colleges and later in predominantly white institutions. Consequently, college enrollment for blacks has seldom been simplistic. Battles over access to higher education have ensued in the streets and the courts. In the courts, the controversy has evolved around such issues as equal access, equal facilities, equal protection, and equal opportunity. Currently, legal and social issues still challenge U.S. universities. Black student achievement, then, has been shaped by America's historic backdrop. The process of recruiting and retaining students cannot be extricated from the historical context. Historically, black institutions have achieved some level of success in black student retention. In the midst of political, legal, and budgetary challenges, traditionally white institutions continue to explore with uncertainty effective measures that maximize student success.

Offices of Admissions are charged with student recruitment as their primary responsibility. Yet, research indicates that successful institutions thrive because of recruitment partnerships throughout the university community. Namely, faculty, student leaders, support services, and senior level administrators contribute to the process through carefully orchestrated initiatives. Their perspectives on majors and academic opportunities, student programs, and the general merit of the institution have benefited prospective families and academe. Equally important, these same institutional partners play an essential role in student retention. Unfortunately, the re-

Zenobia Hikes is Vice President for Student Affairs and Dean of Students at Spelman College, Atlanta, GA.

sponsibility of retention is often decentralized and unstructured—with various campus constituencies constructing strategies without communicating or collaborating with their campus colleagues. Disjointed university initiatives, then, complicate and challenge the effectiveness of African American student retention.

The problem of lack of or low black student enrollment has been widely recognized for years. According to Daryl Smith (1997), diversity issues have been addressed by higher education since the 1960s. Yet, "three decades later, the issue of access is still with us. In addition to concern about the equitable access, however, there is also concern about the educational persistence and success of underrepresented populations" (p. 1). Also, the lack of full participation of minority students at majority institutions remains an unrealized goal. Without a persistent and aggressive commitment to student success, the United States runs the risk of creating a permanent underclass of citizens and social and economic consequences that adversely affect all Americans (Mingle, 1987).

It is clear that access and persistence are positively impacted by financial assistance and scholarships (St. John, 1991). However, designing an appropriate retention strategy for African Americans entails more than financial and academic support. It demands racial, social, and institutional considerations. As financial assistance has been proven to positively impact black student enrollment, its value is understood. Looking more deeply for other success factors, Tinto's (1987) Student Integration Model suggests that students who become integrated academically and socially are more likely to be successful. African American students are less likely to remain at an institution if services and activities for African Americans are not in place. This chapter examines internal and external factors that impact African American student achievement and presents a holistic approach to student retention. First, student retention is framed in the historical context of black access to higher education. Next, the chapter explores current factors, inside and outside academia, that impact retention. Also considered is the importance of the cultural affiliation of black students on white campuses through race-specific organizations and cultural centers. Next, specific successful retention initiatives at a private historically black liberal arts college and a traditionally white public university will be examined. Both these institutions have been ranked number one in African American student retention. Finally, a coupled model that incorporates the admissions process, academic support, the co-curricular experience, and the external community is presented.

The Historical Context

Thomas (1981) explains that the historical context is essential because the current status of blacks in the academy cannot be fully appreciated without an examination of past events that have shaped their present educational experiences." She further notes that when Jim Crow was the overriding norm in America, it was also the mode operating in education. As microcosms, universities mirror larger society. Consequently, both the historical framework and sociopolitical context are relevant in examining a race-specific, coupled approach.

Education before Emancipation

Twenty Africans were brought to North America in 1619 as slaves. By the year 1860, black slaves numbered 4 million (Bennett, 1966). Given the mandates against educating blacks during slavery, the accounts of slave education are limited.

Puritans and Quakers were responsible for the first forays into U.S. education for slaves. With the disintegration of Puritan theology in the early eighteenth century, Quakers became the strongest allies for black slaves. And New England blacks were described as "the best trained and the most articulate of all the Negroes in the New World" (Franklin, 1947).

On the other hand, it is widely known that the South did not share the interest in educating slaves. Though there were a few accounts of schools in the South—such as the Abolition Society School in Wilmington, Delaware, and schools in Richmond, Petersburg, and Norfolk—the slave codes prohibited teaching slaves in the South to read and write. Legislation was passed in slave states perpetuating the oppression of blacks. As examples, Virginia prohibited teaching reading and writing to blacks in 1819; Georgia declared it illegal for any whites to teach blacks to read or write in 1831; and Mississippi declared unlawful any gathering of five or more blacks to thwart attempts at education in 1832 (Gutek, 1986).

Though slaves were forbidden to read, write, or speak articulately, some slave owners and their children did teach slaves privately—Frederick Douglass was one well-known recipient (Franklin, 1947). Despite the abject cruelty and lack of opportunities for education, twenty-nine black Americans managed to earn baccalaureate degrees in the period between 1619 to 1850 (Humphries, 1994/1995). And three historically black frontrunning schools were founded during the early to mid 1800s—Cheyney University (PA), Lincoln University (PA), and Wilberforce University (OH).

Post–Civil War Education

Violent confrontations and legislation have characterized black achievement in U.S. universities. An examination of this historical context provides insight into the discussion on challenges faced by African Americans in U.S. academia today. The first significant efforts in black higher education took place during the post–Civil War era. Following the signing of the Emancipation Proclamation, attempts were made to organize educational facilities for freed slaves (Browning & Williams, 1978). Consequently, once slaves were freed, the Freeman's Bureau was established by Congress to give former slaves full citizenship. The Bureau, with federal assistance, philanthropic donations, and missionary giving, established schools throughout the South for blacks (Bullock, 1967; Gutek, 1986). By 1869, approximately 114,000 blacks attended schools established by the Freeman's Bureau (Bullock, 1967).

Unfortunately, gains achieved between 1877 and 1900 were short-lived, as Jim Crow laws again eviscerated black progress (Redding, 1950). And though northern missionaries accelerated the movement to educate freed slaves with more than 200 institutions, sparse financial backing and hasty development meant the end of many facilities by 1900 (Jencks & Reisman, 1968; Pifer, 1973).

The 1890 Mandate

When federal troops withdrew in 1877, the second wave of repression began (Fleming, 1984), and laws limiting black opportunities and educational growth took effect (Browning & Williams, 1978). In 1890, the Morrill Act, a federal mandate, ruled that states must either provide separate educational facilities or admit blacks to white institutions (Fleming, 1984). Justin Morrill, a member of Congress from Vermont, had been successful in getting legislation to establish white land-grant institutions in 1862. (Alcorn State was the only black institution established under the 1862 Morrill Act.) Given the option to integrate under the second Morrill Act in 1890, adamant Southerners opted to establish separate colleges for blacks. The subsequent Morrill Land Grant Act of 1890, then, created sixteen black colleges to educate blacks in mechanical arts and agricultural sciences. However, with the hasty development and the separatist ideology of the day, the facilities in state-supported institutions were never equal (Fleming, 1984; Schwaneger, 1969; Wilson, 1994).

Missionary societies and churches were also developing private black colleges during the same time (Anderson, 1988). Baptists, Methodists, Presbyterians, and Congregationalists were among the denominations that contributed the largest sums of money to higher education for blacks (Fleming, 1984; Myrdal, 1944). Though missionaries established the first colleges, these facilities, like the state-supported institutions, were incomparable to white institutions.

Though the Supreme Court's ruling of separate but equal in the *Plessy v. Ferguson* (1896) decision applied to public accommodations, it also influenced the climate for educational facilities. Renowned historian John Hope Franklin points out that the "expense of maintaining a double system [one black, one white] of schools and of other public institutions was high, but not too high for advocates of white Supremacy . . ." (Franklin, 1947, p. 338). Fleming (1984) asserts that the doctrine also supported the idea of black intellectual inferiority and subsequently endorsed industrial training for blacks as opposed to liberal arts training. She notes that though the DuBois and Washington schools of thought coexisted, a disproportionate amount of public funding was directed into vocational institutions. Consequently, the role of nonintellectual institutions was buttressed and the view of black intellectual inferiority was reinforced. Yet major surveys conducted during this period determined that the liberal arts programs in privately supported institutions were superior by national standards. As a result, black schools came into the public eye and the "Black Ivy League" composed of schools such as Spelman, Morehouse, and Fisk were highlighted for their academic excellence (Fleming, 1984).

Higher Education Access and the Courts

Less than thirty years ago, the majority of African Americans attended historically black institutions (Wilson, 1994). Five historical milestones have contributed to increased black student enrollment: the GI Bill, the *Brown* decision, the Civil Rights Movement, the 1965 Higher Education Act, and the *Adams* decision (Thomas, 1981).

Blacks who moved to the North during World Wars I and II sent their children to historically black institutions in the South, since they could not attend universities in the North. Consequently, southern historically black colleges and universities became popular for blacks across the country.

Though HBCUs were becoming popular for black students around the country, the push continued in the courts for admissions to predominantly white institutions. Until the 1930s, court cases were settled in accordance with *Plessy*. Many of the landmark cases were organized and supported by the National Association for the Advancement of Colored People (NAACP) and paved the way for black access to the academy (Gamson, 1978). Among the notable early cases on the issue of racial segregation in education were *Murray v. Maryland* (1935), *Missouri ex rel. Gaines v. Canada* (1938), and *Sipuel v. Oklahoma State Regents* (1948), which was filed by Thurgood Marshall. Despite the success of *Murray v. Maryland,* southern states, still relying on the "separate but equal" opinion established under *Plessy v. Ferguson,* were quick to establish poorly funded graduate and professional schools at black institutions as a strategy to avoid integration (Gamson, 1978; Hutchinson, 1992).

With the litigation of the day as a springboard, a turning point occurred during the 1940s. Wilson (1994) refers to the 1940s as revolutionary for black access. In the early 1940s, the University of West Virginia admitted an African American graduate student voluntarily (Gamson, 1978). From the mid 1940s to the end of the decade, the changes were precipitated by the GI Bill and the courts. Wilson (1994) notes that, "The GI Bill was passed to keep millions of veterans from flooding the job market . . . despite its utilitarian intent, that GI bill enabled hundreds of thousands of veterans, including thousands of African Americans and Hispanics . . . to attend college" (p. 195).

Another factor that contributed to the significant increase of blacks in colleges and universities is the Higher Education Act of 1965. Under the act, financial aid such as the College Work Study Program, Educational Opportunity Grants, and the Guaranteed Student Loan Program provided grants for students based on need. Followed by the Basic Educational Opportunity Grant Program in 1972, these programs provided billions of dollars in aid and were supplemented by state aid (Mingle, 1978).

Despite the glacial pace of equity for African Americans, a ten-year span marked the most noteworthy milestones—the decade between *Brown* in 1954 and the 1964 Civil Rights Act. Without question, this is the most significant period in black access to higher education. Though the landmark decision in *Brown v. Board of Education of Topeka* (1954) declared racial segregation in public schools illegal, there were also significant implications for colleges. Black colleges were re-examined for imbalances in federal funding (Jaffe, 1968; LeMelle & LeMelle, 1969; Thompson, 1973), and white institutions opened admissions to black students. Under the spirit of the civil rights movement, the complexion of higher education changed dramatically. Between 1950 and 1960, the enrollment of blacks in college skyrocketed from 50,000 to 200,000. Ninety percent of all blacks in colleges during 1960 were enrolled in black colleges and universities (Humphries, 1994/1995). Sixty-five percent selected historically black institutions. The most dramatic shift, enrollment into majority institutions, became apparent in 1980 (Wilson, 1994).

Though the *Brown* ruling was directed to public elementary and secondary schools, nineteen years later its implications for higher education were articulated in *Adams v. Richardson* (1973). Leonard Haynes describes the *Adams* mandate as "the most important legal action to affect the educational aspirations and achievements of blacks and other minorities since the 1954 *Brown* decision" (Haynes, 1981). In spite of strides made during the 1950s and 1960s, a number of predominantly white colleges and universities remained segregated. This landmark case, the result of a suit filed in 1970 by the NAACP Legal Defense and Education Fund, was a mandate for southern and border states to dismantle their racially segregated systems. Though adjudicating *Adams* revealed that predominantly white higher education institutions had not been responsive to blacks' attempting to enter institutions at all levels, in 1987 the *Adams* case was dismissed on technical grounds by Judge John Pratt. An appeals court remanded the case to Pratt's jurisdiction. Despite the state's failure to meet any of the goals set under the mandate, the Department of Education ruled that the states named in *Adams* had demonstrated "good faith" efforts and were in compliance (Wilson, 1994).

Most notable for black student success, Adams had three weaknesses: (a) The mandate never required states to develop plans to strengthen HBCUs as equal partners in the higher education enterprise; (b) aggressive plans were never established to increase participation from blacks on faculties and boards; and (c) higher education desegregation was not envisioned as part of a state's long-range master plan providing constructive approaches (Haynes, 1981).

During the latter stages of the *Adams* case, presidential politics adversely affected the initiatives proposed under the case. Decisions made during the Reagan administration shaped the institutional climate in academia. Wilson contends that Ronald Reagan's election as a U.S. president marked the descent of civil rights and affirmative action (Wilson, 1994). Further, Orfield notes: "Its approach, as it turned out, was one of neglect and open hostility. . . . Abandonment of that enforcement mission during the 1980s has contributed to the well-recorded decline in minority access and enrollment" (p. 10). As a result of this administration's stance on student aid and equal opportunity, the cost of college became prohibitive for many Americans. This, despite the fact that there is a larger pool of prepared high school graduates for whom college could be a reality (Person, 1994; Simpson & Frost, 1993).

Current Factors That Impact Retention

The investigation of black student access to higher education reveals a number of issues that have not been resolved through legislation or over time. From the student's perspective, certainly the most transparent problems can be lack of preparation and lack of financial support. For traditionally white institutions engaged in increasing their black student enrollment, issues both inside and outside the academic community complicate the process. Based on the historical frame of reference, several authors have attributed the low enrollment among African American students to the lack of adequate financial aid, the absence of faculty of color who serve as mentors, and the increase of racist incidents on campuses (Farrell, 1989; Fleming, 1984; Nettles, 1987; Randolph, 1988; Rosa, 1989; Sedlacek, 1987). In addition to these factors, limited institutional funds, racial climate on campus, and the national climate and the courts warrant further examination.

Limited Institutional Funding

An obvious factor that affects both enrollment and retention is financial resources. The current institutional trend in academe is to downsize budgets and personnel (Hollins, 1992; Phillip, 1995a); and inadequate funding levels can challenge race-specific practices (Henley, Powell, & Poats, 1992).

Today's financial climate in institutions has been dramatically shaped since the 1980s through various complications, including rising cost of tuition in the 1980s and the economic restrictions of the 1990s (Ern, 1993; Keller, 1983; Phillip, 1995a). In this environment, some institutions have been pressured to reevaluate and restructure their operations. Special services and recruitment programs for African American students are easy targets for funding reductions and/or elimination. Even further, in a post–September 11th economy, when university endowments have plummeted, salary increases are minimal, and operating budgets remain stagnant, special programs that support black student achievement are likely to become more scarce. Further, academic support programs and early warning systems, too, face scrutiny. This increasingly strained financial climate taxes initiatives to recruit and retain diverse populations.

Racial Climate on Campuses

Despite the civil rights movement, African American students are still plagued by violence and prejudice on predominantly white campuses. This factor appears to have an adverse effect on black student enrollment at majority institutions.

In 1994, the American Council on Education reported that campus climate was cited as a major obstacle to students of color in attaining degrees. Campus climate was mentioned by 49 percent of the students surveyed, and African American families are concerned about the racial climate on predominantly white campuses (El-Khawas, 1994). In other findings, the National Institute Against Prejudice and

Violence has monitored hateful incidents on campuses since 1985. They report that up to 25 percent of students of color experience harassment, slurs, and other hateful acts including graffiti and cross burnings on white campuses. This figure is disturbing by any standard.

The lack of culturally enriching activities for underrepresented students contributes to a negative campus climate. Taking pride in one's culture is central to achieving cultural diversity. And for majority institutions who expect students to become integrated into mainstream America, the view is diametrically opposed to a diversity perspective and requires a broader understanding (Henley, 1990).

The National Climate and the Courts

In "Achieving Cultural Diversity: Meeting the Challenges," Henley, Powell and Poats (1992) point to the federal climate as a major impediment in obtaining diverse student populations. They contend that the "political tyranny" evident in the policies of both the Reagan and Bush administrations cultivated a climate that opposes diversity.

Building on the foundation constructed by Reagan, Bush opposed the civil rights legislation proposed by Congress for two years, referring to it as a "quota bill." This action was taken despite the fact that the bill contained the same language as the Americans with Disabilities Act signed by Bush in 1990. Bush finally signed the civil rights bill in 1991 once David Duke, an ex-Ku Klux Klansman running for governor of Louisiana, aligned himself with the Republican Party. The Bush administration discontinued its references to race and, instead, adopted a tone of moderation.

Finally, researchers have described the climate of national intolerance that also has implications for higher education. In "Yesterday Once More: African Americans Wonder If New Era Heralds Return of Jim Crow Era," Mary Christine Phillip (1995b) asks the poignant question: "Why is it that African Americans are forced to relive their history over and over again?" (p. 10). After significant civil rights gains in the 1950s, 1960s, and 1970s, a number of U.S. scholars and citizens are outraged by the federal court and legislative actions that resemble those from the Jim Crow era. Among the scholars, Dr. Mary Frances Berry (Phillip, 1995b), the Geraldine Segal Professor of American Thought, History, and Law at the University of Pennsylvania, acknowledges the parallels. She asserts that the 1990s were characterized by attempts to curtail black representation in government, attacks on affirmative action, elimination of education and job-training programs, cuts of funds for summer youth jobs and programs, and welfare reforms.

An examination of earlier civil rights cases reveals parallels with current cases. Reminiscent of *Sipuel, Gaines,* and *Plessy,* the recent affirmative action cases have been criticized by civil rights activists and appear to construct what Phillip (1995b) refers to as the New Jim Crow Era. In particular, three higher education cases, which have gained national attention, are indicative of the political shift. Unlike the civil rights era, the recent cases are not concentrated in the South. The political shift that became popularized during the Reagan and Bush administrations is now evident across the country. Among the most recognized are *Podberesky v. Kirwan* (1995), California Proposition 209, and *Hopwood v. Texas* (1996).

Podberesky, commonly referred to as "Banneker," is a class action suit filed against the University of Maryland at College Park by Podberesky, a former student. Daniel J. Podberesky charged that the University of Maryland's Benjamin Banneker academic merit scholarship for African American students denied him his rights under equal protection of the Constitution and was, therefore, unconstitutional because it was based on race (*Business Officer,* 1994; NACAC, 1995a). After a U.S. appeals court ruled that Banneker scholarships were unconstitutional because they were only offered to blacks, the University of Maryland modified its minority scholarship program. The Banneker scholarship was combined with the Francis Scott Key Scholarship Program, which is open to all students without regard to race (NACAC, 1995b).

On the West Coast, the next landmark event was Proposition 209. In 1996 California residents voted to forbid the use of race as a criterion for admission into the University of California (UC) system (NACAC, 1995a, 1995c). More than forty years after Governors Barnett of Mississippi and Wallace of Alabama upheld segregation in the South, Governor Pete Wilson spearheaded the California Civil Rights Initiative. Wilson, supported by an African American regent, Ward Connerly, directed the campaign to eliminate affirmative action not only in college admission, but also in hiring. Urged by Wilson, the Board of Regents voted to remove affirmative action in its nine institutions in the UC system. Though California's UC system had been among the country's diverse institutions (52 percent white, 23 percent Asian, 12 percent Latino, and 4 percent African American), Locke (1997) reports that following the vote on the proposition, the racial makeup of UC classrooms and administrative has changed.

A landmark affirmative action case originated in the Southwest with *Hopwood v. Texas* (1996). Cheryl Hopwood filed the case, along with four white students who were denied access to the University of Texas law school. The plaintiffs' "Texas index" scores (combined standardized test scores and grade point averages) were a few points higher than those of Mexican American students admitted (Rodriguez, 1996). They argued that their rights under the Fourteenth Amendment had been violated, since the Mexican American students were admitted. In this decision, two members of a three-judge panel of the Fifth Circuit Court of Appeals (which includes Louisiana and Mississippi) ruled that the University of Texas must eliminate any consideration of race in the admissions process. Following the ruling, the outcry came from civil rights groups for the full Fifth Circuit to hear the appeal. Initially, the *Hopwood* decision only applied to institutions in Texas, Louisiana, and Mississippi; however, the decision sparked legislative and legal attempts to end affirmative action in at least a dozen states including Illinois, Florida, Colorado, Oregon, Michigan, and South Carolina ("Affirmative Action," 1996). Further, separate lawsuits were filed in federal courts against the University of Washington School of Law and the University System of Georgia (Lederman, 1997).

Predictably, following the elimination of affirmative action in the California and Texas systems, enrollments dwindled. In fact, only one black law student enrolled in the University of California's Boalt Hall law school and only one also at the University of Texas. In 1997, the single student is reminiscent of *Sweatt* in 1950 and Meredith in 1962. Eva Paterson, a civil rights attorney in Northern California who received the Boalt Hall Distinguished Alumna Award, characterizes the new segregation movement when she comments on the honor, in light of the political shift. She says, "Pretty ironic, isn't it?" It is likely that students selected better offers from private universities because of their concerns that experiences would not be pleasant (Locke, 1997).

In this climate, African American students are experiencing the same kind of alienation as their predecessors. Though two cases against the University of Michigan are at the center of recent affirmative action discussions, there are sure to be more. These new cases, which parallel the historic ones, elicit an unsettled environment.

The Cultural Affiliation of Black Students on White Campuses

African American students and their parents bring to the college search process a particular cultural framework and historical perspective; subsequently, African Americans are more likely to consider institutions where African American issues and culture are raised and addressed. For more than a century, historically black institutions have been able to provide environments where students thrive and special attention is focused on providing cultural programming, student organizations, and race-specific issues. These experiences, which contribute to student success, are lessons worth replicating on white campuses.

Adjustment on White Campuses

Colleges are a reflection of U.S. society (Altbach & Lomotey, 1991; Fleming, 1984; Harper, 1975; Willie & McCord, 1972). Consequently, U.S. colleges, like larger society, suffer the effects of turbulent U.S. history and poor race relations. In light of this historic chasm, several studies have examined black identity in Euro-centered environments. During the civil rights era, Erickson (1967) found that young blacks sought to counter negative circumstances with positive elements of African roots and social activism. Fleming (1984), in her research on blacks in colleges, observed that black students establish their own social and academic environment when they do not feel accepted by the majority culture and attempt to achieve unity with other black students to combat racism.

William Sedlacek (1987, 1989, 1993) addresses the difference in the black student's experience and cultural construct. In "Employing Noncognitive Variables in the Admission and Retention of Nontraditional Students," Sedlacek proposes eight noncognitive variables to address the person from a "nontraditional background." He lists "Understands and Deals with Racism" as one of the variables in adjusting to historically white campuses. He further asserts that the "nontraditional" (underrepresented) student who understands and who is willing to combat the existing system is better equipped to handle racism that still exists in white institutions.

The Importance of Black Student Organizations

Afrocentric programming has played an essential role in the cultural affiliation of black students. Black student organizations were an outgrowth of the civil rights movement following the assassination of Dr. Martin Luther King, Jr.; most were founded in 1968 and 1969. In some of the most salient early research on black student adjustment and cultural affiliation at white colleges, Willie and McCord (1972) found that black students expected less prejudice and more integration. However, their study of 384 black students indicated that these students turned to other black students for social activities and validation out of mistrust and discomfort.

Today black student organizations and special interest groups have become established political organizations on white campuses. Stewart, Haynes, Brown-Wright, and Anderson (1996) confirm the importance of African American student organizations on white campuses today. Their observation is predicated on the research that students of color experience a broad range of social, psychological, and academic problems on majority campuses. Black students use "African American student unions and organizations to satisfy specific cultural and social needs" (p. 4). Organizations related to the academic major are vital as they "fill an academic void in situations where African American students are left out of the informal networks and mentoring relationships that help majority students survive academically and professionally" (p. 4). The involvement in Afrocentered activities is misinterpreted, perceived by some as an attempt to avoid participation in "mainstream" activities. However, these organizations have provided a cultural and social outlet and serve to complement the other activities in which black students participate. Culturally enriched activities can enhance a negative campus climate and subsequently increase retention (Henley, Powell, & Poats, 1992).

Cultural Environments as Comfort Zones

Some U.S. campuses offer cultural and ethnic-specific comfort zones for students. Namely, Hillel provides an opportunity for Jewish students to worship and celebrate their heritage, ethnic-specific cultural and political organizations are available for Latino students, and cultural and special interest events are offered for Asian American and Native American students. Though African Americans seek admission into the larger community of the university, research shows that ethnically centered programs and activities provide a means of affiliating with other African Americans (Person & Christensen, 1996).

Research supports the findings of previous studies on the value of Afro-centered experiences in constructing comfort zones at white colleges and universities. In a 1996 study, Person and Christensen (1996) investigated the impact of black student culture on recruitment and retention. The study revealed that there was a distinct black culture and smaller subcultures on campus. Ninety percent of the participants were strongly in favor of an identifiable black community to support them academically and socially, as well as to contribute to ethnic identity development. Further, the students considered university support services, counseling, summer bridge programs, and black organizations essential in their development.

Students create their own cultural environment, when they do not feel comfortable within the mainstream. And this cultural affiliation with ethnic-specific organizations and programs impacts both recruitment and persistence (Person & Christensen, 1996). Black student's affiliation with race-specific organizations, then, not only benefits the student, but also enriches the institution. Through these organizations black students align themselves with an institution (Fleming, 1984; Monroe, 1973; Ramseur, 1975; Stewart, Haynes, Brown-Wright, and Anderson, 1996).

Retention Initiatives

For more than a century, historically black institutions have successfully recruited, retained, and graduated leading professionals in countless fields. Accounts are plentiful of those with and without means who came to these institutions and were shaped and nurtured by those dedicated to their success. Absent the historical baggage of discrimination and incendiary campus climates, historically black colleges and universities focused on a range of strategies to produce graduates who achieve.

Similarly, a series of techniques that accentuate the African American student's race and heritage have been linked to student success. Traditional white institutions have also utilized race-specific programs and marketing for African Americans. Consequently, some have realized success with an Afrocentric student approach.

Retention Strategies at a Historically Black College: Spelman College

Second only to the black church, HBCUs are one of the most highly respected institutions among African Americans. Wilson (1994) chronicles the adversity black institutions have encountered. He describes more than 130 years of operating despite discriminatory state funding, poor church support, and hostile white power structures. These institutions have educated students on both ends of the academic spectrum. As virtually the only option for African Americans during much of this period, HBCUs disregarded traditional admissions criteria and became known for educating scholars and for recognizing potential.

In *Blacks in College: A Comparative Study of Students' Success in Black and in White Institutions,* Jacqueline Fleming (1984) maintains that the role of black colleges has not been forgotten despite the fact that the majority of black students enrolled in college now attend predominantly white institutions. Gurin and Epps (1975) credit HBCU with creating the black middle class. In 1975, Jordan (1975) credited black institutions with producing 75 percent of all blacks who earned Ph.D. degrees, 75 percent of all black Army officers, 80 percent of black federal judges, and 85 percent of black physicians.

Over the years, the merit of HBCUs has come from a number of sources. Goldman (1963) states that black institutions are more closely connected with the problems of their students and equipped to resolve them. McGrath (1965) found that psychological and social factors encourage students to gravitate to black colleges. Pifer (1973) asserts that some black students simply seem happier at black institutions. Gurin and Epps (1975) draw the same parallel. They maintain that students opt to attend colleges where their personal development is fostered and conflict and isolation, often experienced on white campuses, are minimized. Fleming (1984) acknowledges the role of black colleges in raising black conscientiousness and political activism. Allen (1992), after surveying students at eight HBCUs and six predominantly white institutions (PWIs), report African Americans at HBCUs had higher aspirations, higher grade point averages, and a higher level of involvement in campus social activities than their counterparts at majority institutions. In an examination of students' experiences at predominantly white institutions, Watson and Kuh (1996) determined that African Americans at HBCUs benefited more through campus involvement than their counterparts at PWIs.

Spelman College is a small, single-sex liberal arts college located in Atlanta. The College has a long-standing reputation for graduating successful students. Since it is consistently receives high ratings in retention, its strategies warrant investigation.

History and Campus Climate.   Founded by Sophia B. Packard and Harriet Giles, Spelman College is one of the nation's most highly regarded colleges for women. Packard and Giles were commissioned by the Women's American Baptist Home Mission Society of New England to the study the living conditions "among the freedmen of the South" (Spelman College Bulletin, 2000/2001, p. 5). Appalled by the absence of educational opportunities for black women, the missionaries returned to Boston to seek support. On April 11, 1881, they opened a school in the basement of Atlanta's New England Friendship Baptist Church with $100 provided by the congregation of the First Baptist Church of Medford, Massachusetts. Most of the first eleven students were freed women, determined to learn to read the Bible and write well enough to send letters to their families in the North.

In 1882, Packard and Giles returned to the North for additional support. At a church meeting in Cleveland, Ohio, the missionary educators were introduced to John D. Rockefeller, who emptied his wallet during the collection and questioned the women's intentions and commitment.

When Packard and Giles returned to Atlanta, they took an option on a property site that had been previously used as barracks and drill ground for federal troops after the Civil War. The property was subsequently transferred to the "Atlanta Baptist Female Seminary," and in February 1883, the school relocated to its new nine-acre site. On the third anniversary of the founding of the school, the name of the school was changed to "Spelman Seminary" in honor of Mrs. Rockefeller's mother.

In addition to stabilizing a challenging financial situation, the Rockefeller gift gave Spelman recognition that otherwise might have taken years to garner. Financial support from other sources helped to broaden the school's involvement in community, social, and church work (Spelman College Bulletin, 2001–2002).

Today, Spelman is nationally recognized as a selective admission institution for African American women. The college was ranked in first place by Day Star as the top institution for African Americans in 1998 (LaVeist & Whigham-Desir, 1999), and it has historically had the second largest number of students admitted to medical school in the country. Spelman's retention rate is ranked the highest among HBCUs (Hurd, 2000).

Afrocentric Admissions Strategies.   The nature of the college admissions process at Spelman is Afrocentric. The college uses standard practices to recruit talented students nationally and internationally. Primary markets include the South, the Northeast, and the West Coast. Spelman is also a popular choice for students from Jamaica, Trinidad, and African countries. In 2001, the college graduated its first Japanese students, and students from European countries study at Spelman from year to year. Yet, women of African descent remain the overwhelming majority. Admitted students are well prepared academically with honors and AP courses as part of their high school curricula.

Given Spelman's history and legacy, students seek a unique historically black experience for women. Therefore, the focus in admissions centers on the academic rigor, but also on the traditions and customs of the campus. Graduates from predominantly white and predominantly black high schools enroll at Spelman seeking the experience. Publications and other materials are Afrocentric. Students "see themselves" in publications and on the website.

Outreach.   The college has maintained a long-standing relationship with schools, agencies, and nonprofits in the metropolitan Atlanta area. For example, relationships with INROADS and TRIO programs contribute to the pool of well-prepared prospective students.

Another form of outreach that benefits both recruitment and retention are academic summer programs, hosted each year by Spelman. Namely, programs such as the Atlanta Public Schools Summer Math and Science Enrichment Program, the Howard Hughes Summer Research Fellows, and Bridges (for precollege and college students) are among the feeders. In addition, summer bridge programs are a mainstay for admitted students in health careers. Though preparation for the major course of study is the concentration during the summer, the college's history and its opportunities are a component of precollege bridge programs. Sisterhood is a value that students and other members of the college community reinforce. Students, then, matriculate aware of campus support services and familiar with faculty and staff members.

Student Involvement.   One of Spelman's strongest assets is an active student population that comes to college having been involved in a wide range of co-curricular experiences. There are more than ninety organizations for approximately 2,000 students. Students are typically involved in at least two or three organizations. These students enrich the recruitment and retention process through their investment in other students.

As with other colleges, on-campus preview programs afford a more realistic view than that relayed by printed pieces and virtual tours. Spelman features two such campus programs—*A Day in the Life at Spelman* and *Spel-bound*. A Day in the Life is an overview program for prospective students and their families. Currently enrolled Spelman students participate in student panels, conduct tours, and engage with interested students. At Spel-bound, a yield activity for admitted students, up-per-class students host admitted students in their residence hall rooms. The weekend includes academic and social activities—with sisterhood as the focus. Students, too, are involved as ambassadors conducting admissions tours and interacting with the more than 17,000 annual visitors to the campus.

And as a capstone to the enrollment experience, currently enrolled students serve as Student Orientation Leaders (SOLs). These Student Government Association officers, Program Board members, resident assistants, and international peer leaders remain with an assigned group of first-year students for ten days of orientation. During that time, entering students participate in an African rites of passage parting ceremony whereby first-years leave their parents and join their new family of students and administrators. Students also lead pep rallies teaching cheers, assist in history and tradition sessions, and attend talent shows and a block party. At the end of orientation, SOLs have dinner with their first-years and place personalized handmade gifts for them on tables in the dining hall. These bonding activities connect the entering students to the college community and allow currently enrolled students to take ownership in the enrollment of students.

Other College Support.   In keeping with the coupled, holistic approach to retention and student success, departments work together in the best interest of the student. In the Student Affairs department, Housing and Residence Life, Counseling Services, Health Services, Public Safety, and the Dean of Students Office often collaborate as appropriate. This interdepartmental communication is an effective method in addressing student issues. Further, Student Affairs works closely with the Academic Dean and Financial Aid. Should a student decide to withdraw, she must meet with the Vice President for Student Affairs along with the Academic Dean and a representative from financial aid.

The nature of a small liberal arts campus lends itself to familiar dialogue about students. Students' problems that may lead to withdrawal are brought to the fore both formally and informally.

Academic Support.   Though the college admits well-prepared students, retention strategies at Spelman have been described as intrusive. An Associate Dean works with first-year and sophomore students and the Academic Dean with juniors and seniors.

If students are provisionally admitted, they are monitored by the Learning Resource Center immediately. Each student is required to meet once or twice a week with Learning Resources and attend Academic Success Workshops. Provisionally admitted students are not allowed to take more than three courses. Of the provisional admits, 80 to 85 percent are removed from probation after the first semester. For these students, this gradual introduction to Spelman's academic rigor contributes to their success.

Another method used to strengthen the academic experience is the Early Warning Process. After the fourth week of each semester, the faculty receives a request to submit the names of students whose performance is below "C" work. Deficiency notices are then submitted to the Registrar and the Academic Dean's office. Once a student receives the notice, she is encouraged to meet with her professor and academic advisors, visit the Learning Resource Center, and meet with a tutor. Although the system is a good monitoring system, it is not used uniformly by all professors.

Students whose grade point average falls below 2.0 have their course load reduced to nine hours in addition to being placed on probation. If the student does not make satisfactory progress at the end of the year, she is dismissed by the College.

Another way that the educational experience and exposure is broadened is through First-year Convocation and Sophomore Assembly. First-year students attend convocations regularly and are exposed to local and national speakers. These required programs provide an extension of the learning that takes place in the classroom. Sessions with the academic advisor are held twice a semester. In addition, first-years attend supplemental courses in Academic Integrity and in other areas topics to strengthen their experience. Though Convocation is open to the entire College community, students must attend one Convocation and may pick among three others. The focus of Sophomore Assembly is personal development. Areas include career planning, time management, and public speaking.

Using a model whereby students are clustered in programs according to their major, Spelman has been successful in graduating students who participate in these academic support programs. Namely, the Health Careers Program was initiated in 1971 to advance the professional areas of medicine, such as dentistry, osteopathy, optometry, podiatry, pharmacy, veterinary medicine, and physical therapy; the Model Institutions for Excellence for science, engineering, and mathematics (SEM) education; and the Women in Science and Engineering Scholars Program. Each program provides counseling, academic support, career information, internships, and market trends that support student retention and preparation of solid professionals in various fields.

Symbolism and Cultural Artifacts.   At Spelman, symbols are an inescapable part of the institution's landscape. The campus's history oval is lined with national Historic Register buildings that acknowledge its missionary founders, Packard and Giles, and the Rockefeller philanthropy. The mostly stately is Sisters Chapel. This Greek Revival edifice was dedicated by John D. Rockefeller in 1927. Students learn early in their relationship with Spelman that Sisters Chapel has been the center of many historic and noteworthy public events. (For example, Dr. Martin Luther King's body lay in state in Sisters Chapel and was visited by mourners from around the world.) Behind Sister's Chapel is Bessie Strong Hall, built in 1917. Students recognize this upper-class residence hall from the television series *A Different World,* which was about black college life.

Spelman's recent success has been fortified by one of the largest gifts to any institution. In 1988, Bill and Camille Cosby contributed $20 million to the college. A portion of this generous gift was used to construct a modern academic building named in honor of Dr. Camille Cosby. These visible campus structures symbolize the longevity of the institution yet reinforce its regard among leaders today.

Other symbols include the Women's Research and Resource Center that has among its goals the curriculum development in women's studies and research on women of African descent. The Center also coordinates the Toni Cade Bambara Writer/Scholar/Activist Internship Program and the Sojourner Truth Women's Studies Collective.

Finally, several times a year (i.e., orientation, reunion, graduation) photographs of noted alumnae are displayed on a wall in the Student Center. The photo gallery traces the college's beginnings and marks years of graduating successful women. These Afrocentric symbols and artifacts at Spelman College validate students and their ability to succeed and enable them to connect with the culture.

Retention Strategies at a Traditionally White Institution: University of Virginia

Given the history of higher education in the United States, black students interested in traditionally white institutions approach the search process differently. Their perceptions and experiences affect retention. Unlike most white students, many African American students inquire about the institution's racial climate, the black student population, and the black social life on campus, in addition to its academic and social support mechanisms. These inquiries are often made in response to racial incidents, feelings of alienation, and African American student attrition on predominantly white campuses.

Despite a tumultuous history that dates back as far as slavery, the University of Virginia (UVa) has been nationally recognized as a leader in recruiting, retaining, and graduating African Americans. This highly selective public university has the highest retention rate in the country among its peer institutions (Brotherton, 2001). *The New York Times* considers UVa a success story in black student recruitment and retention (*The New York Times,* 1996). Authors attribute these retention results to Afrocentered and multicultural efforts, which have helped to change the temperament of the campus climate and the racial composition of the student population.

History and Campus Climate.   Thomas Jefferson established the University of Virginia in 1819. Jefferson not only founded the institution, but also secured the funds from the General Assembly for its construction and maintenance, presided over the body that determined the location, formulated the plans for operation, made the architectural drawings, watched every stage of development through a spyglass from the mountaintop at Monticello, supervised construction on the grounds, and served as the first Rector of the governing board.

Though the Jefferson legacy is the cornerstone of the university, its significance is different for African Americans. The African American view of Jefferson is often one of slaveowner and historical hypocrite—the Jefferson whose definition of democracy did not include people of African descent. Numerous African American administrators at UVa acknowledge that Jefferson does not hold the same interest for black students. The early history of people of African descent at the university is oppressive. Africans were on the Grounds (the word for "campus" at UVa) in the 1800s, but as slave labor. The father of the university also fathered children with at least one slave, Sally Hemmings (Gordon-Reed, 1997; Jordon, 1993).

The ideological chasm is apparent in an editorial written by Pat Collier and Heoulole Mohallim, Chair and Chief Financial Officer, respectively, of the Black Student Alliance at UVa:

> It is the position of the BSA that more than one culture is a constant in the University community, thus the welcomed coexistence of the two is the optimal goal. Members of BSA are of the strong belief that this is our University; Mr. Jefferson may have founded it, but our ancestors built it.
>
> In addition, the money of taxpaying African-American residents of this state supports this institution. Thus, we feel no need to integrate into an establishment with which we undeniably are connected. The effect of our primary purpose is to foster an environment on Grounds that is open and receptive to different cultures and ethnicities.
>
> . . . The topic of race always has been at the forefront of University social issues. Race played a major role in the creation of the University of Virginia. Mr. Jefferson created an institution that educated only white males on the labor of African slaves. Consequently, race was the reason why students of color were banned from this institution for nearly 150 years. Race was the reason why Walter Ridley (the first African-American male admitted to the University of Virginia) was prohibited from living on Grounds. Race was the impetus behind the creation of the Office of African American Affairs 21 years ago. (Collier & Mohallim, 1997, p. 2)

A highly selective public institution, the University of Virginia has a stellar academic reputation and holds the highest retention rate for African Americans among its traditionally white peer institutions (Hurd, 2000).

Afrocentric Admissions Strategies.   A *New York Times* article (1996) begins, "The University of Virginia, once known for its Confederate flag-waving football fans, is being recognized for its success in retaining and graduating black undergraduates." Today this institution's success is enviable.

Though the University of Virginia has received national recognition for recruitment and retention of African Americans, people on both sides of the Afrocentric idea present varying arguments. Some members of the UVa community are adamant and argue that the institution has not done enough. They question the University's being upheld as the model, since the African American population in the state of Virginia is 18.8 percent and the percentage of African American students at UVa is 11 percent ("The States," 1997; University of Virginia, 1997–98).

Following the recommendations of a Minority Affairs Planning Committee to establish an Office of Minority Affairs, several key players laid the foundation that has contributed to the well-established program of today. Both the development of a formal plan and the consistency with which professionals performed both recruitment and retention responsibilities is telling.

A venerable debate in recruiting African Americans is whether only African Americans can recruit African Americans. In UVa's paradigm, African Americans committed to attracting and retaining students went beyond the Grounds. Former admissions administrators indicate that they were given autonomy to implement the appropriate strategy and were respected for their expertise. Yet, the nature of the work requires the support of colleagues.

It appears that at institutions where black admissions professionals are in small number, a tangible commitment from white colleagues is a necessity and contributes to the success of the efforts. In fact, one could argue that UVa is engaging in practices that attempt to broaden the involvement of majority staff in admissions strategies for African Americans beyond a cursory level.

African Americans in admissions offices at PWIs experience a workload that is atypical for white counterparts, yet far too familiar to other African Americans in comparable positions on white campuses. That is, other professionals are assigned specific tasks that are cyclically driven (student search, international student recruitment, special on-Grounds programs). Consequently, there are "peaks and valleys" associated with their primary responsibility. However, the individual who is the point person for African Americans works with constant "peak" periods. In addition to the standard admissions tasks (recruitment travel, reading applications, campus programs), African Americans respond to calls following Afrocentric letters sent to families, work with current student representatives, develop race-specific programs on campus, and conduct outreach activities in the community throughout the year.

Further, African American admissions counselors often assume the "nurturing" role of mentor or advisor once the recruited student enrolls. This Afrocentric paradigm (tying in the specific issues and concerns of African Americans students) is apparent on campuses around the country, yet hardly recognized by white peers in the same office. The mentoring responsibilities can be taxing without the support of other colleagues. One administrator asserts that though African American students often see and have contact with African American professionals, it is also important that Caucasian colleagues welcome students to predominantly white campuses, as theirs are largely the faces black students will see on a daily basis.

Outreach. A number of measures were undertaken to contribute to the community and to introduce younger students to the University. The institution engages in special outreach programs with the junior high schools to cultivate an academically stronger pool of future African American applicants. In these settings, students are informed that UVa is a "tough school" and that it's important to "take honors and AP [advanced placement] courses." By advising junior high students that the University of Virginia is a "difficult school," the institution intends to cultivate an academically prepared student body.

Both the admission office and the University have a relationship with summer bridge and college simulation experiences that target students of color. Namely, relationships are maintained with Upward Bound, LEAD (for students interested in business careers), and engineering programs such as FAME and CHROME. When admitted, these students have more realistic expectations and better preparation than others not enrolled in outreach programs.

Student Involvement. An admissions group was established specifically to attract more black students to the University of Virginia. Today, the Black Student Admission Council (BSAC) is a vital part of the Afrocentric recruitment process. Working closely with the admissions staff to perform several tasks, its longevity and structural organization appear to contribute to its effectiveness. To ground the council, the minority recruitment/admissions staff generally selects two co-presidents. The remainder of the membership chooses the executive body. A hosting committee chair ensures that prospective students who visit overnight have sleeping accommodations in a UVa student's room. The hospitality committee for the Fall Fling open house programs greets families and provides information and parking instructions. The correspondence committee chair is in charge of the phone-a-thon, where admitted African Americans are called in the spring. The organization is large enough that eight to ten different students rotate to make calls during the evening. This committee also participates in a write-a-thon with personal, handwritten letters in response to inquiries regarding majors. Members of the BSAC also participate in various outreach programs.

Afrocentric Administrative Support Initiatives. As a coupled approach, the Afrocentric recruitment methods at UVa are supported by a substantial Afro-centered support mechanism. It is essential to note that support, in this context, does not speak to academic deficiency, but rather to networking, counseling, cultural affirmation, and guidance. The Office of African American Affairs and three other offices serve as the primary points of contact for African American students.

The Office of African American Affairs.   The Office of African American Affairs (OAAA), which was established in 1976, has five goals: (a) to provide a supportive environment through direct contact with African American students, (b) to enhance the sensitivity of the larger community by ensuring that academic components and social programs are reflective of African American culture, (c) to provide information and support to the parents of African American students by strengthening the Parents Advisory Association, (d) to monitor and assess the university's climate and ensure full participation of African Americans in the university's community, and (e) to enhance relationships in the Charlottesville/Albemarle communities through civic involvement and activities.

Located in the Luther P. Jackson House, the OAAA offers three primary services that interface with the role of the admission office and contribute to retention. Specifically, programs and services include the Peer Advisor Program, the African American Student/Faculty/Administrator Mentoring Program, and the Parents' Advisory Association. The Luther P. Jackson Cultural Center coordinates cultural, educational, and social events specific to African culture (University of Virginia, 1997a).

Peer Advisors.   In 1993, the University of Virginia's Peer Advisor Program was recognized by the American Association of University Administrators for "exemplary practice in achieving campus diversity" (University of Virginia, 1997a). The mandatory program is designed to assist African American first-year and transfer students in making their transition to the university. Second-, third-, and fourth-year students who have maintained a 2.8 grade point average and are involved in Student Life organizations may apply to become peer mentors. Students must submit a writing sample as part of the selection process and serve as role models and leaders for first-years.

Once selected, peer advisors are thoroughly trained and informed of their dual role as admissions personnel and retention officers. During the summer, peer advisors write letters to the students with whom they have been matched. The letters appear to be an important part of the enrollment process as they not only connect the student with the peer advisor, but the letters also represent the University's commitment. Parents' questions are wide-reaching. Some inquire about racial climate as well as academic and social environment. In fact, peer advisors have changed the minds of black families who planned to cancel their acceptances.

The peer advisor's retention function begins once the new students are on Grounds. To reinforce the letters they have written during the summer, peer advisors meet with new students early on. During the Harambee Program (a one-hour orientation about the Office of African American Affairs), new students see their peer advisors again and learn about the program. As an African-centered component of orientation, Harambee has featured original poetry and prose, instrumental renditions, performances by the gospel choir, and skits by peer advisors. This showcase of peer advisors as role models is not a part of the general session.

Also beneficial to parents during orientation weekend is the candor of President Casteen. As part of the program for all students, the Office of African American Affairs hosts a welcome program and reception for African Americans. President Casteen attends the event and considers it among his priorities. Also, other African American faculty members and administrators attend this event and are introduced. This "visible presence" of African Americans in significant positions, as well as the president's visible support, has been important for students.

University personnel indicated that the special orientation and the efforts of the peer advisors help the students to establish community early. During the school year, the peer advisors sponsor universitywide programs, including weekly study halls and academic workshops.

Faculty Mentoring.   The Faculty Mentoring Program was established in 1995 "to help students of color achieve academic, intellectual, and personal success at the University of Virginia." In the program, a diverse faculty of all races serve as volunteer mentors for students beyond the first year. Though there is no selection criteria for students, the OAAA does match faculty with students according to common interests. The program's goal is to have students "look forward to intellectual stimulation, academic support, career guidance, and friendship" (University of Virginia, 1997b).

Other University Support Vehicles.   In addition to the services provided through the Office of African American Affairs, there are three primary vehicles through which students receive support—the Office of the Dean of Students, the Minority Engineering Program, and the Transition Program. Though each is not an African-centered office—that is, exclusively for students of African descent—African Americans comprise a significant portion of the students utilizing their services.

Academic Support.   In addition to Afrocentered social and cultural support mechanisms, academic support systems for students of color and first-generation students are available. The Office of Minority Programs in the School of Engineering and Applied Science has as its objective to increase the recruitment and persistence of undergraduate and graduate African American, Native American, and Hispanic students who are pursuing degrees in engineering and the applied sciences (Office of Minority Programs, 1996). The program's undergraduate components include developing recruitment activities with the admission office, tutoring assistance, academic monitoring and advising, summer bridge opportunities, corporate exposure through Project View, and student organizations that target special needs and interests of students of color in engineering.

Though not African-centered, another academic program designed for first-generation students also serves African American students at UVa. During the early 1970s, Professor William Elwood, the award-winning producer of the film *The Road to Brown,* was instrumental in establishing the first Summer Transition Program. The program (which was required in institutions statewide under the Virginia Plan for desegregation) sought to smooth the transition to college for first-generation students and to aid in academic preparation ("Professors Elwood and Sedgwick Retire," 1997). Though the program has changed since its inception, the longevity of the academic support remains central for African American students.

Symbolism and Cultural Artifacts.   Rainsford (1990), in "The Demographic Imperative: Changing to Serve America's Expanding Minority Population," speaks to the value of symbols in recruiting African Americans to predominantly white campuses. He posits, "Much of what colleges do consciously reflects the majority culture of our society. If an institution seeks to make a place for minority persons, attention to symbols is important" (p. 98).

At UVa, many symbols are crafted around its historic inception and the Jefferson legacy. Research during the site visit reveals that African Americans do not revere this history in the same way as some members of the majority culture. African Americans do, however, identify with several symbols on Grounds—both tangible and intangible. The most significant tangible symbols are three interrelated buildings—the Luther P. Jackson House, which houses the administrative offices for the Office of African American Affairs and the Nat Turner Library; the Luther P. Jackson Cultural Center, which offers performances, lectures, and workshops; and the W. E. B. DuBois Center, where meetings and programs are held. Through its cultural programming and enriched academically centered programs, these facilities appear to connect students and administrators to African-centered culture, issues, and achievement at the University of Virginia.

Despite an intense history, African Americans have crafted their own Afro-centered symbols through which they have affiliated with the university. It can be argued that these Afrocentered symbols have served to affirm their culture and heritage, while providing a social haven that visually diminishes the impact of being in the minority on a majority campus.

Summary of Significant Findings

Though Spelman College and the University of Virginia appear to be polar opposites in several areas, parallels can be drawn. Both hold number one retention rankings—Spelman among HBCUs and the University of Virginia among PWIs (Hurd, 2000). Each institutes initiatives that contribute to black student success. Many are African-centered. The Spelman story is one rich in the history and legacy of academic excellence. Students are inspired by the fact that many successful black women have been graduated by the institution, and it has remained a center committed to justice and the advancement of women for more than a century. While former slaves were the first educated at Spelman, the University of Virginia's history includes slaves who worked on the campus. Yet, despite its past, the university's prestigious faculty, the culture of free inquiry, and the facilities all contribute to student growth. Talented black students seek admission to UVa and benefit from race-specific and Afrocentric initiatives. Through admissions, student life, the faculty, and administrative support, student success is buttressed by a race-specific integrated approach to achievement.

Seven primary themes emerge in examining the two institutions: (1) a seamless transition between recruitment and retention, (2) an exceptional professional commitment beyond assigned tasks, (3 and 4) longevity and consistency of approach and personnel, (5) the building of a community through an African American presence, (6) viewing students as partners, and (7) the cultivating of allies within the university community.

First, the *transition between recruitment and retention was almost seamless.* Professionals appeared to have an equal interest in both components of student enrollment, despite their own specific functions.

Second, and a component of the "seamless" philosophy, was the *commitment from individuals who appeared to go beyond their assigned tasks.* At Spelman, much of the commitment appears to be grounded in the HBCU and black experience. These experiences shape the understanding that black students are achievers. And it is the role of those in the community to contribute to their success. Among black faculty, staff, and allies at the University of Virginia, the personal commitment to and investment in African American students takes many forms. Members of the University community dedicate themselves to multiple approaches and points of contact on and off campus.

Themes three and four are *longevity and consistency of approach and personnel.* During the early 1980s, UVa developed a recruitment plan. Over the years, the plan has been modified, as necessary, yet the core of the plan is still carried out today. This formal effective plan has served as a guide and also impacts relationships with the academic and administrative departments. Spelman has many academic programs based in the major areas that have functioned since the 1970s. And at both institutions, professionals and key members of the community have longevity. This consistent cadre contributes to student achievement through networks inside and outside the university community (pre-college program advisors, alumni, business and civic leaders, and educators).

The fifth theme that emerged is *building community through an African American presence.* Certainly at Spelman, women are surrounded daily by role models who reinforce the idea and likelihood of success. Further, this validation is ensured through the curriculum, convocations, and guest lecturers. At UVa, the African American presence is a theme that is echoed in various settings—peer advisors, orientation, and academic programs. And Afrocentric measures are used to build community and strengthen the affiliation with the institution.

The sixth theme that emerges is *students as partners.* In both institutions, talented black students are connected to recruitment, orientation, academic programs, and programming. The "endorsement" of currently enrolled students appears to send a favorable message to prospective families and serves to support current students.

Finally, the institution's emphasis on *cultivating allies* is evident in admissions and other segments of the university community. For Spelman, as a historically black institution, the mission of education women of African descent is clear. As a small private liberal arts college, support from allies for the college's mission must be broad-based. The University of Virginia's allies now include black alumni who previously felt alienated based on their experiences and others who advocate for enhanced black student recruitment and retention efforts.

Spelman College traces its beginnings to two missionary educators from New England who were dedicated to teaching former slaves. The noble charge of educating the descendants of Africa has continued for more than a century. Today, academically talented students achieve some measure of success with Afrocentric and other integrated strategies to support their success.

Although black students at UVa have comparable academic credentials and socioeconomic levels as their white counterparts, the contrast among cultures is vivid. Yet, on a campus where some students still speak of "Mr. Jefferson" in the present tense and others speak of him with disdain, UVa has managed to develop a formula, evident in the emerging themes, that has benefited its recruitment and retention of African Americans. The formula is one clearly evident in the historically black college and university experience.

The Coupled Model

A Coupled Afrocentric Approach

In her work, *Why Are All the Black Kids Sitting Together in the Cafeteria? And Other Conversations of Race,* Beverly Daniel Tatum addresses the need to speak frankly about racial identity. She notes that "Black students practice their 'language' in Black student unions and cultural centers and at college dining halls on predominantly White campuses all across the United States" (Tatum, 1997, p. 77). Tatum further finds that outside of the educational setting, in the corporate cafeterias, Black men and women are sitting together "to connect with someone who looks like them and shares the same experiences" (p. 88).

The Afrocentric approach to student recruitment and retention, then, addresses the particular issues, culture, and social concerns of the black student. In this context, it is defined as an approach whereby enrollment efforts on and off campus are developed collaboratively to openly acknowledge the black experience and accentuate an institution's Afrocentered cultural advantages and academic opportunities. Characteristically, in recruitment, admissions letters, publications, bus trips, recruitment travel, academic programs, campus organizations, and community outreach are designed to focus exclusively on African Americans. This race-specific approach employed at majority institutions has contributed to student success.

Employed by admissions and others within the university community, the approach uses the familiar context of the black student's heritage and comfort zones in presenting race-specific offerings, activities, and programming. Different from other strategies, the Afrocentric approach directly addresses the issues and interests of both prospective and currently enrolled black students. Institutions have used this open, race-specific technique to directly address the social environment, racial climate, and academic opportunities, all of which have been inflammatory and prohibiting matriculation and success.

To maximize student success, it is important to couple or integrate strategies campuswide. This approach maximizes resources and reaches the student through an expansive, holistic approach. The cultural center is used as a context. As the black student's life has many aspects, including the impact of race, the race-specific approach has some merit.

Authors who have used race-specific approaches at predominantly white universities have recognized that the particular social and cultural issues of African Americans on campus are as important as the academic issues (Harris, 1994; Roberson, 1991). Not only do the discipline-based programs (such as engineering, education, and the sciences) affect retention, but the involvement of currently enrolled students and others in the university community contributes to retention and campus relationships. Recruitment, then, is intermingled with and coupled to retention through black college students and the university community (Harkema, 1990; Roberson, 1991).

The Coupled Model for Majority Institutions

Based on the success of the University of Virginia and the lessons learned from other historically black colleges and universities, the coupled model has aided universities in the successful education of African American students (see Figure 2.1).

Institutional Commitment.   Researchers argue that before substantial change can occur in enrollment and retention, institutional commitment must be an integral part of the process. Endorsement of campus initiatives is generally effective when supported by the president. Recently, the climate nationally has presented challenges for race-specific support programs. Consequently, the endorsement of the president and senior administrators at majority institutions remains important. Smith (1997) maintains that "Numerous factors have been cited as integral to organizational change to achieve a pluralistic college or university. Heading the list are leadership, mission, faculty and staff diversity, and overall institutional commitment to the goal" (p. 43).

Interoffice Realm.   Apart from the foundation laid by commitment by senior administrators, the interoffice realm is an invaluable component of the coupled model. Its emphasis is organizational climate, staffing, institutional mission, and institutional goals (enrollment, retention, and cultural). This realm is relevant for both historically black and traditionally white universities. As African Americans are often

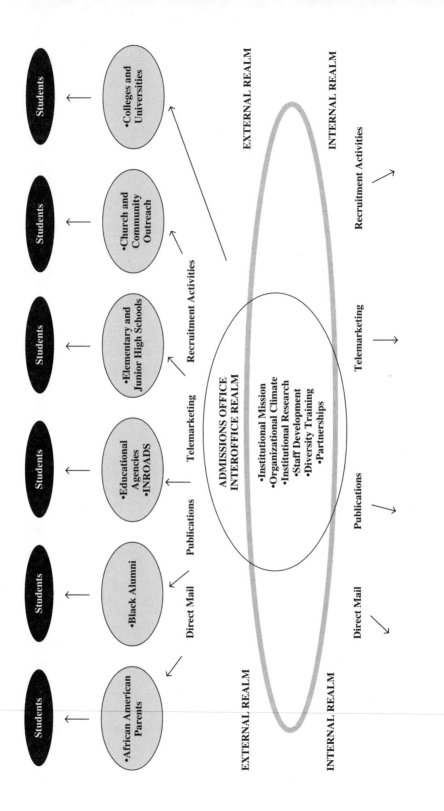

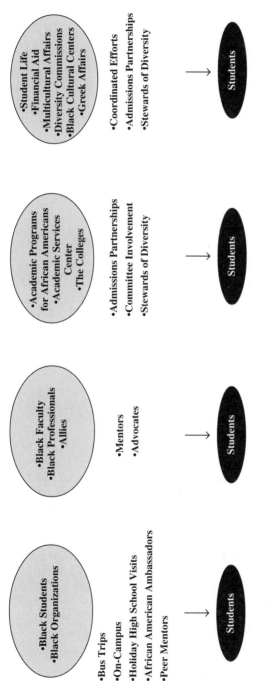

FIGURE 2.1 Coupled Afrocentric Recruitment and Retention Model: Interoffice, Internal, and External Realms of Interaction

scarcely represented in the admissions offices at PWIs, sensitive white colleagues are needed as allies and active members of a recruitment team for people of color.

Both professional and support staff should be included in discussions on sensitivity in answering phones and communication with black students and families. In traditionally white institutions, the open dialogue regarding issues of race also contributes to a change in organizational climate. Black and white issues and concerns are not secrets.

Staffing and Climate Recommendations

1. Develop a comprehensive recruitment plan that incorporates the university's vision and goals, outlines a strategy for the next five years, and includes internal and external constituencies. The enrollment plan should be guided by demographics and an investigation of new markets.
2. Establish a multicultural recruitment team in the admissions office. Members of the team should be sensitive to black students, knowledgeable of African-centered cultural and social issues, and full partners in black student recruitment.
3. Engage in ongoing training of support and professional staff to effect change in the organizational climate and to cultivate allies. Special emphasis should be given to customer service on the telephone and in person.
4. Hold monthly support staff meetings. The meetings serve to inform personnel on admissions initiatives and the diversity agenda.
5. Invite guest speakers from black student groups and other diversity-centered units to professional and salaried staff meetings. This effort is intended to demystify black student activities and connect staff with black student recruitment and retention.

Internal Realm.   Once the in-house operations in admissions are in order, with training mechanisms for salaried and professional staff, a formal plan, and endorsements from senior level administrators, the structure can be carried out in the internal realm. The internal realm consists of four sectors within the university community: (1) black students and organizations; (2) black faculty, professionals, and other allies; (3) academic (including academic programs for African Americans, the Academic Services Center, and academic departments); and (4) administrative support services (including financial aid, the Office of Multicultural Affairs, the Commission on Racial and Cultural Diversity, Career Services, and the Center for Black Culture).

Recommendations for Student Organizations

1. Partner with black student organizations to mentor entering students through an African-centered program that links entering students with upperclassmen. Communication between mentors and mentees can occur during the summer.

2. Partner with Admissions, Support Programs, and other departments to connect entering students and provide a support network for continuing students.
3. Seek allies in the administration to support cultural events and engage in issues of interest to black students.

Recommendations Working with Faculty, Professionals, and Other Allies

1. Establish a cadre of professionals and faculty to serve as allies to black students. Institutions report success when professional and faculty mentors are connected to students. Include matching and closing receptions as part of the activities.
2. Develop an effective informal means of communication with the faculty and staff of color on campus. A listserv to announce increased enrollment, special events on campus, and student leader recommendations engages the community.

Academic Recommendations

1. Establish and enrich academic support programs based in the majors (engineering, education, business, the sciences, etc.) to strengthen students' academic performance. Programs include academic advising, regular meetings, tutoring, networking opportunities, and experiential learning.
2. Establish formal and regular communication with the academic programs for students of color and the Academic Services. A committee to convey admissions strategies can strengthen linkages between summer bridge programs and currently enrolled students.
3. Advocate the inclusion of racial/ethnic materials in courses for the good of all students. Humphreys and Schneider (1997), Astin (1993), Villalpando (1994), and Duster (1995) report the growth of courses that promote social responsibility and their positive effect on racial understanding as well as students' overall satisfaction with college.
4. Use early warning systems for first-year students whose grades drop below a 2.0.

Student Support Recommendations

1. Initiate and formalize an ongoing dialogue with departments that impact the quality of student life: (a) financial aid, (b) student affairs, (c) multicultural affairs, and (d) the cultural centers. Cultivate these and other partnerships with stewards of diversity.
2. Establish and/or seek membership in commissions on racial and cultural diversity and other related committees to broaden the link between recruitment and retention.
3. Work cooperatively and actively as committee members with career services, multicultural centers, and others who engage in race-specific activities.

External Realm.   Universities have made significant inroads into the community via civic organizations, educational agencies, and the black church. Community partnerships have taken years to cultivate through college awareness visits (not specific to the institution), service on boards, and on-campus programs. Educational agencies and organizations, especially those offering preparatory programs for students, serve a particular advantage. And certainly, students who participate in these precollege prep programs are good prospective students.

Based on the historical context of predominantly white universities in the United States and the need to broaden the base of allies, six sectors are proposed that can yield new markets of successful students, serve as a pipeline for students in preparatory classes, and fortify the institution's reputation in the community. A contact person from the admissions office should be assigned to one or two of the sectors. The outreach sectors are (1) black parents, (2) black alumni, (3) educational agencies, (4) churches and community groups, (5) schools, and (6) colleges and universities. Admissions, then, should work with the academic departments to solidify these partnerships and "grow their own" future students.

Recommendations for Working with Black Parents

1. Establish a black parents' association. The University of Virginia has used its Black Parents Association for fundraising, networking, and recommending new students.
2. Work with the cultural centers to co-sponsor events where black parents are currently targeted.

Recommendations for Working with Black Alumni

1. Establish partnerships with black alumni. Traci Harris (1994) contends that black alumni will support prospective black students despite their own college experiences. Black alumni may prove instrumental in referrals, as participants during campus visits, and during phone-a-thons.
2. Invite black alumni to race-specific programming on campus and assign a function. Alumni members also strengthen the pool of professionals for networking opportunity and professional development talks.
3. Communicate with all black and Latino alumni at the beginning of the year to initiate interest and support in the recruitment and retention endeavors.

Recommendations for Working with Educational Agencies

1. Broaden the market base by communication with educational agencies that target students of color and first-generation students.
2. Establish formal contacts with directors of educational agencies and meet with each on an annual basis.

Recommendations for Working with Churches and Community Organizations

1. Establish a ministerial alliance among black pastors in the local area. Work to develop a citywide college awareness program, co-sponsored by the university and held in a local church. The program can be designed such that a middle school program is given at one church and the high school component is held at another. The locations can rotate each year.
2. Establish personal contact with an individual who is responsible for announcements and newsletters or a youth minister at local churches. The names of the contact and minister should be verified annually.
3. Communicate regularly with local churches by letter announcing events of interest to African Americans.
4. Develop partnerships with the NAACP, the Urban League, and other organizations to provide college awareness programs for the organizations' youth.
5. Network with community organizations through annual banquets and awards dinners sponsored by the groups.
6. Invite religious and community leaders on campus for an annual event to discuss the university, black student achievement, and enrollment and to meet with students.

Recommendations for Working with Schools

1. Cultivate a younger student population in the elementary and middle schools.
2. Develop a counselor program that will more closely connect African American guidance counselors and counselors in largely black high schools to the institution. The program should include a communication strategy, such as the scholarship nomination process from the school and on-campus visitation programs.

Concluding Thoughts

For more than a century, historically black institutions have used multiple approaches to impact student success. Many of these efforts have been grounded in the historical context of the black experience and use the students' racial background as a frame of reference. Traditionally white institutions also find that when the issues of race are directly addressed and when the holistic approach to student achievement takes into consideration the student's race, retention is positively affected.

As student recruitment requires campuswide support, so does retention. To maximize student success, campus-efforts should be coordinated, coupled, and well communicated. When coupled or integrated with other departments on campus, these Afrocentric or race-specific strategies have proven successful. When effective Afrocentric models are examined, several themes emerge: the importance of senior level administration's *commitment to institutional change, a seamless transition between recruitment and retention, the coexistence of Afrocentrism and Eurocentrism in student recruitment, the commitment of African Americans who view themselves as change agents, the cultivation of allies, students as "owners," connecting the community to the university, and the need to communicate with "stewards of diversity" in the university community.*

Sedlacek (1993) makes the case for considering different cultures and backgrounds in the admissions process. He acknowledges that U.S. universities were largely designed for white middle- and upper-class males. The same case must be made to contribute to the students' success. It appears that even institutions whose historical framework includes slavery and desegregation battles can make strides in black student success. Even when institutions appear to have little in common, progress toward student success can be made using a similar coupled Afrocentric approach.

What is recommended, then, is a new paradigm. For some campuses, the traditional approach still exists, based on a largely white male middle-class population of the past. Yet, paradigms must shift with the dynamics of a new population. Institutions can and should choose to take a progressive stance that speaks to social justice, equality, racial identity, support, and the contributions of other races. In that way, historically black colleges and universities and traditionally white institutions weave a common thread in the fabric of student success.

REFERENCES

Adams v. Richardson, 480 F. 2d 1159 (D. C. Cir. 1973).

Affirmative action: Hopwood and beyond. (1996, June). *Perspective,* 4–5.

Allen, W. R. (1992). The color of success: African-American student outcomes at predominantly white and historically black colleges and universities. *The Harvard Educational Review, 62*(1), 26–44.

Altbach, P., & Lometey, K. (1991). *The racial crisis in American higher education.* New York: State University of New York Press.

Anderson J. D. (1988). *The education of blacks in the south, 1860–1935.* Chapel Hill: The University of North Carolina Press.

Astin, A. W. (1993). Student involvement: A developmental theory for higher education. *Journal of College Student Development, 25,* 297–308.

Bennett, L., Jr. (1966). *Before the Mayflower: A history of the Negro in America, 1619–1964.* Baltimore: Penguin Books.

Brotherton, P. (2001, October 25). It takes a campus to graduate a student. *Black Issues in Higher Education,* 40.

Brown v. Board of Education of Topeka, 347 U.S. 483 (1954).

Browning, J., & Williams, J. (1978). History and goals of black institutions in higher education. In C. V. Willie & R. R. Edmonds (Eds.), *Black colleges in America.* New York: Teachers College Press.

Bullock, H. A. (1967). *History of Negro education in the south: From 1619 to the present.* Cambridge, MA: Harvard University Press.

Business Officer. (1994, January). Judge approves race-based scholarships at University of Maryland. *Business Officer, 27,* 8.

Collier, P., & Mohallim, H. (1997, November 20). Defining BSA's purpose, politics. *The Cavalier Daily*, p. 2.

Duster, T. (1995). They're taking over! And other myths about race on campus. In M. Berube & C. Nelson (Eds.), *Higher education under fire: Politics, economics, and the crisis of the humanities*. New York: Routledge.

El-Khawas, E. (1994) *Campus trends 1994*. Washington, DC: American Council on Education.

Erickson, E. (1967). The concept of identity in race relations: Notes and queries. In T. Parsons & K. Clark (Eds.), *The Negro American*. Boston: Beacon Press.

Ern, E. (1993). Managing resources strategically. In M. J. Barr (Ed.), *The handbook of student affairs administration* (pp. 439–442). San Francisco: Jossey-Bass Publishers.

Farrell, C. S. (1989, February 2). AAUP conference focuses on recruitment of minority students and faculty. *Black Issues in Higher Education*, 32.

Fleming, J. (1984). *Blacks in college: A comparative study of students' success in black and in white institutions*. San Francisco: Jossey-Bass.

Franklin, J. H. (1947). *From slavery to freedom*. New York: Alfred A. Knopf.

Gamson, Z. F. (1978). Civil rights and race relations. In M. W. Peterson et al. (Eds.), *Black students on white campuses: The impacts of increased black enrollments* (pp. 11–19). Ann Arbor: The University of Michigan Press.

Goldman, F. H. (1963). Integration and the Negro college. In F. H. Goldman (Ed.), *Educational imperative: The Negro in the changing south*. Chicago: Center of Liberal Education for Adults.

Gordon-Reed, A. (1997). *Thomas Jefferson and Sally Hemmings: An American controversy*. Charlottesville: University of Virginia Press.

Gurin, P., & Epps, E.G. (1975). *Black consciousness, identity and achievement*. New York: Wiley.

Gutek, G. L. (1986). *Education in the United States: A historical perspective*. Englewood Cliffs, NJ: Prentice-Hall.

Harkema, P. M. (1990). *Development of a black student enrollment: Enrollment management efforts and organizational culture in three church-related liberal arts colleges*. Unpublished doctoral dissertation, Michigan State University.

Harper, E. D. (1975). *Black students: White campuses*. Washington, DC: APGA Press.

Harris, T. A. (1994, Summer). Marketing for black alums. *The Journal of College Admissions*, 5–11.

Haynes, L. L., III. (1981). The Adams mandate: A format for achieving equal educational opportunity and attainment. In G. E. Thomas (Ed.). *Black students in higher education: Conditions and experiences in the 1970s*. Westport, CT: Greenwood Press.

Henley, B. (1990). United through diversity week: Promoting diversity and addressing racism. *NAPSA Journal*, 27(4), 313–318.

Henley, B., Powell, T., & Poats, L. (1992). Achieving cultural diversity: Meeting the challenges. In M. Terrell (Ed.). *Diversity, disunity, and campus community* (pp. 1–25). Washington, DC: National Association of Student Personnel Administrators.

Hollins, C. (1992). Where do we go from here? *Containing Cost and Improving Productivity in Higher Education*, 75, 115–19.

Hopwood v. Texas, 95-50062 (1996).

Humphreys, D., & Schneider, C. (1997). Curricular changes gain momentum: New requirements focus on diversity and social responsibility. *Diversity Digest*, 1(2), 1–5.

Humphries, F. S. (1994/1995, Winter). A short history of blacks in higher education. *The Journal of Blacks in Higher Education*, 6, 57.

Hurd, H. (2000, October 26). Staying power: Colleges work to improve retention rates. *Black Issues in Higher Education*, 42–46.

Hutchinson, D. J. (1992). Unanimity and desegregation: Decision-making in the Supreme Court, 1948–1958. In P. Finkelman (Ed.), *Race, law, and American history 1700–1990: The struggle for equal education* (pp. 87–182). New York: Garland Publishing.

Jaffe, A. J. (1968). *Negro higher education in the 1960s*. New York: Praeger.

Jencks, C., & Reisman, D. (1968). *The academic revolution*. New York: Doubleday.

Jordan, V. E., Jr. (1975). Blacks in higher education: Some reflections. *Daedalus*, 104, 160–65.

Jordon, E. L. (1993, February 26). Champion of liberty, slavery: Racial issues. *Daily Progress* (in Jefferson 250 newspaper insert), p. 31.

Keller, G. (1983). *Academic strategy: The management revolution in American higher education.* Baltimore: Johns Hopkins.

LaVeist, T., & Whigham-Desir, M. (1999, January). Top 50 colleges for African Americans. *Black Enterprise,* 71–80.

Lederman, D. (1997, March 21). New lawsuits may help determine what's legal in affirmative action. *The Chronicle of Higher Education,* pp. A34–A35.

LeMelle, T., & LeMelle, W. (1969) *The black college: A strategy for relevancy.* New York: Praeger.

Locke, M. (1997, July 13). Minorities dwindle at schools where affirmative action ends. *News Journal,* p. A10.

McGrath, E. J. (1965). *The predominantly Negro colleges and universities in transition.* New York: Teachers College Press.

Mingle, A. R. (1978). *Black enrollment in higher education: Trends in the nation and the south.* Atlanta: Southern Regional Education Board.

Mingle, J. R. (1987). *Trends in higher education participation and success.* Denver: Education Commission of the States.

Missouri ex rel. Gaines v. Canada, 305 U.S. 337 (1938).

Monroe, S. (1973, February). Guest in a strange house: A Black at Harvard. *Education-Saturday Review,* 45–48.

Mount Holyoke. (2002c). *Beverly Daniel Tatum.* Available Internet: http://www.mtholyoke.edu/offices/comm/profile/tatum.shtml

Murray v. Maryland, 182 A 590 (1935): 169 Md 478 (1937).

Myrdal, G. (1944). *An American dilemma: The Negro problem and modern democracy.* New York: Harper & Row.

National Association of College Admissions Counselors (NACAC). (1995a, March). Affirmative action and the college admission process—where do we go from here? *NACAC, 33,* 1.

National Association of College Admissions Counselors (NACAC). (1995b, April). University of Maryland modifies scholarship program. *NACAC, 33,* 1.

National Association of College Admissions Counselors (NACAC). (1995c, August/September). University of California regents end affirmative action in college admission. *NACAC, 33,* 1.

Nettles, M. (1987). *Financial aid and minority participation in graduate education.* Princeton, NJ: Educational Testing Service.

The New York Times. (1996, December 1). University helping blacks to graduate, p. 43.

Office of Minority Programs. (1996). *Office of Minority Programs School of Engineering and Applied Science* [Brochure]. Charlottesville, VA: University of Virginia.

Orfield, G. (1989). *The Reagan administration's abandonment of civil rights enforcement in higher education.* Washington, DC: The Joint Center for Political Studies.

Pascarella, E. T., & Terezini, P. T. (1991). *How college affects students: Findings and insights from twenty years of research.* San Francisco: Jossey-Bass.

Person, D. R. (1994). Black and Hispanic women in higher education. In Francisco Rivera-Batiz (Ed.), *Reinventing urban education* (pp. 303–326). New York: IUME Press.

Person, D. R., & Christensen, M. C. (1996, Fall). Understanding black student culture and black student retention. *NASPA Journal, 34,* 47–56.

Pifer, A. (1973). *The higher education of blacks in the United States.* New York: Carnegie Corporation of New York.

Phillip, M. C. (1995a, February 23). Shrinking resources and calls for accountability are forcing tough lessons on higher education and challenging the institution to reinvent itself. *Black Issues in Higher Education,* 9–13.

Phillip, M. C. (1995b, July 27). Yesterday once more. *Black Issues in Higher Education,* 10–14.

Plessy v. Ferguson, 163 U.S. 537 (1896).

Podberesky v. Kirwan, 38F. 3d147 (4th Cir, 1995).

Professors Elwood and Sedgwick Retire from UVA. (1997, Fall). *Profiles in Excellence: The Newsletter of the Walter Ridley Scholarship Fund, 3*(9), 2, 8.

Rainsford, G. N. (1990). The demographic imperative: Changing to serve America's expanding minority population. In D. W Steeples (Ed.), *New directions in higher education: Managing change in higher education* (pp. 91–100). San Francisco: Jossey-Bass.

Ramseur, H. (1975). *Continuity and change in black identity: A study of black students at an interracial college.* Unpublished doctoral dissertation, Harvard University.

Randolph, L. B. (1988, December). Racism on college campuses. *Ebony,* 126–130.

Redding, S. (1950). *They came in chains.* Philadelphia: J. B. Lippincott.

Rickard, C. E. (1991, Summer). Why effective admission programs make universities strong. *The Journal of College Admission, 132,* 2–4.

Roberson, A. M. (1991). Minority student recruitment issues in managing enrollment. In A. Galsky (Ed.), *The role of student affairs in institution-wide enrollment management strategies* (pp. 48–61). Washington, DC: National Association of Student Personnel Administrators (NASPA).

Rodriguez, R. (1996, August 6). Life after Hopwood. *Black Issues in Higher Education,* 8.

Rosa, P. M. (1989). *Equity and pluralism: Full participation of blacks and Hispanics in New England higher education.* Boston: New England Board of Higher Education. Ann Arbor, MI: University Microfilms.

St. John, E. P. (1991). The impact of student financial aid: A review of recent research. *Journal of Student Financial Aid, 21*(1), 18–32.

Schwaneger, H. (1969). *The history of higher education in Delaware.* Unpublished Ph.D. dissertation, University of Pennsylvania.

Sedlacek, W. E. (1987). Black students in white colleges and universities: Twenty years of research. *Journal of College Student Personnel, 28,* 484–495.

Sedlacek, W. E. (1989). Noncognitive indicators of student success. *The Journal of the National Association of College Admission Counselors, 125,* 2–10.

Sedlacek, W. E. (1993). Employing noncognitive variables in admissions and retention in higher education. In *Achieving diversity: Issues in the recruitment and retention of underrepresented racial/ethnic students in higher education* (pp. 33–39). Evanston, IL: National Association of College Admission Counselors.

Simpson, R. D., & Frost, S. H. (1993). Who goes to college and why? In *Inside college: Undergraduate education for the future* (pp. 39–66). New York: Insight Books/ Plenum Press.

Sipuel v. Oklahoma State Regents, 322 U.S. 631,632 (1948).

Smith, D. G. (1997). *Diversity works: The emerging picture of how students benefit.* Washington, DC: Association of American Colleges and Universities.

Spelman College Bulletin, 2002–2003. Available Internet: www.spelman.edu.

The States. (1997, August 29). *The Chronicle of Higher Education 1997–1998, Almanac Issue,* 38–107.

Stewart, G., Haynes, B., Brown-Wright, D. A., & Anderson, D. (1996, July/August). African-American student associations: Misunderstood, but critical in retention. *Access, IV/V,* 4–5.

Tatum, B. D. (1997). *"Why are all the black kids sitting together in the cafeteria?" And other conversations on race.* New York: Basic Books.

Thomas, G. E. (1981). *Black students in higher education: Conditions and experiences in the 1970s.* Westport, CT: Greenwood Press.

Thompson, D. C. (1973). *Private black colleges at the crossroads.* Westport, CT: Greenwood Press.

Tinto, V. (1987). *Learning college: Rethinking the causes and cures of student attrition.* Chicago: University of Chicago Press.

University of Virginia. (1997a, November). Available Internet: http://www.virginia.edu/~oaa/goals.html .

University of Virginia. (1997b, November). Available Internet: http://wsrv.clas.virginia.edu/~xy2m/Courses.html

University of Virginia. (1997–98). *University of Virginia prospectus*. Charlottesville: University of Virginia Admission Office.

Villalpando, O. (1994). *Comparing the effects of multiculturalism and diversity on minority and white students' satisfaction with college*. Paper presented at the annual meeting of the Association of the Study of Higher Education, November, Tucson, AZ. ERIC Document No. ED 375721.

Watson, L., & Kuh, G. (1996). The influences of dominant race environments on student involvement, perceptions, and educational gains: A look at historically black and predominantly white liberal arts institutions. *Journal of College Student Development, 37,* 415–420.

Willie, C., & McCord, A. (1972). *Black students at white colleges*. New York: Praeger.

Wilson, R. (1994). The participation of African Americans in American higher education. In M. Justiz, R. Wilson, & L. Bjork (Eds.), *Minorities in higher education* (pp. 195–209). Phoenix: American Council on Education and the Orys Press.

3 Successful Mentoring Strategies within Historically Black Institutions

Cynthia Neal Spence
Spelman College

Successful mentoring strategies employed by historically black institutions (HBCUs) cannot be fully discussed without a close examination of the history and mission of these distinct institutions. It is in the very fiber of their existence that successful mentoring is expected and practiced by faculty and staff at HBCU. Their founding missions dictated that mentoring would be a core expectation and core activity.

HBCUs, founded in the middle to late 1800s to literally make a way out of no way for blacks in northern areas above the Mason-Dixon line and newly freed blacks in the South, developed human infrastructures to support and guide their students through the uncharted territory of structured education.[1] In their very beginnings, most of these institutions provided education to all levels, including elementary. Drewry and Doermann (2001) comment that "at a time when southern Blacks constituted 94 percent of black American population, and when 90 percent of them could not read or write, the effort to establish simultaneously elementary schools, secondary schools, and colleges where none had previously existed created a unique situation with a unique set of problems" (p. 34). The founding missions of each of these institutions shared the common goal of "uplifting the race." Once barred from reading, blacks throughout the country became the beneficiaries of the benevolence of missionaries, religious groups, ex-slaves, and free blacks. The reality that education

---

[1]According to research of Drewry and Doermann (2001), the first record of a black institution awarding a baccalaureate degree is in 1865. Ashmun Institute, which was renamed Lincoln University in 1866, awarded the first baccalaureate degree in 1865.

Cynthia Neal Spence is Associate Professor of Sociology and former Dean of the College at Spelman College, Atlanta, GA.

was the key to individual and social transformation never eluded blacks. The desire to read and write was often so desperately sought that slaves risked their lives to learn these skills. They knew that these abilities were obviously tied to some form of freedom. If they had not been, their slave masters would not have so vigorously or vigilantly forbade the activity. Neither threats nor discouragement could quell the insatiable thirst for learning.

Educational opportunities created by the early historically black institutions required broad-based learning, attention to varying learning styles, basic remediation, and one-on-one tutoring. Their missions united these very special educational institutions in a political and social quest to gain equality of opportunity for their students and graduates. Common missions necessitated the development of faculty/student relationships that expanded the role of teachers beyond mere purveyors of knowledge to career and academic advisors, personal consultants, role models, and surrogate parents. The teacher-as-mentor model was adopted and has prevailed as a most effective tool to transform the lives of those who enter these institutions as students. The character traits traditionally associated with mentoring became embodied in the work of founders, teachers, and staff of the early historically black institutions. These characteristics continue to run through the veins and arteries of today's distinguished HBCUs.

The absence of educational opportunity for blacks compelled concerned members of society, black and white, to construct physical structures and adopt a steely resolve that would sustain generations of African Americans as they made the slow ascent from slavery and segregation and prepared to take their rightful places in society. The need for one-to-one supervision and guidance necessitated that teachers place specific attention on the successful mentoring strategies that have produced countless graduates who have gone forward to assume positions of leadership in all occupational arenas and as social change agents.

Mentorship is a term with broad application in contemporary society. The term is said to have originated in ancient Greek society. Mentorship in the ancient Greek system of education referred to the system of developing protégés to take on the roles of their superiors. The act of mentoring suggests a concerted initiative to guide and direct the paths of those under one's tutelage or supervision. This ancient Greek word is said to have been first broadly introduced in Homer's *Odyssey*. The National Academy of Sciences guide *Advisor, Teacher, Role Model, Friend: On Being a Mentor to Students in Science and Engineering* (1997) characterizes the mentor as a wise and trusted counselor who is expected to protect and care for and assume a parent's patria position in the absence of one's paternal guardian. Reference is made to Homer's use of the concept mentor through the character Athena: "Athena, in the guise of Mentor, became the guardian and teacher of Odysseus's son Telemachus." Marian Wright Edelman (1999) notes the special role of Mentor in her most recent book *Lanterns: A Memoir to Mentors*. Edelman acknowledges the role assumed by Athena when she impersonates Mentor, the faithful friend of Odysseus. Athena inspires and imparts wisdom and encouragement to Telemachus as he departs for unknown challenges on his way to find his father (p. xvii). Contemporary mentors serve in this same capacity. They provide guidance, support, and direction to protégés who may lack the foresight, exposure, or intuition needed to attain certain goals.

Whether the founders of historically black colleges were familiar with Homer's conception of mentor is neither known nor documented. What is known is that HBCUs have been in the business of developing students through informal and formal mentorship programs for the past 150 or more years. Although educational opportunities have changed for blacks in that time, 16 percent of all black college and university students who choose to attend college select historically black institutions. Today, 103 institutions, varying in size, geography, and emphasis, exist to primarily educate African American students.[2] Students attending these institutions range from those who could, on the basis of college entrance examination scores and high school grade point averages, attend any school in the United States to those whose test scores and high school grade point averages mandate remediation at some level. Students representing every socioeconomic level walk the campuses of these 103 institutions. Young women and men who are world travelers, together with those who have never traveled beyond their local communities, take their places at these institutions. Young men and women who know nothing but low expectations come together with those for whom excelling is the only expectation. Students ranging from those with parents who hold the highest graduate and professional degrees to those with parents who did not complete high school come to these institutions in search of the intellectual and personal tools that will enable them to achieve goals that many of their parents and guardians could only imagine. Unlike 150 years ago, they do not come freshly emerged from shackles and legal segregation. However, many do come as by-products of de jure integrated but de facto bifurcated school systems that resulted in inferior educational experiences. HBCUs recognize the varying experiences of their students and await their arrival each year as they continue the legacy of their founders to make a way out of no way for some and to provide platforms for reaching the highest heights for others. This chapter will focus on successful mentoring strategies employed at historically black colleges and universities. Specific attention will be placed on informal and formal mentorship structures. The success stories of selected HBCUs will frame the entire analysis as we examine specific cases and look more broadly at the impact of mentoring on students within the United Negro College Fund institutions.[3]

The success of these institutions cannot be discussed without a parallel discussion of the impact of formal and informal mentoring structures. Mentorship models can be developed in any institutional structure. Effective mentorship models within

---

[2]Statistical data taken from position paper developed by William Gray, President United Negro College Fund, *Washington Post,* 1997.

[3]United Negro College Fund institutions are historically black private, primarily liberal arts institutions. There are thirty-nine (39) institutional members.

HBCUs share one very important characteristic—a sincere belief in the ability of students of African descent to succeed against all odds. Students entering historically black institutions are made to believe that higher education is their destiny and that there are faculty and staff who inhabit the halls of the academy who will guide and assist them as they journey together. This belief and faith have sustained historically black institutions, their faculty, staff, students, and graduates for the past 150 years.

The Success Story of HBCUs

> In short, he was there for us through thick and thin, focused not just on our learning in the classroom but on our learning to stand up and feel empowered to act and change our own lives and the community and region in which we lived. He taught us to be neither victims nor passive observers of unjust treatment but active and proud claimants of our American birthright.
>
> —Marian Wright Edelman, *Lanterns: A Memoir to Mentors,* 1999, p. 32

The above quote reflects Marian Wright Edelman's memory of a significant mentorship relationship she shared with Professor Howard Zinn, a professor of history at Spelman College. Ms. Edelman, an alumna of Spelman College and President of the Children's Defense Fund, shares her memories of three very special mentors she had while a student at Spelman College: Professor Howard Zinn, Dr. Benjamin Elijah Mays (former President of Morehouse College), and Charles Merrill (a benefactor of both Spelman and Morehouse Colleges).

When speaking of the impact of Dr. Mays on her life, Ms. Edelman reflects on the many lectures, discussions, and both formal and informal interactions he provided during her tenure as a student at Spelman College. Lessons on life, service, and passionate commitment to uplift the race, to social change, and to excellence framed these interactions. Dr. Mays believed in his students and their abilities to overcome obstacles associated with racial segregation and injustice.

Her experience under the mentorship of Charles Merrill affirms the reality that mentorship relationships can occur between black students and white mentors. Mr. Merrill, a white wealthy benefactor of Spelman and Morehouse Colleges, has supported the institutions in many ways but has placed particular importance on study abroad. Mr. Merrill believed that intellectual and personal transformation is tied to one's ability to escape provincialism and create a worldview. Since the late 1960s, Mr. Merrill has annually provided scholarship funds to Spelman and Morehouse Colleges to support study-abroad opportunities. Marian Wright Edelman studied in Europe as a Merrill scholar. When reflecting on her relationship with Mr. Merrill, she recounts that as a recipient of the Merrill scholarship, "Charles E. Merrill, Jr. opened up the world to me . . . he did not just give me a scholarship; he gave himself in long conversations, letters and visits" (1999, pp. 32–33). Marian Wright Edelman observes that although students need mentors with whom they can identify on racial, cultural, and social levels, this view nevertheless coexists with the fact that all people, regardless of race, class, and gender, have something to share and to teach. The success of a mentorship relationship rests less in the ability of one to mirror by race and gender the one being mentored and more in the spirit of support and belief in the ability to accomplish a transformation in the one being mentored (1999, p. 34). Interracial mentorship relationships can be and often are just as effective as intraracial relationships. It is important to bear in mind, however, that the mentor is not a missionary, but a guide who will gain in direct proportion to his or her commitment to share.

Any roll call of successful African American leaders of the twentieth century will almost without exception be accompanied by a roll call of allegiances or connections to some historically black college or university. Although HBCUs enroll only about 16 percent of all African American college students, one-third of all African American college graduates who receive an undergraduate degree receive it from a historically black institution (Gray, 1997).

Although more African American college-bound students attend historically white institutions, the persistence rate of African American students at historically black institutions is greater than at historically white institutions. These rates can actually be explained by a number of factors. Retention begins at admission. The standards for admission vary from institution to institution. However, historically white institutions with significant populations of black students generally will admit black students whose entrance credentials would suggest a strong chance of academic success.

When analyzing the impact of affirmative action strategies in higher education, Bowen and Bok (1998) found that among highly selective historically white institutions, "the large majority of these black applicants handily outscored not only the average black test-taker, but also the average white test-taker" (p. 18). They do, however, acknowledge that there was still a difference of approximately 186 points between the average SAT score of white admittees and black admittees. Thus, white college students attending highly selective institutions on average score about 186 points higher than their black counterparts attending these highly selective institutions. Remembering that the average represents a combination of the lowest and highest scores affirms that these black students, in most cases, have many other white counterparts attending the same institution with very similar SAT profiles. Were these students white there would arguably be no adverse assumption about their abilities. The most significant finding of the Bowen and Bok (1998) research is that the black students who persist at these institutions and graduate often find more varied and meaningful ways in their post-graduate years to contribute to society than their white counterparts (p. 281). Even in the face of this reality, many African American students attending historically white institutions are made to feel as if they do not belong or that they are only there because of affirmative action. It is assumed by many faculty members that their presence necessitates some form of remediation and/or reduction in standards. This myth often impedes the potential for developing effective mentorship structures for African American students attending historically white institutions. The perpetuation of this myth often results in a missionary approach to mentorship rather than a collegial approach. Interracial mentorship opportunities are often lost because of mutual assumptions made by potential mentors and students of color. Barriers to effective interracial mentorship must be addressed by our historically white institutions.

When surveying colleges across the country to determine the best fit for African American students, *Black Enterprise* magazine (1999–2001) has listed historically black institutions for the past two years as the number one destinations for African American students. Spelman College and Morehouse College have traded the number one positions for the past two years.

More than fifteen years ago, the subject of black student adjustment was the theme of a book authored by Jacqueline Fleming, entitled *Blacks in College* (1984). Fleming's research yielded several interesting conclusions. Most prominent among them was the issue of "fit." A student must believe that he or she belongs. Student success is tied to the level of engagement in the academic as well as nonacademic realms. Fleming's research concluded that one major factor lacking for African American students at historically white institutions is the absence of an abundance of role models who look like them. This absence is compounded by the reality that oftentimes at these institutions minority faculty members are in such demand that their ability to develop strong mentorship ties with minority students is compromised. The video documentary *Shattering the Silence* (Nelson, Stanley, & Pellett, 1997) speaks of the cultural tax placed upon minority faculty in majority institutions. Because of their race and/or ethnicity, they are placed on numerous committees, serve on all diversity initiatives, advise minority students, and attempt to remain engaged in scholarly pursuits. Given this consuming web of responsibility, it is sometimes difficult for these faculty to develop quality mentorship relationships with students. In many ways they are experiencing the same sense of the "other" as their students. This is not to suggest that this is always the case or that it is impossible for nonminority faculty to serve as mentors. It is quite common in historically black institutions and historically white institutions alike for students to develop mentorship relationships with nonminority faculty.

Successful mentorship is not an exclusive property of historically black institutions nor is it the sole province of faculty/student relationships that are intraracial. The fact is that many of our HBCUs are actually more racially diverse than historically white institutions. According to Bill Gray, President of the United Negro College Fund, "eleven percent of students attending historically black institutions are white compared with the 6 percent of students at other colleges who are black. About 20 percent of faculty at historically black institutions are white, while only 2 percent of faculty at other colleges are black" (1997). Thus, mentoring at historically black institutions is often occurring between a non-African American faculty member and an African American student. This is an important point because some faculty at historically white institutions might incorrectly assume that they are incapable of forming mentorship relationships with minority students because of racial or ethnic differences. One key difference between the mentoring that occurs between white faculty members on historically black college campuses and black students is that the white faculty members do not operate within environments that question the presence of these students on their campuses. White faculty teaching at historically black institutions are confronted daily with the reality that not only do the students belong at the institution, but that they are a legacy of thousands of achievers who have come before them.

Xavier University

Xavier University in New Orleans, a historically black university and a member of the United Negro College Fund, has achieved the rank of the number one institution in the nation for sending women of African descent to medical school. Spelman College is number two in the nation. Xavier University is also recognized as providing the most African American physics, chemistry, and biology graduates in the country. When asked to explain the success formula at Xavier, faculty and staff refer to the expressed belief in their students' ability to succeed. Their approach has been characterized as the "nurture and assist" model (Fletcher, 1997). This is a recognized mentorship model.[4] The philosophy of nurture and assist is embraced at the top by the president and woven throughout the fabric of the institution. President Norman Francis is quoted as saying, "It is not who comes in. What is important is who graduates from the institution" (Fletcher, 1997).

At Xavier, as well as most of the HBCUs, mentorship is tied to the formal advising program as well as other programs that are specifically designed as mentorship programs. Mentorship relationships are developed through the formal advising structures that exist at these institutions that pair students with a faculty advisor representing their intended major upon entry. Faculty advisors are strongly and continuously encouraged to get to know their advisees beyond the perfunctory information about class scheduling and course sequencing. Students in Xavier's premedical program are required to check in with advisors on a weekly basis to give progress reports.[5]

The use of peer mentorship programs is quite active at Xavier University, as well as other at historically black institutions. Peer mentors sometimes represented as upper division students are paired with incoming students. These peer mentors are pursuing the same majors and careers as their mentees. Structured and unstructured opportunities for the peer mentoring engagements to occur are created

---

[4]It is quite common for historically black institutions to use the verb *to nurture* to describe the intrusive guidance provided to their students. For some, the expectation of nurturing is often debated within the discussion of how to best prepare students for the real world where individuals may not be as committed to ensuring their success.

[5]Information obtained from telephone interview with Dr. Elizabeth Barron, Vice President of Academic Affairs, at Xavier University (August 30, 2002).

throughout the academic year. Peer mentors serve as guides for their younger coun-terparts as they navigate not only the academic environment but the social environ-ment as well.

Xavier, like other historically black institutions, adopts the African proverb, "It takes a village to raise a child." Historically black institutions believe that it takes an entire community to ensure the success of their students, and they are keenly aware of some of the impediments to academic success facing their students. Per-sonal and social adaptation concerns are recognized and addressed through formal and informal mentorship networks. It is not uncommon for professors at HBCUs to become connected to parents and other family members of students if the need arises.

In addition, parental influence is quite significant in the equation for academic success. Parent orientation sessions at many HBCUs focus on how best to gain co-operation from parents as the institution "assumes the driver's seat" in their children's lives. This is quite necessary because often, until the point of college entry, the parents/guardians have been the most significant mentors in the student's life.

Spelman College

At Spelman College, women are told at the point of entry that they are expected to occupy the spectrum of the professional ranks and to take on the role of social change agents throughout their world communities. They are told that they are the chosen ones to take on the mantle of the thousands of outstanding women who have preceded them. In addition to faculty advising, several structured mentorship pro-grams have been designed to ensure a successful transition through and after col-lege. Spelman College is among the top ten institutions in the country to send African American women on to graduate and professional schools. Effective advis-ing and faculty/student research mentorships and peer mentorship programs con-tinue to support initiatives designed to increase the number of Spelman women in graduate and professional schools.

In the sciences, Spelman women are expected to fully immerse the ranks of science professionals as doctors, scientific researchers, and public health profession-als. Students are exposed to research and research mentors very early in their ca-reers. The Office of Health Careers and Science departments coordinate mentorship activities. The Spelman Women in Science and Health (SWSH) organization is a mentorship program that pairs students with health professionals. Aside from at-tending special seminars, the students shadow the health professionals during the academic year and summer months. Alumnae science and medical professionals are brought to campus to speak to students to share their stories. It is also quite common for alumnae to form mentorship relationships with Spelman students. Some of these relationships are through structured initiatives within the Health Careers Office, while others are unstructured. In addition, peer mentoring takes place through a big sister program. Senior and junior health career majors sign up in the Health Careers Office to serve as big sisters to first- and second-year students.

The National Science Foundation designated Spelman College as a Model Institution for Excellence (MIE) in 1994. This recognition was granted in response to Spelman's success rate in producing students pursuing graduate degrees in the areas of science. Funding was specifically targeted to help strengthen the science infrastructure to augment support for curriculum and activities to increase the number of students majoring in the sciences and going on to pursue graduate degrees. A very special component of the MIE grant to the institution was an internship program that pairs students with faculty in research projects. These faculty/student collaborations allow for mentoring relationships that sustain students throughout their tenure as undergraduates and when they enter graduate schools. A similar program exists within the mathematics department. The Center for Engineering, Science, and Mathematics (CESAM) pairs students interested in math, engineering, and science with faculty engaged in research in these areas. In addition to exposing students to more in-depth research of a topic, faculty/student research mentorship programs create opportunities for faculty and students to work in a collegial manner around common interests. These relationships conform to the standard conceptual definitions of mentoring. The faculty mentor serves as a guide and/or guardian of the student as she develops and navigates the challenges and opportunities associated with the pursuit of higher education.

Throughout the Spelman environment, students and faculty work closely together in various configurations of mentorship. Spelman College established a research associates program several years ago with funding from the Pew Charitable Trust Fund and then later through the Eli Lily Foundation. The Research Associates Program was created as another version of faculty/student mentorship centered on scholarly research. Faculty from all disciplinary areas were provided with an opportunity to have a student serve as a research assistant. Generally, faculty preparing for the tenure review process were given first pairing priority. The program had a two-fold mission—to assist junior faculty in their pursuit of tenure and to establish a vehicle to strengthen student engagement with faculty. The work of Jacqueline Fleming (1984) noted the significance of student engagement with faculty as a major contributor to student persistence and retention.

Spelman women interested in social science research are offered opportunities to participate in a number of mentorship/research programs including the MBRS (Minority Biomedical Research Support), MARC-HURT (Minority Access to Research Careers, Honors Undergraduate Research Program), and NIMH-COR (National Institute of Mental Health-Career Opportunities in Research) programs designed for students interested in pursuing careers in mental health. MARC is a program designed for students interested in pursing careers in biomedical, natural, and social science research. These programs pair students with faculty mentors engaged in research in the respective areas. Students involved in these research programs form significant relationships with faculty researchers engaged in cutting-edge projects. These programs are crafted to intellectually and personally invigorate students. The mentoring associations follow them through their undergraduate careers and beyond.

Spelman College has also taken advantage of the external corporate environment in the development of mentorship programs. The former Corporate Mentors Program paired students with corporate executives throughout the city of Atlanta. Students would shadow corporate executives during business hours, attend special events hosted by the corporations, visit their corporate mentors in their homes, and participate in various facets of the corporate mentors' lives in order to gain full exposure to the life of corporate executives. Students were selected in their junior year and participated in the program to the point of graduation.[6]

Morehouse College

Morehouse College has produced African American leaders representing all occupational sectors of society. One of the most famous graduates of Morehouse College is Martin Luther King, Jr. During his tenure at Morehouse College, Benjamin Elijah Mays served as President. Dr. Mays was President of Morehouse for twenty-seven years, from 1940 to 1967. He was considered the consummate mentor to generations of Morehouse men. One could even say that the often-touted "Morehouse Mystique" was created during the tenure of Benjamin Elijah Mays.

Martin Luther King, Jr., Morehouse class of 1948, considered Benjamin Elijah Mays as a primary mentor. In reflecting on his role as a mentor to Martin Luther King, Jr., Dr. Mays wrote:

> Many times during his four years at Morehouse, he would linger after my Tuesday morning address to discuss some point I had made—usually with approval, but sometimes questioning or disagreeing. I was not aware how deeply he was impressed by what I said until he wrote, *Stride Toward Freedom,* in which he indicated that I had influenced his life to a marked degree. In public addresses, he often referred to me as his spiritual mentor. (Carter, 1996)

This quote from Dr. Mays demonstrates that mentorship can be so informal that unstructured interactions between students and faculty and administrators can yield the same level of mutual bonding and engagement as very formal structured mentorship programs.

Today, Morehouse College continues in the tradition of Dr. Mays and other leaders preceding and succeeding him. The overall guiding principle remains to produce men who are prepared to take on our nation's and world's challenges in all arenas. Structured mentorship programs pair students with faculty and alumni of the

---

[6]The Spelman College Corporate Mentorship Program was a private grant-funded initiative that was supervised by a former member of the Spelman College administrative staff. Efforts to restore the program are being discussed and planned.

institution. The Crown Forum Series is a speaker series designed to expose students to world leaders who are effecting social change in all sectors. These sessions help to provide a foundation for mentorship activities that occur at a variety of levels from faculty/student relationships to peer mentoring and alumni mentoring networks.

In addition to being successful in producing graduates who go on to excel in a variety of disciplinary areas, Morehouse has also been able to successfully prepare students for one of the most prestigious scholarships in the world—the Rhodes scholarship. During the past decade, two Morehouse men have been selected as Rhodes scholars. A mentorship model frames the early identification of potential Rhodes scholarship recipients. These young men are identified by the administration by way of faculty/staff recommendations. They are attached to a faculty or staff person such as the Vice President for Academic Programs and the mentorship or "grooming" commences. Much like Athena, the mentor serves as a guide to the potential scholar. The guide exposes the student to opportunities and relationships that will help to facilitate his preparation for the Rhodes competition.

Morehouse College also inaugurated an Executive Mentorship Program several years ago. The program based in the departments of Economics and Business focuses "on educating students to the changing expectations of leadership in the coming decades" (Harris, 1996, p. 6). The Executive Mentorship Program functions very much like the former Spelman College Corporate Mentorship program. The corporate mentor exposes the student to all facets of corporate culture and life. Students and their corporate mentors interact within both the business and home environments.

At Morehouse, just as with other historically black institutions, faculty advisors often become mentors to their advisees. While obviously not confined to HBCUs, faculty advising at these schools nevertheless receive high priority. It is impressed upon faculty that they often are the most influential adults in students' lives during their matriculation. Students depend on them for academic as well as personal guidance in many instances.

Andrew Mellon Minority Undergraduate Fellowship Program (MMUF)

Historically black institutions are responsible for producing a disproportionate share of graduates going on to pursue doctoral degrees. Although only about 16 percent of black students attend HBCUs, nearly 45 percent of those obtaining doctoral degrees are graduates of historically black institutions. These statistics represent students who were identified by faculty and/or staff and encouraged to dream dreams and pursue goals that might otherwise never have been considered as options (Gray, 1997).

Within the past ten years, many of these individuals have been beneficiaries of the Andrew Mellon Foundation Mellon Minority Undergraduate Program. The

UNCF/Mellon Minority Undergraduate Program, based at Spelman College, is a mentorship program for minority students interested in pursuing a Ph.D. in the areas of the humanities, mathematics, physics, anthropology, and sociology. Student fellows at UNCF institutions are a part of the UNCF/Mellon Fellows Program. In any given year, a total of fifty undergraduates attending various UNCF institutions are involved in mentorship activities with faculty members on their campuses whose primary goal is to create a new generation of Ph.D.s.

The overall premise of the Mellon Minority Undergraduate Fellowship Program is that if students are mentored early in their careers as undergraduates, they will be better prepared to enter graduate school and better prepared to persist in graduate school. Interested students are selected during the second semester of the sophomore year. Each is paired with a faculty mentor who is responsible for working with the student to assist the student in the pursuit of the Ph.D. The student and faculty mentor work together on a major research project. Together, they identify a topic, develop a bibliography, and prepare a scholarly research paper that is reflective of their particular area of inquiry. Faculty mentors are expected to provide opportunities for students to gain classroom experience by preparing and delivering a lecture or leading a discussion. Also, the faculty mentor works with the student to identify graduate schools and is expected to help facilitate graduate school visitations. Mentors and students attend conferences together and make joint presentations. In addition, student fellows spend the summer between their sophomore and junior years at a summer institute designed to expose them to the life of scholarly activity. Fellows develop research prospectuses under the supervision of graduate student mentors and faculty directors. They interact with graduate student mentors throughout the summer institute and learn the language and experiences of graduate school education. In the summer between the junior and senior years, fellows are provided a stipend of $3,000 to use toward the furtherance of their scholarship or graduate school preparation. During each academic year of the fellowship, stipends are provided for the student fellow and the mentors.

The UNCF/Mellon Undergraduate Fellowship Programs enjoy a phenomenal success rate. Since its inception in 1989, eight students attending UNCF institutions have received Ph.D.s. Another 45 are in the pipeline to receive Ph.D.s within the next several years. Seventeen have received the masters degree, with 25 pending M.A. degrees. Mellon Minority Undergraduate Fellows throughout the UNCF network have benefited from the close one-on-one guidance from faculty mentors. These fellows will assume their roles in our nation's institutions of higher education as faculty who know the power and influence of successful mentoring relationships with students.

The UNCF/Mellon Undergraduate Fellowship Program is probably one of the most successful mentorship programs not specifically targeting students majoring in the biological or physical sciences. The linchpin to the program's formula for success has been the early identification of interested students and the subsequent pairing of these students with interested faculty teacher/scholars. Its formal structure replicates informal structures that have prevailed throughout HBCUs for over a century.

Mentorship models like the Mellon Minority Undergraduate Fellowship program are easily duplicated and adapted for various interest areas and functions. Currently, nineteen of the thirty-nine UNCF institutions have faculty and students participating in the mentorship program. Mentors and coordinators come together once per year to share their mentorship stories and to celebrate the accomplishments of their protégés.

The UNCF/Mellon Programs are a subset of Mellon Minority Undergraduate Programs operating at thirty-four historically white colleges and universities, including the University of Cape Town in South Africa. Operating under the same principles of faculty-student research partnerships, the total number of Ph.D.s produced by the UNCF and MMUF programs will approach 100 at the end of the 2002–2003 academic year.

Proven Successes and Strategies

A review of the data and anecdotal information provided in this chapter points to some very specific themes that support effective mentorship models at historically black institutions.

Connection to College Mission

The most effective initiatives in higher education are those that can be traced to the mission and purpose of the institution. Seamless ties to the mission of an institution provide very clear blueprints for implementation of programmatic efforts. Although the term mentorship does not appear in the mission statements of these institutions, inherent in their institutional structures is the framework for informal and formal mentorship opportunities. A commitment to successful mentoring has been imbedded in the institutional infrastructure of historically black institutions.

Appreciation for Diversity

A second significant theme is the recognition and appreciation for the diversity that exists within the African American student populations that inhabit HBCUs. Students representing varying secondary educational experiences, class, and cultural experiences come together at these institutions to pursue a singular goal of reaching beyond their dreams. They wish to exceed the experiences of those who preceded them. Faculty and staff at historically black institutions prepare to meet these students where they are and expose them to the knowledge, skills, experiences, and expectations of their chosen disciplinary and career interests. Faculty and staff come prepared to serve multiple roles as teachers, role models, counselors, and confidants to these students. The institutions commit to aiding students in their quests to live out their destinies. Successful mentoring strategies must be sufficiently adaptable to respond to the diversity of an ever-changing student population.

Faculty/Student Scholarly Engagement

The third theme that resonates among the various mentoring programs at HBCUs is the intellectual engagement and exchange between faculty mentors and students. It is quite significant that most of the mentoring programs discussed in this chapter focus on student/faculty research mentorships. The dual and mutual benefits of these partnerships help to sustain the interest of both faculty and student participants. Mentorship initiatives at HBCUs do not exist solely for the growth and development of the student. Faculty participants experience intellectual and personal growth from these associations as well.

Mentorship Support Structures

A fourth theme relates to the supporting activities that provide firm foundations for successful mentoring. Speaker series, special seminars, and shadowing experiences all enhance mentorship programs. Students also benefit greatly from small informal group discussions with mentors. It is the informal interactions that are sometimes the most meaningful to students and faculty/staff participants.

External Resources Support

A fifth theme focuses on the use of external sources of support to sustain mentorship initiatives. Alumni, corporate executives, and friends of the college can all provide guidance and support to students. These groups are often in search of opportunities to give back to their communities. Mentorship programs become mutually beneficial investments.

Peer Mentorship

Last, but certainly not least, is the value of peer mentors. Peer mentoring programs are quite successful. The pairing of upper division students with lower division students is successful on a number of levels. Students often feel more comfortable expressing their anxieties and concerns with peers. These peer mentors are able to share their experiences navigating curricular requirements, finding research programs, and identifying faculty/staff mentors. Successful mentoring strategies are guided by the assumption that students can excel. Mentors must demonstrate a sincere belief in the student's ability to succeed. Successful mentoring strategies employ the "nurture and assist" philosophy apparent throughout the many successful initiatives at Xavier University, Spelman College, and Morehouse College.

Concluding Thoughts

Mentorship is a term that is widely used in a variety of settings. Although the focus of this chapter has been effective mentorship strategies at the undergraduate level, mentorship models exist outside of academia. It is quite common to hear of corporate mentorship programs for junior level employees. Many national professional and social organizations have established mentorship programs for elementary and high school students. When one examines the proliferation of mentorship programs and various models, the common denominator that links all programs together is the intention to create opportunities for those whose history and/or experience has not guaranteed equal access. Thus, whether the impediment to access is based on race, class, gender, exposure, perceived intelligence, or skill, mentorship programs are effective mechanisms to help navigate the playing field.

At historically black institutions, structured and unstructured mentorship programs have sustained, supported, and propelled thousands of African American students to positions of leadership and authority in our nation's classrooms, courtrooms, hospitals, and corporate boardrooms. Internal and external mentors have accepted the call to "lift as they climb." In doing so, they have ensured that generations that follow will be able to accept the baton and continue a great tradition of mentorship.

This chapter has focused on the history of mentorship models within the historically black college community. Historical and contemporary models have been discussed and highlighted. The most successful programs succeed using a variety of mentorship structures. As historically white institutions continue to define and develop their own mentorship structures, the following components should be considered:

- Faculty advising structures that require monthly interaction with advisees.
- Peer mentorship programs pairing upper division students with first- and second-year students.
- Parent orientation programs that effectively introduce parents to the expected academic and social experiences of their sons and daughters.
- Faculty/student research partnerships that are mutually beneficial.
- Professional mentors representing selected career areas of students.
- Alumni/ae mentorship programs pairing students with alums representing similar academic career interests.
- Graduate school mentorship structures involving graduate students at all levels.

REFERENCES

Bowen, W. G., & Bok, D. (1998). *The shape of the river: Long term consequences of considering race in college and university admissions.* Princeton, NJ: Princeton University Press.

Carter, L. (Ed.). (1996). *Walking integrity: Benjamin Elijah Mays, mentor to generations.* Scholars Press.

Drewry, H. N., & Doerman, H. (2000). *Stand and prosper: Private black colleges and their students.* Princeton, NJ: Princeton University Press.

Edelman, M. W. (1999). *Lanterns: A memoir to mentors.* Boston: Beacon Press.

Fleming, J. (1984). *Blacks in college.* San Francisco: Jossey-Bass.

Fletcher, M. A. (1997, May 10). "Xavier's desk-side manner is prescription for medical school: Small black college nurtures achievement." *Washington Post,* p. A2.

Gray, W. H. (1998, July 9). "The case for all-black colleges." Response to 6/29/98 *Wall Street Journal* article by Christina Duff. *Washington Post.*

Harris, A. (1996, Fall/Winter). Mentoring a priority at Morehouse. *The Alumnus,* 6.

National Academy of Sciences. (1977). *Advisor, teacher, role model, friend: On being a mentor to students in science and engineering.* Washington, DC: National Academy Press.

Nelson, S., Stanley, W., & Pellett, R. (1997). *Shattering the silences* (video documentary). New York: Ford Foundation.

4 Strategies for Effective Oral Communication

Marshalita Sims Peterson
Spelman College

Oral communication skills may be viewed as "curriculum as conversation," highlighting the significance of effective skills of sending and receiving messages. Curriculum implementation as "conversation" constitutes process and application linked to communication style, rhetorical structure, content presentation, and cultural contexts in the educational domain. Curriculum implementation is useful only when the sharing of information is facilitated and enhanced by true and meaningful exchange of ideas specific to content and pedagogy. Pedagogical philosophy, however, must speak to *culturally relevant pedagogy* and, ultimately, communication and linguistic differences relating to African American students in higher education. It is critical to note that "cultural connections" between students and teachers reflect "communication connections" and provide the impetus for the teaching and learning process. Studies indicate an increase in academic achievement of students when instruction is modified and congruent with the cultures and communication styles of culturally diverse students. Cultural mismatch theory suggests that when communication between the student and teacher is not culturally congruent, there can be adverse outcomes for students. This cultural mismatch or incongruence is a significant factor relating to academic achievement of African American students.

Effective teaching practices *must* include culturally relevant pedagogy for African American students. Ladson-Billings (1995a, 1995b) associates culturally relevant pedagogy with a critical "pedagogy" that empowers students intellectually, socially, emotionally, and politically. Cultural referents are used to impart knowledge, skills, and attitudes. Applebee (1996) identifies education as a process of mastering new traditions of discourse, including sharing information and understanding the roles and relationships of home, school, and community. Often, the components of communication, linking culture and the academy, become increasingly specialized and formal as a student moves through the education system with focus toward academic disciplines.

Marshalita Sims Peterson is Chair of the Department of Education at Spelman College, Atlanta, GA.

The most fundamental and important functions of schools are achieved through communication. Cazden (1988) notes three key reasons why communication is central to educational institutions:

> First, spoken language is the medium by which teaching and learning take place, and in which students demonstrate to teachers much of what they have learned. Second . . . the teacher is responsible for controlling all the talk that occurs while class is officially in session—controlling not just negatively, as a traffic police officer does to avoid collisions, but also positively, to enhance the purposes of education. . . . Third, and perhaps least obviously, spoken language is an important part of the identities of all the participants. (pp. 2–3)

While much attention is given to communication effectiveness at the younger levels (kindergarten through grade 12), equal focus is essential at the college/university level. The old paradigm of college education centered on the transfer of faculty knowledge to passive students. There was little acknowledgment of the individual student specific to his or her experiences, culture, learning style, or communication patterns. The new paradigm of college education views teaching as one way to help students actively construct their own knowledge and engage in communication of that knowledge through various avenues.

Communication is identified as the classic way in which humans make meaningful connections with each other. Communication must be embraced as a "notion of community," because there is a community among speakers and listeners. The social aspect of speaking and listening is consummated by effective communication as both the speaker and listener alternate from one role to another. Without communication, there can be no community. The higher education "community" identifies some common and wide-range expectations through general admissions requirements. Students, however, bring varying levels of communication, because social variations and culture impact communication competence and performance. One can easily be consumed by the "higher education setting" and devote little attention to critical elements of communicating with those of whom professors serve. Much focus can be given to "content" as opposed to the "presentation of content" during the weekly 50 to 75 minutes of instruction. As the facilitator and guide, the instructor has the key responsibility of effectively communicating the intended message. Teachers must demonstrate significant skill in communication to guide students toward meaningful discussions as contributors and even as leaders. The essential role of teachers is linked to communication, understanding and acknowledging communication styles of students, and curriculum implementation. Irvine (1990) argues for the importance of teachers' making a difference in the lives of students. She concludes that teachers are significant others in their students' lives, thereby affecting their achievement and self-concept, particularly African American students.

Effective communication in teaching requires that professors have a clear understanding of content and how to share the material with students in a way that they come to own and understand. Stronge (2002) states that communication of content in teaching is far more than just talking about objectives. Teachers must ensure that students are engaged in the two-way teaching and learning process. Ultimately, being an effective communicator is about repackaging and delivering a message so that the student can receive, respond, adapt, and use the information productively. Lisa Delpit (1995) stresses that education, at its best, hones and develops the knowledge and skills each student already possesses, while at the same time adding new knowledge and skills to that base. Delpit stresses that classroom learning should be structured such that students are able to strengthen their *communication* proficiencies and to share these with classmates and teachers.

Verbal skills are highly valued in the black community, because there is a rich oral tradition characterized by concrete narratives, episodic framework, action verbs, and prosodic structures. Students of all cultures bring to college varied experiences, different performance levels, as well as different communication competencies. It is clearly obvious that all African American students in higher education do not display identical oral communication skills, just as those skills vary with students of color during the kindergarten through twelfth-grade years. There are, however, key elements that appear to be central to effective communication and effective instruction for African American students in higher education. Strategies may be general enough for application to any student, yet specific enough to greatly impact the process of teaching and leaning particularly for African American students in higher education.

Theoretical Framework

A general definition of communication includes the transmission of ideas, thereby symbolizing a medium of interaction. Human communication is identified as meaning occurring when individuals involved in the communicative event understand the intent underlying the words used. Socialization and meaning of communication involve a dynamic process. The basic communicative act identified by Zelko and Dance (1978) involves stimulus, perception, interpretation, decision, encoding, message, response, and channel. Gallagher (1991) identifies language as a primary means by which we make interpersonal contact, socialize, and regulate our interactions.

Porter and Samovar (1991) describe communication as a matrix of interacting social acts. These acts occur in a complex social environment that reflects the way people live and how they come to interact with and get along in their world. This social environment is culture, and if we are to truly understand communication, we must also understand culture (p. 10).

Anderson, Anderson, Ballentine, and Howes (1964) summarize the significance of oral communication skills: "The ability to use the spoken word to accurately communicate thought or express feeling is the most significant skill developed by individuals in the highly complex social organization of modern life"

(p. 45). Taylor (1990) defines communication as the act of sharing information involving a speaker and a receiver. The ability to communicate, to use language as a tool, is related to all aspects of living. Communication skills are relevant to communication competency. Communication competency reflects language and linguistic form in social behavior as a mode of action. The term *communication competence* was introduced by Hymes in 1967 and refers to all modes of social and grammatical behavior. The original meaning of competence proposed by Chomsky in 1957 indicated the speaker's knowledge of the rules requisite to appropriate language. Extension of communication competence includes knowledge of appropriate and effective language use in social contexts. Chomsky further defines communication competence as the speaker-hearer's knowledge of his or her language.

> The speaker-hearer is an autonomous individual in a completely homogenous speech community, who knows its language perfectly and is unaffected by such grammatically irrelevant conditions as memory limitations, distractions, shifts of attention and interest, and errors in applying his/her knowledge of the language in actual performance. (p. 3)

Geneva Smitherman (1977) associates communication competence with linguistic and semantic appropriateness and the ability to employ rhetorical strategies to create a desired mood or effect on the audience and to move that audience in the desired direction. Communication competence is also expanded to include a process through which interpersonal impressions are shaped. These interactions and satisfactory outcomes are derived from an interaction. Competence is related to actual performance and is characterized by four features: Competence depends upon one's available repertoire of experience; competence requires that the individual make critical choices from his or her repertoire; competence takes place when suitable behaviors are aligned with performing desirable tasks; competency is sustained when individuals can evaluate their performance behaviors objectively. Allen and Brown (1977) define communication competence as involving an awareness of the transactions that occur between people.

Scholars have highlighted concomitant terms of effectiveness, ability, and interaction. Sptizberg (1983) defines communication competence as an impression resulting from three perspectives, which are the context, behaviors of the relational interactions, and characteristics of the individuals involved. Such competence is dependent upon the participant's view during targeted situations or settings. Littlejohn and Jabusch (1982) define communication competence as the ability and willingness of an individual to participate responsibly in a transaction in such a way as to maximize the outcome of shared meaning. Duran (1983) defines communication competence as a function of one's ability to adapt to differing social constraints. He further details communication adaptability as the ability to perceive socio-interpersonal relationships and adapt one's interaction goals and behaviors.

Bochner and Kelly (1974) developed a model of interpersonal competence inclusive of three skills groups, including the ability to formulate and achieve an objective, the ability to collaborate effectively with others, and the ability to adapt appropriately to situational variations. Five observable skills include self-disclosure, descriptiveness, empathetic communication, owning feelings and thoughts, and behavioral flexibility.

Communication Models and Process

Four general skills are included in the communication process, including speaking, listening, reading, and writing. The act of oral communication involves three elements: the listener, the message, and the speaker. The listener is identified as the object of communication, or message decoder.

.The communication process is essential for understanding the relationship between communication effectiveness and communication. Varying models exist that encompass general factors of the communication process. Communication models have been presented by Berko, Wolvin, and Wolvin (1985). The *Linear Model of Communication* reflects a one-directional view of the communication process. The speaker encodes a message and sends it to a listener, who decodes the message. The speaker then observes specific desired responses from the listener. This model is a simple speaker-listener process. The *Interactional Model of Communication* represents increased and ongoing communication interaction. The speaker encodes a message and sends it to the receiver. The receiver decodes the message and provides feedback to the source. The Interactional Model is a two-directional process involving receiving, sending, and receiving in a continual manner. The source is aware of possible communitarian difficulties and responds to feedback. The *Transactional Model of Communication* is based upon communication transaction as a simultaneous transaction between participants. In this model, the communicators interchange roles through the communication act, constituting a multidirectional process. Both communicators serve as sender and receiver during the encoding and decoding transaction.

Communication research places emphasis on the sender-receiver concept, with the sender determining the desired behavior of the receiver. Focus is given to the outcome of the process and interactions. Person A represents the sender-encoder and Person B represents the receiver-decoder. Both persons bring their frames of reference to the communication interaction. Such reference or experiences are a compilation of the person's attitudes, values, education, and culture. For effective communication to occur, there is overlapping of both persons' experiences. Communication can occur at one or more levels in a system, including intrapersonal, interpersonal, organizational, and/or communication systems. Communication processes include acquiring, processing, generating, and/or disseminating.

Communication processing requires awareness of language usage and behavior for response and interaction. Additional elements needed for communication processing include adequate vocabulary and language compatibility, thereby accommodating perception and comprehension. Level and Galle (1988) elaborate on effective communication processing and contextual variables. These variables include the objective of the message, the relations needs of the sender and receiver, attitudes of the sender and receiver, receiver's time span of attention, and the relevant sociocultural system. DeVito (1985) defines communication as the act, by one or more persons, of sending and receiving messages that are distorted by noise, occur within a context, have some effect, and provide some opportunity for feedback. Universal elements of communication include context, source(s)-receiver(s), messages, noise, encoding processes, decoding processes, feedback, and effect.

Translation is the ability to put what you say in the most proper, fitting, assertive, and powerful words possible. The four basic elements of the communication process are content, coding, sending, and decoding. *Content* includes the specific components of vocabulary, sequencing, details, main idea, and summary. *Coding* refers to transforming the message into words associated with meaning. *Sending* involves transmitting the message. *Decoding* is the responsibility of the hearer, as it is in direct proportion to the effectiveness of the content, coding, and sending.

Speech and Language Components

Speech components include articulation, voice, and fluency skills. Language skills can be identified in three specific areas: content, form, and use. Language *content* emphasizes semantics, direction concepts, comprehension, and reasoning skills. Language *form* focuses on syntactical structure inclusive of grammatical context, sentence expansion, and complexity components. Language *use,* also termed *pragmatics,* highlights performance of language content and form in varying settings. Skill areas in language use include topic initiation, topic maintenance, topic relevance, eye contact, response appropriateness, conversation turn-taking, and social amenities.

Conversation

Conversation is a complex process that involves social and psychological objectives that are advanced by systematic strategies and discourse devices and cues that are critical to comprehension. Conversation is identified as a mutually structured activity between the speaker and the listener. Conversation, discussion, or "talk" is identified as the most important form of communication. Discussions are conversations with a definite and stated purpose that are guided or controlled in some way to achieve a prescribed goal. The complexity of socialization and the importance of conversation are significant variables to communication in the classroom setting. Applebee (1996) makes the connection between school and conversation. He asserts that academic settings should be organized to help students enter into culturally significant domains for conversations.

Ethos and Communication

Ethos is identified as the perceived degree of character or credibility that a person believes exists in another person or object. To develop one's ethos, a teacher must communicate effectively with his or her students in the classroom. Because communication involves interaction, the teacher's pedagogy or engagement of instruction must manifest itself through a communication process that helps the teacher to be perceived as credible (Nussbaum, 1992). Communication exchange is central to the speaker/listener construct, which impacts and most often dictates communication competence and comprehension in the classroom setting. Frymier and Thompson (1992) assert that whether at the conscious or unconscious level, the individual's perception of the teacher's credibility has a tremendous impact on both how he or she reacts to the teacher and on how effective the teacher will be as an educator and communicator.

Nonverbal Communication

More than 93 percent of the messages teachers send to students are nonverbal. The African American culture relies on nonverbal communication, which accompanies and confirms verbal communication. Effective communication depends on consistency among the component parts of the message including the words spoken, voice, face, eyes, and body. When the instructor's facial expressions, tone of voice, and bodily posture say one thing and his or her words say another, the words are disconnected. When body, voice, face, and words are synchronized, one's words are taken at face value. Maintaining eye contact denotes an interest and a desire to connect with students.

Stereotype Threat

Steele (1999) notes that *stereotype threat* is the threat of being viewed through the lens of a negative stereotype, or the fear of doing something that would inadvertently confirm that stereotype. Stereotype threat is associated with external variables, including the situational threat of being negatively stereotyped regarding intellectual functioning and communication skills. The experience for African American college students can be directly associated with communication performance and participation in the classroom. Students may feel an apprehension in the classroom to engage in conversation and contribute to class discussion based on direct or indirect communication messages from the teacher. An inviting classroom environment conveys a statement of support and value of students emphasizing a learner-centered approach. Examination of the Texas Learner-Centered Proficiencies includes Learner-Centered Communication. Key elements of this approach are applicable to the higher education setting for black students including:

- The teacher must demonstrate effective professional and interpersonal communication skills.
- The teacher must work to create an environment in which taking risks, sharing new ideas, and innovative problem solving are supported and encouraged.
- The teacher should be a compelling communicator, incorporating techniques of inquiry that promote communication in the classroom setting.

African American Culture and Communication

Boykin (1986) identifies nine interrelated dimensions of African American culture:

1. Spirituality, an approach that views life as essentially ritualistic rather than mechanistic, with the conviction that nonmaterial forces influence people's everyday lives.
2. Harmony, the notion that one's fate is interrelated with other elements in the scheme of things, such that humankind and nature are harmonically conjoined.
3. Movement, an emphasis on the interweaving of rhythm, percussiveness, music, and dance as central to psychological health.
4. Verve, a propensity for relatively high levels of stimulation and for action that is energetic and lively.
5. Affect, an emphasis on emotions and feelings together with a special sensitivity to emotional cues and a tendency to be emotionally expressive.
6. Communalism, a commitment to social connectedness, which includes an awareness that social bonds and responsibilities transcend individual privileges.
7. Expressive individualism, the cultivation of a distinctive personality and proclivity for spontaneous and genuine personal expression.
8. Oral tradition, a preference for oral and auditory modes of communication in which both speaking and listening are treated as performances and in which oral virtuosity (the ability to use alliterative, metaphorically colorful, graphic forms of spoken language) is emphasized and cultivated.
9. Social time perspective, an orientation toward time as passing through a social space rather than a material one, in which time is seen as recurring, personal, and phenomenological.

Examination of communication skills is critical to the dimensions of oral tradition, communalism, and expressive individualism. Effective communication, therefore, is dynamic in nature and in application. Dandy (1991) highlights three points specific to distinctive features of African American communication. First, there is variation among African American speakers. All African Americans do not use all of the distinctive features. Certain features may be prominent in the speech of African Americans indigenous to particular parts of the country and may not be found in the speech of others. Any given speaker may not use all the features all of the time, while another may use all of the features. Second, several of the features are shared with other dialects of English, including those spoken in the Caribbean, South America, the Sea Islands, the Appalachian Mountains, and various other regions of the United States. Last, distinctive features are not limited to syllables, words, and sounds, but also extend to how words are used and how they are interpreted by others, all of which relate to culture.

Gay (2000) asserts that culture provides the tools to pursue the search for meaning and to convey understanding to others. Communication, therefore, cannot exist without culture, culture cannot be known without communication, and teaching and learning cannot occur without communication or culture. To understand communication, one must understand culture. Culture is identified as the rule-governing system that defines the forms, functions, and content of communication. Communication is also governed by the rules of the social and physical contexts in which it occurs. Communication styles are systems of cultural notions and the means through which thoughts and ideas are expressively personified. The absence of shared communicative structures and discourse systems makes it difficult for culturally diverse students and teachers to genuinely comprehend each other and for students to fully display their intellectual abilities.

African American communication styles may be often characterized by overt demonstration of involvement through movement and sounds, a prescribed method for how performer and audience react, total involvement of the participants; the tendency to personalize by incorporating personal pronouns and references to self, and use of active verbs coupled with adjectives and adverbs with potential for intensification. Prosodic structure of speech often reflects the way information is organized for presentation. These observable aspects of African American communication style provide leads for teaching innovations (Anokye, 1997).

Strategies for Effective Communication/Discourse

Specific strategies for effective/enhanced communication for African American students in higher education include the following:

- Contextualization approach
- Interactive/Participatory approach
- Communal approach
- Paraphrasing and repetition
- Phrasing, pausing, and pacing
- Listening skills
- Topic discourse variance
- Nonverbal communication/Body language

Contextualization Approach

Contextualization clues refer to verbal and nonverbal signs that help speaking partners relate what is said during conversation to past experiences and presuppositions. Contextual cues facilitate speaking partners' highlighting some parts of conversation more saliently than others. Listeners can then assess what is really intended in the conversation. Professors should utilize contextual engagement involving personal connections, experiences, applications, associations, and referents. They should also create and cultivate a social context for increased communication and task engagement. Black students benefit from skill focus strategies, including components of vocabulary, main idea, details, and summary to facilitate problem solving and critical thinking. Problem solving and critical thinking are best facilitated through contextual engagement, because students are provided opportunities to absorb, process details, summarize, synthesize, and analyze information being presented.

Interactive/Participatory Approach

Student participation/engagement is most effective utilizing deliberate activities facilitating interaction. Interactive/participatory style of communication is one of the major communication styles among African Americans. This communication style is often referred to as *call-response*. Call-response reflects oneness, interdependence, and participation. Call-response seeks to bring together the speaker and the listener. Smitherman (1977) describes call-response as a spontaneous verbal and nonverbal interaction between speaker and listener in which all the speaker's statements (calls) are answered by expressions (responses) from the listener. The response may occur during the call or immediately after the call is given. Response provides acknowledgment. Without acknowledgment, communication does not exist (Asante, 1987). Call-response requires immediate feedback from students. Call-response is also an effective technique used by professors for establishing and maintaining rapport with students. Impromptu utterances should be recognized as opportunities for heightened classroom discourse for the community of speakers and listeners.

Communal Approach

Classroom context refers to the interaction among people in the setting. As the demands for participation vary from context to context, so may the conversation structures that facilitate communication in the classroom. The experience in the classroom should reflect a culture of learning and exchange, which supports a collective or common presence of cultural expressiveness. A group-centered approach promotes achievement and interaction among African American students, allowing for cooperation and collaboration. Professors must provide an environment where students feel safe voicing their opinions and asking questions for the purpose of fostering learning and critical thinking.

Paraphrasing and Repetition

Use of rewording/rephrasing assists in comprehension and facilitates listening, memory, and processing skills for both the student and professor. Restating information provides opportunities for expanded discussion of content prompting sharing, questioning, and analysis. Repetitions should be employed and not avoided as they facilitate intrinsic connections for students and most often naturally lead to enhanced listening. Use of repetition following paraphrasing signals an indicator of "impact," identifying key elements for content emphasis and accuracy.

Phrasing, Pausing, and Pacing

Phrasing and pausing are critical elements to listener processing and ultimately student engagement and participation. Professors utilizing effective phrasing strategies generally speak only *one* thought per sentence, pause, and say another sentence. Phrasing and pausing also facilitate the emphasis on important points and signal critical transitions between ideas and making connections. Variance of oral presentation speed (pace) is also critical to students internalizing and focusing on information presented. Studies indicate that most people can process approximately 750 words a minute. Since most people speak about 150 words a minute, it is essential that the professor avoids a belabored, monotonous pace and tone by varying the pace during presentation of information. Even though phrasing, pausing, repetition, and paraphrasing are significant to effective oral communication skills for African American students, it is critical that the professor is aware of the significance of pacing, employing appropriate rhythm patterns, including slowing down or gearing speed for content emphasis.

Listening Skills

Students generally spend a significant amount of time listening to the professor's lectures. A limited period of time may be allocated for discussion, which is often at the end of the class session. This highly structured, controlling, and authoritative method of teaching is more suitable for analytic learners and less suitable for global learners. Listening involves attention and focus, as well as expenditures of energy. Listening is not only the student's responsibility, but the professor's responsibility as well. Observation of student responses can guide the instructor to modify his or her presentation. The professor can facilitate increased communication and ultimately critical listening by assessing student responses in contextual remarks; identifying the main points; questioning; probing for expanded discourse, sequential structures and detail; and noting the relationship and sequence of information presented.

Topic Discourse Variance

Topic-centered discourse involves discussion of *one* issue during the timeframe/period of conversation. This strategy facilitates focused and engaged discussion.

Topic-centered discourse also involves arranging facts and ideas in logical, linear order from discrete to whole. *Topic chaining discourse* involves narrative linguistic style and elaboration. *Topic association discourse,* which is more complex, is episodic, thematic, enriching, and integrative. This discourse style involves creativity with embedded details. As communication is bidirectional, the professor should utilize topic-centered discourse, topic chaining discourse, and/or topic association discourse during class discussion for enhanced communication.

Nonverbal Communication/Body Language

Effective communication depends on consistency among *all* the component parts of the message. These components include the words spoken, voice, face, eyes, and body. When the professor's facial expression, tone of voice, and body posture say one thing and words say another, the words and meaning are discounted. This incongruity may be perceived by African American students as a disconnect relating to emotional content. One component of emotional content includes the student's assessment of the teacher's conviction. Does the teacher really believe what he or she is saying? Is the professor truly engaged in the exchange of information? When students judge the emotional content, they give much weight to vocal quality, facial expression, body movement, and words of the professor. When body, face, voice, and words are harmonized, the professor's words are received with greater validity. Body language does not play the lead role in communication, but it is significant to the overall element of effective communication for African American students.

Reflective Communication

A self-reflective approach, specific to communication skills, is essential to communication effectiveness and professional development. The intended message can be easily distorted by ineffectiveness in performance and use of content vocabulary, sequential construct, syntactical choices, rate of speech, fluency, intonation, and pragmatic components, all of which contribute to classroom discourse. General functional skills of communication include response clarity, response organization, content accuracy, voice production, descriptive language, volume control, topic maintenance, topic relevance, vocabulary adequacy, feedback response, fluency control, facial expression, eye contact, gesturing, and listening skills. The following descriptors provide a general self-assessment guide of indicators for oral and nonverbal communication skills.

- Response clarity: Distinctness and explicitness in verbal response facilitating comprehension for the listener.
- Response organization: Systematic arrangement in verbal presentation of content.

- Content accuracy: Concrete, precise discussion of information relating to preparation.
- Voice projection: Enthusiasm, expression, and vocal expression evidenced during conversation.
- Descriptive language: Adequacy in oral expression of persuasion, summation, qualifying content.
- Volume control: Degree of loudness or intensity of sound displayed during conversation.
- Topic maintenance: Continuance of discussion/conversation with elaboration of response.
- Topic relevance: Continuing conversation on related issues of discussion.
- Vocabulary adequacy: Inventory/Index of words and phrases within one's field of knowledge appropriate during conversation.
- Feedback response: Verbal/Nonverbal reaction to the message also involving comprehension elements and response clarity and organization.
- Fluency control: Smoothness of word phrasing during oral language.
- Facial expressions: Signals observed by facial appearance during conversation situations.
- Eye contact: Establishment of direct alignment of eye relationship between conversation participants.
- Gesturing: Motions of body links as a means of expressions and emphasis.
- Listening skills: Hearing with thoughtful attention for comprehension.

Concluding Thoughts

Presentation of content is facilitated by effective communication, which is an essential component of the teaching/learning process and curriculum implementation. Communication utilizing the following elements and strategies is most effective for African American students: contextualization approach, interactive/participatory approach, communal approach, paraphrasing and repetition, phrasing/pausing/pacing, listening skills, topic discourse variance, nonverbal communication/body language. Fundamental characteristics of teachers as effective communicators are essential to academic success of African American students in higher education. Teachers must be committed to the teaching and learning process and continually engage in reflection relating to culturally responsive pedagogy and curriculum implementation. They must be knowledgeable about the content and the students they teach. They must make content relevant and provide connections and meaningful linkages to student experiences. The effective teacher must also facilitate critical thinking, engage students in the learning process, and empower students to think. The effective teacher must encourage communication among students, facilitate contextualization, engage students in the process of inquiry and critical discourse, and give students a voice in the learning process.

Variability, presentation, and communication of content to African American students in higher education provide the foundation from which students are engaged and intellectually stimulated. These elements serve as a springboard, challenging students to incorporate critical thinking, problem solving, analysis, research, and reflection in the teaching and learning process. The enacted curriculum, reflective of communication with a purpose, lends itself to cognitive, social, intellectual transformations as a result of the interactions between students and teachers. It is therefore essential to utilize effective communication to *engage* the mind, not to merely persuade it.

REFERENCES

Allen, R. R., & Brown, K. L. (1977). *Developing communication competence in children*. Skokie, IL: National Textbook.

Anderson, V. D., Anderson, P. S., Ballentine, F., & Howes, V. M. (Eds.). (1964). *Reading in the language arts*. New York: Macmillan.

Anokye, A. D. (1997). A case for morality in the classroom. *The Clearing House, 70*(5), 229–231.

Applebee, A. (1996). *Curriculum as conversation*. Chicago: The University of Chicago Press.

Asante, M. K. (1987). *The Afrocentric idea*. Philadelphia: Temple University Press.

Berko, R., Wolvin, A., & Wolvin, D. (1985). *Communicating: A social and career focus* (3rd ed., Boston: Houghton Mifflin.

Bochner, A. P., & Kelly, C. W. (1974). Interpersonal competence: Rationale, philosophy, and implementation of a conceptual framework. *The Speech Teacher, 23*(4), 270–301.

Boykin, A. W. (1986). The triple quandary and the schooling of Afro-American children. In U. Neisser (Ed.), *The school achievement of minority children*. Hillsdale, NJ: Lawrence Erlbaum Associates.

Cazden, C. B. (1988). *Classroom discourse: The language of teaching and learning*. Portsmouth, NH: Heinemann.

Chomsky, N. (1957). *Syntactic structures*. The Hague: Morton.

Dandy, E. (1991). *Black communications: Breaking down the barriers*. Chicago: African American Images.

Delpit, L. (1995). *Other people's children: Cultural conflict in the classroom*. New York: The New Press.

DeVito, J. A. (1985). *Human communication: The basic course* (3rd ed.). New York: Harper & Row.

Duran, R. L. (1983). Communicative adaptability: A measure of social communicative competence. *Communication Quarterly, 31*, 320–326.

Erickson, H. (1972). *Communication and the technical manual*. Englewood Cliffs, NJ: Prentice Hall.

Frymier, A. B., & Thompson, C. A. (1992). Perceived teacher affinity-seeking in relation to perceive teacher credibility. *Communication Education, 41*, 399–399.

Gallagher, T. M. (1991). *Pragmatics of language: Clinical practice issues* (pp. 11–41). San Diego, CA: Singular Press.

Gay, G. (2000). *Culturally responsive teaching: Theory, research, and practice*. New York: Teachers College Press.

Howard, T. (2001). Powerful pedagogy for African American students: Case of four teachers. *Urban Education, 36*(2), 179–202.

Hymes, D. (1967). Models of the interaction of language and social setting. *Journal of Social Issues, 23*, 8–28.

Irvine, J. J. (1990). *Black students and school failure: Policies, practice, and prescriptions*. New York: Greenwood Press.

Ladson-Billings, G. (1995a). But that's just good teaching! The case for culturally relevant pedagogy. *Theory into Practice, 34*(3),159–165.

Ladson-Billings, G. (1995b). Toward a theory of culturally relevant pedagogy. *American Educational Research Journal, 32*(3), 465–591.

Level, D. A., & Galle, W. P. (1982). *Managerial communication.* Plano, TX: Business Publications.

Littlejohn, S., & Jabusch, D. (1982). Communication competence: Model and application. *Journal of Applied Communication Research, 10,* 29–36.

Nussbaum, J. F. (1992). Effective teacher behavior. *Communication Education, 41,* 167–180.

Porter, R. E., & Samovar, L. A. (1991). Basic principles of intercultural communication. In L. A. Samovar & R. E. Porter (Eds.), *Intercultural communication: A reader* (6th ed., pp. 5–22). Belmont, CA: Wadsworth.

Smitherman, G. (1977). *Talkin and testifyin.* Boston: Houghton Mifflin.

Spitzberg, B. H. (1983). Communication competence, knowledge, skill, and impression. *Communication Education, 32,* 324–327.

Steele, C. (1999). Stereotype threat and black college students. *Atlantic Monthly.*

Stronge, J. (2002). *Qualities of effective teachers.* Alexandria, VA: Association for Supervision and Curriculum Development.

Taylor, O. (1990). *Cross-cultural communication: An essential dimension of effective education* (2nd ed.). Washington, DC: Mid-Atlantic Center for Race Equity.

Zelko, H., & Dance, F. (1978). *Business and professional speech communication.* New York: Holt, Rinehart & Winston.

5

A Shared Role

Alternative Assessment of Student Learning at Historically Black Colleges and Universities

Joya Anastasia Carter
Georgia State University

Louis A. Castenell, Jr.
University of Georgia–Athens

> *For many years now, there are those of us who have charged that mass-produced standardized professional test and materials are ill suited to the needs of most African American students, in part because certain false assumptions are made about the students and their culture.*
>
> —Hilliard, 1997

As institutions of higher education (HE) confront the challenges of student assessment in a rapidly changing society, historically black colleges and universities (HBCUs) have an opportunity to lead the discussion in the twenty-first century. The transformation of society is placing a demand on HE to become more inclusive of

Joya Anastasia Carter is Assistant Professor of Inclusive Education at Georgia State University. Louis A. Castenell, Jr. is Dean of the College of Education at the University of Georgia.

serving students of underrepresented groups, and the HBCU perspective offers strategies of assessment that are paramount in embracing this influx of cultural diversity. The institutional climate within HBCUs provides an insightful framework for facilitating agendas that align assessment with current sociopolitical factors, historical and cultural reference points, and demographic societal change.

The 2000 Census reflects a dynamic change in the profile of U.S. society. Hodgkinson (2002) reports that by 2010 Latinos are projected to account for 43 percent of the U.S. population, the numbers of Asian and Pacific Islanders will increase by 64 percent in the next twenty years, and the numbers of African Americans and Native Americans will remain stable (i.e., African Americans 12% and Native Americans 1%). More than 60 percent of the population growth in the next twenty years will be Latinos and Asian, about 40 percent Latinos and 20 percent Asian. According to many demographers (Olson, 2000), the U.S. population could be so diverse by 2050 that no race or ethnic group would be a majority. A current illustration of this is California, which currently does not have a single majority group.

A review of literature indicates that these demographic trends directly impact today's PK–16 institutions in the form of an overwhelming correlation between the increasing diversity within schools and the increasing disparity in the existing achievement gap between white and minority students (Bainbridge & Lasley, 2002; English, 2002; Green, 2001). It is inferred that structures in (higher) education continue to operate from a traditional dominant paradigm—that is, isolation, independence, competition (Miller & Stayon, 1999)—and fail to use culturally responsive curriculum and assessment—that is, authentic practice, portfolio assessment (Huba & Freed, 2000)—in serving the growing diversity of students.

Recently, test companies such as Educational Testing Service (ETS) go on record asking institutions not to place heavy emphasis on their tests without considering other insightful indicators such as grade point average and authentic participation in schools and/or communities (Reising, 2000), thus acknowledging that standardized test and measures fail as reliable evaluations of performance and often sort students inappropriately. As we continue to change demographically, it will be increasingly necessary to identify multiple ways to assess varied talents and gifts, such as the naturalistic/authentic measures used at HBCUs.

The tradition of HBCUs is to cultivate alternative strategies for improving academic performance of African American students (Anderson, 1988). HBCUs are important resources, as evidenced by the fact that 40 percent of all African Americans who obtained undergraduate degrees received them from HBCUs (Garibaldi, 1991). These institutions have a long history of successfully teaching African American students who were said to be unprepared for higher education based on criteria for admission to most majority institutions. Perhaps Bertman (2000) stated it best, ". . . what one group sees and cherishes, another fails to recognize; what is important to some is meaningless to others" (pp. 105–106).

The vast majority of African American leaders who now serve on state boards, in local and national government, as CEOs in the private sectors, in the U.S.

Presidential Cabinet, and as higher education faculty graduated from HBCUs. Wagener and Nettles (1998) report that 35 percent of the African Americans who have obtained terminal degrees attended an HBCU for baccalaureate studies. For example, African Americans make up 8 percent of all full-time university faculty; half of these people are employed at HBCUs. The proportion of black faculty at majority white institutions is 2.3 percent, virtually the same as twenty years ago (Wilson, 2002). Concomitantly, the number of African American and Latino undergraduates in major institutions has increased over the past decade by 32 percent and 98 percent respectively (Nettles & Perna, 1997). However, retention and graduation rates remain low when compared to others (Carter & Wilson, 1997). More specifically, there is a 71 percent dropout rate for African Americans compared to 55 percent for whites and a 20 percent gap between graduation rates of whites and blacks in majority institutions.

In light of the changing times of HE—the density of minorities and the increasing gap in academic achievement—there is a need for investigating alternative measures of academic performance. As we seek to improve both the learning and its assessment of African American students, the HBCU perspective can be instrumental in providing leadership. The following sections highlight a plethora of assessment strategies offered by individuals affiliated with HBCUs in the southern region of the United States.

In focus group discussions, three faculty members, three students, and three higher education administrators talk about how they perceive their individual and collective roles in effectively assessing the learning performance of African American college students within the context of HBCUs. We have withheld the identities of these individuals (and respective institutions, as well as the names of their institutions) because our interest is on the voice represented through the lived experiences of each distinct group of people. Each perspective provides insight for others concerned with creating alternative forms of assessment that consider current sociopolitical factors, historical and cultural points of reference, and demographic societal change. This sampling of personal accounts at the very least contributes new dialogue to the roles of faculty, students, and the higher education institution in assessing student performance.

The Role of Faculty

The faculty voices represented in our focus group approached pedagogical and assessment practices from sociocultural and political perspectives. In essence, their curricula are influenced by their concerns related to inequities of power and access for the larger African American community. As faculty acknowledged their cultural epistemologies (or ways of perceiving their place in or about the African American community), important connections are established in how they think about student assessment for improving teacher instruction and ultimately student learning. The group posed several quandaries based on the notion of being socially conscious: How do faculty conceptualize their role and responsibilities with students having membership in underrepresented groups? And, how do these faculty understandings interact with assessing student learning?

To answer these questions, faculty address conscious-raising assessment strategies that match teaching styles to learning styles, engender authentic forms of assessment, and include teacher self-evaluation. Here's an excerpt from a faculty member sharing his teaching philosophy:

> I think of and evaluate myself as a teacher of change agents because all of my students are readily involved in questioning and challenging the societal constructs that directly or indirectly marginalize people of color. . . . Although I'm a professor of science education, I want to raise a certain level of consciousness and empowerment or agency as students develop skills in my course and have the potential to transform society.

Several faculty members illustrated roles in social action and reported teaching from a constructivist perspective that attempts to place students within the center of their cultural reference point—the African American community. By engaging in culturally relevant pedagogy, students are said to develop confidence as well as agency in their own understandings and actions in generalizing course content beyond the boundaries of the schooling context. The intent of this faculty member is to foster a transformative education:

> My course syllabi and overviews, assignments, tests, and so on reflect my teaching philosophy as a transformative educator. I help students make their own meaning out of my courses and relate it to the community at large. Most times I have to customize instruction, create a variety of test formats, and basically individualize the learning objectives of the course.

Moreover, faculty are concerned with the prior knowledge and understandings that African American students bring into the learning context. In order to effectively assess content knowledge, the core course objectives and benchmarks are aligned with students' frames of reference. Faculty draw these connections from prior knowledge to new understanding by taking inventory of students' interests, community concerns, lived experiences, and future aspirations—just to name a few. Here is an example:

> For me the students' zones of proximal development also include lived experiences, learning styles, and interests. For example, the basis for assessing say Kendra's content knowledge is the relationship between how well my teaching aligns with her cognitive style and her learning performance. If I don't know my students' starting points and build from there, it's nearly impossible for me to adequately assess their growth.

A Context for Compatible Instructional and Learning Styles

Notably, the majority of students at HBCUs share the African American cultural reference point; however, faculty indicated a tremendous diversity of dispositions and learning styles within and across students. While acknowledging that each student has a preferred mode of thinking about and organizing information, faculty suggested that it is most often from a nontraditional orientation, for example, collaborative, community-referenced. Therefore, faculty design and implement a variety of nontraditional learning opportunities to better equip students for success in their courses. In short, when multiple strategies are used, multiple students are given opportunities to operate out of their dominant orientations to learning:

> I have an obligation to use a variety of teaching styles in order to meet the needs and demands of the variety of different types of learners taking my courses. If I don't recognize this responsibility, I'm just as guilty as the majority universities that operate from a one-sided paradigm. HBCUs are historically and traditionally gifted to be in tune to needs of African American learners.

Several faculty approach the matter of matching instructional style to learning style by administering formal and informal learning style and/or personality type inventories and questionnaires. These rubrics are said to provide the insights needed for designing compatible methods of assessment and to better help faculty position *what* students learn in the context of *how* students learn:

> I have recently started using informal and formal cognitive inventories such as Myers Briggs and the Kolb Learning Inventory. . . . My class size is usually less than fifteen, therefore small enough that I can tap in on the individual dispositions of my students and how they are perceiving my class. If not by simply observing them in class, I'll talk with them after class, at games, or arrange to meet with each of them individually during my office hours. It helps my teaching when I develop a strong relationship with them in and outside the classroom context.

A Context for Authentic Assessment

Faculty asserted that student knowledge is acquired in a context that is relevant. For that reason, faculty endeavor to create opportunities for thoughtful exercises that prompt students to critically analyze how course content is relevant and has implications for life-based experiences. There are examples of authentic practice being infused throughout the learning community at HBCUs. Students are said to actively engage in material through observations, modeling, and interacting with the community, while reflection, problem posing, and critical thinking remain key. Another faculty member explained how his students are located within an authentic contextualized curriculum where student assessment efforts are more entrenched in the process of learning instead of the content:

> I'll admit that some of my students have a predisposition for lecture notes, rote memorization, and regurgitation of material, so sometimes it's hard to really facilitate the higher order thinking and more complex learning. But when I emphasize authentic

material such as project-based products and explain that they will be graded on the group process and dynamics, students almost always excel.

If opportunities for student learning in the authentic community of reference are not available, faculty then create a context in courses whereby students reflect on course content using such venues as narratives, case study vignettes, and role plays. Instructional material is used that encourages students to examine authentic learning situations from multiple perspectives—that is, beyond the dominant views presented in manufactured textbooks and curricula. As students become actively involved, course content is generalized to the broader community of reference, and this process becomes the preparation for assessment, explains this faculty member:

> At HBCUs it's a given that most or at least many of our black students are interactive, interpersonal, and noncompetitive. That's part of the traditions of the black college experience. So, to assess students without this consideration—say, in a rather individualistic framework—is doing our students a disservice. No matter the course I'm teaching, whether is it's a child development course or the senior seminar, I infuse practical real-life experiences as well as challenging provocative scenarios.

At a later point, this same faculty member provided an example of an assessment activity (found in Appendix A):

> Last week I created an intertexting activity to test students' understanding of the readings. The students read a slew of articles on disability, and they were then asked to create a matrix that allowed the characters of each article to speak and respond to the voice in another article. Students analyzed and problematized the situations . . . the textbooks and instructor's guides in my field don't get that creative.

A Context for Teacher Evaluation

Faculty make decisions about assessment by examining the effectiveness of their own teaching and the fundamental connections between what students are learning. Simply put, the faculty ask themselves, How successfully are students accomplishing the intended instructional goals? And, is the assessment of these objectives aligned with learning performance? Several faculty are involved with institution-wide professoriate projects:

> Our university has a program for improving university teaching. We're each charged to produce a teaching portfolio—that is, if we choose to participate in the group. This portfolio offers a frequent and systematic place for me to reflect on my teaching and also receive feedback from my colleagues. We'll revisit course goals and objectives and redesign each others' syllabi from time to time. . . . There's talk of having this group or parts of this group required for all faculty in conjunction with our annual review of our scholarly performance goals.

Faculty reported using critical self-reflection in helping them reexamine how well learning goals are identified, instructional plans are implemented, and students are led in accomplishing course objectives. Other useful reflective activities include, but are not limited to, developing journals and teaching dossiers as well as soliciting formal peer observations and student feedback:

> As long as I'm resigned to implementing innovative forms of student instruction and assessment, I'm going to have to use equally progressive ways to evaluate myself. The standardized methods of teacher evaluations—the likert scale questionnaires given at the end of the semester—don't really account for the multilevel teaching and learning in my classroom and seldom even inform my instruction.

Needless to say, the purpose of teacher evaluation is to improve student learning, and this is done by obtaining sources of information that will inform pedagogy. The faculty report that a positive change occurs when they self-evaluate on an ongoing basis and make decisions on what and how material is added and/or taken away from a given course.

Summary Points

- Examine your own sociocultural views and pedagogical philosophies based on the students' reference points and course context.
- Provide relevant assessment that reflects students' lived experiences, interests, and learning styles.
- Engage students in authentic assessment by providing practical and collaborative learning opportunities.
- Create opportunities to self-evaluate teaching, while using various sources of information to improve course design.

The Role of Students

Students at HBCUs are operating from a metacognitive process of planning, monitoring, and evaluating their own thinking. By critically reflecting on one's own understandings, actions, choices, and patterns of learning, students are taking ownership for their personal growth. This section presents self-assessment strategies of students engaging in personal, critical reflection of their own processes of learning through personal profiling, peer-assisted assessment, and portfolio development. This student explains the process he started as an underclassman:

> Freshman year my big brother and (peer) mentor taught me how to track how I was doing in courses without having to ask the professor. He showed me how to chart all my course objectives, assignments, and tests and then monitor my progress. This way, I'm not surprised at the end of the semester and I know what I'm learning and can identify if I need someone to intervene.

The Art of Personal Profiling

In the process of personal profiling, students make decisions that aim to draw connections between lived experiences and the schooling context, decisions that, in fact, faculty may not be able to make for them. The focus group student-participants acknowledged a vision and reference point to learning objectives that included experiences within and outside course context. Students reported documenting autobiographical sketches that position their learning performance as a holistic, ongoing and continuous integrated process. For example, this student demonstrates the critical goal of monitoring and reflecting on progress:

> I'll write sloppy paragraphs in my notepad every night on just about anything—personal feelings, thoughts, questions, presumptions about assignments. I use this space to work through my ideas and experiences in my own words without fear that an instructor is going to grade me on it.

Personal profiling, also referred to as learning autobiographies, are written in journals, diaries, or logs and trace the acquisition of skills, understandings, beliefs, or attitudes about schooling. Student-participants note activities, personal motivations, emotions, involvement of other people, turning points, and disappointments or frustrations that unfold during the learning process. Routinely, students are able to surmise conclusions about their own learning patterns, preferences, and processes and inevitably make decisions about their overall progress on work. Another student explains how she thinks about strategies:

> I took a study skills course last semester that helped me learn how to gage how I learn best. The instructor explained that the learning styles of blacks and whites can sometimes be completely different. It felt good to know that there's a reason why it's harder for me to learn in certain classes, even though I still have to find the strategy that works best for me.

A high level of efficacy is associated with learning as a result of the students' recalling prior knowledge and developing a greater awareness of current performance and new concepts. The act of personal profiling promotes confidence, perseverance, and motivation. Perhaps this student said it best: "I feel good and delight in the fact that I'm able to see connections unfold between information that's in a cultural and community angle. It's a given that some types of knowledge are more important and interesting to me as a young Sister (African American) and I'm more eager to pursue them if they make sense to me."

The Art of Peer-Assisted Assessment

Student-participants viewed peer-assisted assessment and mentoring as a catalyst for individual and collective learning. They recognized that positive academic performance is interactive and therefore allows the sharing of others' diverse experi-

ences to clarify their own perspectives and assist in their own self-growth and development. At regular intervals students engage in reflexive and reciprocal activities
that promote collaborative/mutual support, guidance, encouragement, coaching, and
tutoring, all reportedly in an effort to promote each other's positive academic performance. An example of these peer-assisted assessment strategies is described:

> We'll share stories with each other because we are all in some form of transition and
> trying to figure out our place. I think it's an awesome benefit to have my friends read
> my essay on the origin of hip hop lyrics—you know how recording companies are sell-
> ing out—and have them actually understand what I'm talking about. Then I'll have to
> take responsibility in helping them also.

This vignette illustrates a peer group that is framed in a sociopolitical context,
facilitating personal development while at the same time acknowledging the understandings of the broader social issues operating in the community. Another student-
participant expounded in greater depth his experience in an Afrocentric peer program
where students support each other through spiritual principles of self knowledge and
empowerment:

> I'm involved in a student group that is formed around six African principles. We meet
> once a week in the student union and frame our conversation around African philoso-
> phies. . . . One of the principles is *Umoja,* which represents like unity, group work, and
> our responsibility to the group. We have such a sense of community and solidarity or
> harmony in our vision for doing this group. We didn't start it, but our leader, who's an
> upperclassman, always says that we are our brother's keeper! Each week we kind of
> report in on our academic stuff, but we have fun, too. . . . Another principle is *Kuumba,*
> which means creativity and talent. We do numerous meaningful social activities like
> the feed-the-hungry program. Every student I know at this school is involved in a ser-
> vice project.

At another point, the student further described the ongoing sense of reciprocity
within the Afrocentric-based peer group:

> *Kujichagulia,* or nurturing, is important because we contribute to each other through
> our own self-pride and determination. We kind of pump each other up. When I'm hav-
> ing issues, somebody in the group cheers me up and helps me work through my phase.
> Everything matters. Like with *Imani,* it's our faith in a higher power or group purpose.
> But my favorite aspect of the group is *Nia,* or independence. It's like each of us is
> trying to recognize our individual purpose . . . it's a great process.

Further information on the Afrocentric Mentoring Paradigm can be found in Harris
(1999), who explains the interconnectedness of the student perspective and this
paradigm, which employs *Nguso Saba* (Karenga, 1977) principles as supportive
strategies for African American students. This model provides strategies grounded
in peer support—spiritual, psychological, social, personal, and academic mentoring—to enhance success.

The Art of Portfolio Development

Portfolio development is an alternative assessment tool that facilitates students' active role participation in shaping their learning processes and performance outcomes through critical self-reflection. It is a nontraditional measure in that it provides a broader holistic view (approaches learning from broader perspectives) of direct *performance outcomes* versus indirect outcomes, such as test scores. It recognizes the diversity of learning and what is important and relevant from the point of view of the student:

> The portfolio review was useful in helping me make connections between the theory of courses and real-life practice. It also helped me see what components of a course are similar to components of other courses. I play a certain role in my own education that kind of makes it real to me.

The student-participants described their portfolios as a three-ring notebook or an electronic collection of course artifacts that demonstrate skills and accomplishments. Each piece of evidence included in the portfolio is explained through critical thought, such as written reflections in which students evaluate their own learning for the products in the folder. The supporting evidence often included in portfolios consists of assignments, papers, projects, homework, lab reports, problems solved, videotapes of presentations, and performances. It's a day-to-day record of progress that demonstrates strengths, improvements, and engagements. Here, a student describes her portfolio:

> My instructor and I establish most of the goals of my portfolio together. We'll meet periodically to discuss portfolio entries and goals. And, I have a rubric to guide me in how to organize the products. But my portfolio is all me and I can be as creative as I want in how and what I select to put in it.

As demonstrated above, students use self-evaluation—personal profiling, peer-assisted assessment, and portfolio development—to construct and critique their own work. They communicate what knowledge has been acquired, what has been learned, why it's important, and what they can do with this knowledge. This process of clarifying, modifying, and creating in-depth understanding leads to improved metacognitive knowledge that honors the uniqueness of each student's individual strengths, weaknesses, and needs.

Summary Points

- Personal profiling: An autonomous documentation that critically examines and logs developing skill knowledge and competence from a personal perspective.
- Peer assistance: A collaborative approach that promotes, supports, and evaluates a holistic view of learning.

- Portfolio development: A thoughtful collection and documentation of artifacts to illustrate the critical analysis of one's own thinking process and judging of one's own work.

The Role of the Institution

The higher education administrators participating in our focus group identified the use of institution-wide assessment strategies that aim to look at students in comprehensive, holistic ways. The organizational climate of HBCUs generally embodies a student-centered, service-oriented paradigm, in contrast to the more teacher-directed, research-based focus. The underlying priority at HBCUs from the perspective of our higher education administrators is how to best serve students preparing for meaningful future roles as leaders in the African American community. There is an added emphasis on the overall sociopersonal development of students, in addition to their academic achievement.

This section on the role of the institution highlights campus-wide approaches to assessment that include localized instruments and activities, reflecting the socioeducational expectations for students at HBCUs. Here, an administrator talks about her institution's approach in improving student development:

> We have whole-scale campus assessment efforts where the entire academic community works together and discusses overall student development. Because we are creating the African American leaders of tomorrow, it's going to take the whole village to raise a child. . . . We try to design unique approaches to assess students' performance as well as instructors' teaching quality and stray away from uniform measures.

An Interdisciplinary Dialogue

There are campus-wide teams that attempt to examine their university community experiences and practices to foster students' well-rounded social and intellectual growth. HBCUs are organized where programs and departments share faculty and conduct teaching and assessment across disciplines. This multidisciplinary structure allows institutions to collaboratively determine what desired competencies college graduates should individually and collectively achieve. Hence, a clear institutional vision of how to support academic success is presented:

> Our college has a university committee or task force where faculty develop professional development programs on assessment and share information on national conferences, projects, and internal and external grant competitions and awards. We have broad conversations about the vision of our school. . . . I'll also meet across departments on these big issues, because I teach both in the psychology and history departments.

The venue for faculty dialogue across disciplines stimulates strategies of how to share university vision on designing better assessment and teaching while monitoring student progress across programs. The goal is to agree upon institutional priorities, outcomes, and methods. Students become a part of this interdisciplinary conversation:

> All students take a freshman forum that covers the history and values of our institution. This semester-long course provides an interdisciplinary support network for students. . . .

A Learning Institution

The administrators suggested that a climate of talking about assessment fosters positive perceptions of assessment. The formative views of how to improve student learning are more informative than the summative reviews of teaching. A systematic approach to collecting and using assessment information promotes critical thinking and problem solving. This administrator explains how his faculty members come to understand the continuum of alternative assessment strategies:

> The buzzword is "learning communities," but we've been enhancing student learning in creative ways for years through things like block scheduling of courses or multiprogram service learning projects . . . anything to facilitate a climate that challenges the status quo.

The university portfolio was recommended as a vehicle of institutional learning. This tool consists of a campus-wide selection of authentic work, data, and analysis that demonstrates self-examination, reflection, and improvement. The portfolio highlights the use of authentic evidence—artifacts of faculty and student work. It illustrates the actual teaching and learning processes in detail and demonstrates student proficiency and achievement. As described below, it is a multidimensional portrait of student and faculty performance:

> Our college has been using some form of institutional portfolios for some time now. Being that they are performance based, there's an ongoing accumulation of products, such as audiovisual excerpts of field-based projects, microteaching seminars, student material presentations, and grading rubrics.

Given the attention to addressing social and academic outcomes for diverse student profiles, the use of mainstream measures of the effectiveness of U.S. higher education are said to be less appropriate for students and faculty at HBCUs. Poignantly, these measures are often culturally insensitive and irrelevant and often do not adequately account for the impact a student's cultural reference point has on his or her college achievement. HBCUs assume a responsibility for their students' growth—intellectually, personally, and socially:

> Being that many of our students are first-generation college students and come from low-income families, they often have real financial disadvantages. . . . We find ways to increase their access to educational opportunities. . . . Even though some of our

students are from more privileged backgrounds, they too require our emphasis on personal development. . . .

Summary Points

- Employ systemic processes and procedures that assess desired outcomes in light of the institution's mission.
- Facilitate an interdisciplinary integration that allows critical dialogue concerning academic and social processes of pedagogy.
- Develop institutional learning—study for comprehensive understanding and interpretation of the assessment practices.

Concluding Thoughts

The faculty, students, and higher education administrators within our focus groups described alternative assessment from a self-evaluative perspective that included a sociocultural and political reference point. While many of their strategies for assessment of African American students are collaborative in nature, their primary goal involves a personal responsibility for self-reflection. The role of faculty illustrates social action agendas, the role of students indicates a constructivist paradigm, and the role of the institution ascribes to an interactive mission statement.

The participants in our focus groups represented several types of HBCUs, varying from small public to large private institutions. A critical observation is that there is definitely diversity within the larger group of HBCUs. It is implied that those HBCU institutions with greater resources may more easily promote an array of teaching and learning approaches, but consistent throughout the focus groups is the driving theme of alternative assessment.

Appendix: Intertexting Activity

Purpose

Intertexting is an exercise designed to allow the student to develop a rich understanding and feeling for several authors' perspectives. Because the student actually must adopt individual authors' viewpoints or outlooks, it requires the student to know them well.

Procedure

■ Students choose three articles from the selected readings and peruse them for several key points.

■ Students then become the voice(s) in the articles and develop a dialogue across articles using the reference point of each article. In order to do this effectively, it will be helpful to first examine the authors' unique voices, their points of view, even their manners of presenting themselves. Formulating a response to another author requires the writer to leave his or her own perspective and adopt that of the character to whom he or she is responding. It often takes several tries before one begins to achieve success with this task.

■ Your dialogue should be presented in chart form. Please see example provided below as a guide.

Themes	Author/Article #1	Author/Article #2	Author/Article #3
Religion and Culture	Quote	Quote	Quote
Spiritual Humanism			
African American Episcopal			

REFERENCES

Anderson, D. (1988). *The education of blacks in the South, 1860–1935.* Chapel Hill: University of North Carolina Press.

Bainbridge, W. L., & Lasley, T. J. (2002). Demographics, diversity, and K–12 accountability: The challenge of closing the achievement gap. *Education & Urban Society, 34*(4), 422–438.

Bertman, S. (2000). *Cultural amnesia.* Westport, CT: Praeger.

Carter, D. J., & Wilson, R. (1997). *Minorities in Higher Education, 1996–97* (15th Annual Status Report). Washington, DC: Office of Minorities in Higher Education of the American Council on Education.

English, F. W. (2002). On the intractability of the achievement gap in urban schools and the discursive practice of continuing racial discrimination. *Education & Urban Society, 34*(3), 298–312.

Garibaldi, A. M. (1991). Blacks in colleges. In C. V. Willis, A. M. Garibaldi, & W. L. Reed, (Eds.), *The education of African-Americans.* New York: Auburn House.

Green, R. S. (2001). Closing the achievement gap: Lessons learned and challenges ahead. *Teaching & Change, 8*(2), 215–225.

Harris, F. (1999). Centricity and the mentoring experiences in academia: An Africentric mentoring paradigm. *Western Journal of Black Studies, 23*(4), 229–235.

Hilliard, A. G. (1997). Language, culture and the assessment of African American children. In A. L. Godwin (Ed.), *Assessment for equity and inclusion: Embracing all our children* (pp. 229–240). New York: Routledge Press.

Hodgkinson, H. (2002). Demographics and teacher education. *Journal of Teacher Education, 53,* 102–105.

Huba, M. E., & Freed, J. E. (2000). *Learner-centered assessment on college campuses: Shifting the focus from teaching to learning.* Boston: Allyn & Bacon.

Karenga, M. (1977). *Kwanzaa: Origin, concepts, practice.* Los Angeles: Kawaida Publications.

Miller, S. P., & Stayon, V. (1999). Higher education culture—a fit or misfit with reform in teacher education. *Journal of Teacher Education, 50,* 290–302.

Nettles, M. T., & Perna, L. W. (1997). *The African-American education data book: Higher and adult education.* Fairfax, VA: Frederick D. Patterson Research Institute.

Olson, L. (2000). Minority groups to emerge as a majority in U.S. schools. *Education Week,* 17–20.

Reising, B. (2000). High school reform. *Clearing House, 73*(4), 188.

Wagener, U., & Nettles, M. (1998). How three HBCUs succeed in retention. *Change, 30*(2), 18–25.

Wilson, R. (2002). Stacking the deck for minority candidates. *Chronicle of Higher Education, 68,* A10–A12.

PART TWO

Voices from the Field

6 Education, Liberation, and Transformation

Teaching African American Students within a Context of Culture

Joan T. Wynne
Florida International University

> *An important component of African indigenous pedagogy*
> *is the vision of the teacher as a selfless healer intent on*
> *inspiring, transforming, and propelling students to a higher*
> *spiritual level.*
>
> —Hilliard, 1997a, pp. 69–70

When I first read this passage by Asa G. Hilliard III in *SBA: The Reawakening of the African Mind,* I felt as I did when the Berlin Wall fell or when Nelson Mandela had been released from prison. I never thought either would happen in my lifetime. Neither did I think that anyone with a respectable reputation—indeed, a renowned scholar—in a white university would ever have the courage to publicly frame education within a context of spiritual transformation. Seeing that in print, I felt as though somewhere in my psyche, walls had fallen down or a liberator had been set free.

My years in white universities as a student and as a professor had indicated to me that matters of the intellect and matters of the spirit are as separate as church and state. That the purpose of my education might become the "transformation toward a new spiritual level" was certainly never remotely discussed or assumed. Typically,

Joan T. Wynne is Associate Professor of Urban Education at Florida International University at Miami, FL.

scholars who entertain such ideas are relegated to fringe groups in their disciplines. Because of the distortions of fundamentalists on such issues, many academicians may feel justifiably uncomfortable. Nevertheless, for fear of being thought anti-intellectual, or worse, unworthy of academia, I kept the idea of a connection between spirituality and intellectual pursuits suppressed in my conversations with other mainstream professors. My experience in colleges and universities around this issue taught me that Paulo Freire (Freire & Macedo, 1987) was probably right when he suggested that "The intellectual activity of those without power is always characterized as non-intellectual" (p. 122). I found that scholars who openly spoke of the spiritual within a context of intellectual discourse typically were outside the academic circles of power.

Yet as I thought about the writing of this chapter, I kept coming back to Hilliard's wisdom as one of the distinguishing characteristics of effective pedagogy with African American students. I learned it when teaching African American students at an inner-city high school; I learned it when teaching at a premier, all-male, historically black college (HBCU); and I learned it again when working with African American teachers in an urban teacher leadership master's degree program. In all three experiences, there seemed to be an innate sense of the "spiritual" aspirations of an entire people being integral to educational journeys. Jacob Carruthers (1999), a professor of Inner City Studies, concurs in *Intellectual Warfare,* saying that the "Restoration of African civilization is not possible without a return to African spirituality" (p. xv).

As a white woman, I feel presumptuous writing about effective pedagogy for African American students. So I can only offer my story from the perspective of one who first learned about "good teaching" from African American teachers and scholars. Master teachers like Mattie Williams, Dorothy McGirt, Baby Ruth Brantley, and Oliver McClendon took me under their wings my first year out of college, when I taught at an African American high school. They taught me how to expect and demand the best academic performance from all students, especially those living in poverty. Later on, scholars, teachers, and leaders like Alonzo Crim, Lisa Delpit, Robert Dixon, and Asa Hilliard III taught me the theory that explained the practice that had been modeled at Howard High School. Thus, any wisdom I share came from those educators and those places where, no matter the physical structure, the educational process became a "sacred space" (Hilliard, 1997a).

The research literature and my experiences in the classroom indicate that there are specific strategies that create optimum learning conditions for African American students. Yet, some of those studies and experiences have also persuaded me that regardless of the strategies, something far more profound than methodology connects students of African descent with the pursuit of academic excellence. For, along the way as I worked with African American students, I did observe, and probably engaged in, as well, some "bad" instruction that seemed antithetical to what is considered pedagogically sound. Nevertheless, many African American students survived such instruction.

It is only recently, however, that I've begun to understand the reasons that students of African descent can endure ineffective teaching strategies in HBCUs when they often cannot in mainstream colleges. That is not to say that there are not thousands of African American students who, nonetheless, achieve in mainstream colleges without these conditions being present. Rather, they excel in spite of those colleges, not because of them.

Some of the conditions, beyond pedagogy, yet bound within the culture, that I believe facilitate academic success for African American students are:

- The assumption of the spiritual connection to educational pursuits
- The infusion of music into the educational experience
- The explicit discussions of challenging an oppressive society
- The expectation and demand for excellence in the midst of a nurturing environment
- The developing of personal relationships with faculty
- The belief in the collaborative nature of the educational journey

All of these were integral parts of the total Morehouse College experience, an HBCU where I taught for thirteen years. Much of what I now consider a quality educational experience for any student—but especially for African American students—was crystallized for me at that college.

Spiritual Connection to Educational Pursuits

When explaining the ancient education traditions of Africa, Hilliard (1997a), who often spoke at the college, said, "Our educational and socialization process was always situated in a sacred space. This space served to clarify purpose and emphasize the divine nature of the process" (p. 10). At Morehouse, part of that "educational and socialization process" was obligatory attendance at chapel twice a week. In that space, students heard renowned persons of African descent—ministers, scholars, politicians, or heads of state—speak of the ancestral spirits who gave their all so that these young men could be at that college. At the end of such meetings at chapel, students resoundingly sang together the "Alma Mater." When the song's reference to the "Holy Spirit" emerged, all reverently lowered their voices and bowed their heads as they whispered the two words. I had never before experienced, first, a student body who all knew and sang their "Alma Mater," nor, secondly, a secular college that made reference to the "Holy Spirit." This attention to the divine, outside a specific religious context or denomination, poured out beyond the chapel walls. The legacies of spiritualists/educators like Howard Thurman, Martin Luther King, Jr., and Benjamin E. Mays reverberated not only in the chapel but also in the halls of the academy. The memorializing of those legacies is a ritual considered part of the mystique of the college.

Many of my students, whether they were in the writing, literature, speech, or education seminars, unabashedly found appropriate ways to connect their personal spiritual experiences to their writing, speeches, or classroom discussions, no matter the assigned topic. I learned early in my career at Morehouse that "touching the spirit" was a collective assumption throughout the campus. No hesitation there to connect the intellectual with the spiritual. Carruthers (1999) insists that, "The road to African liberation begins at the door of that 'Good Old African Spirit'" (p. xv). And if education is not "liberating," then it becomes, more often than not, propaganda for maintaining the societal status quo.

For mainstream professors in colleges or universities where the spiritual is ignored or shunned, creating opportunities for students to connect their spiritual heritage to discussions of content in a specific discipline is a culturally responsive strategy that can be quite effective in fostering stronger engagement of African American students in college classrooms. In such discussions, the professor is not obligated to validate or dismiss any particular belief system, only to establish a safe space for the students to bring those spiritual analogies into classroom conversations. I once observed a mainstream professor, a professed atheist, sit respectfully quiet as student after student began to connect her spiritual beliefs to the topic at hand. The energy in the room, due to his acquiescence to their desires to connect their own spiritual stories to the abstraction being grappled with, grew into a vigorous, synchronized exploration of the self and the discipline.

Infusion of Music

Part of the spiritual experience at Morehouse was music. The college's award-winning Glee Club usually opened and closed every chapel session. Their sometimes thundering renditions of old spirituals often left me so charged that I, too, felt the call of their ancestors to produce the best teaching performance possible for those who had inherited these heroes' struggle. Moreover, after a number of years attending chapel, I became convinced that the messages and music, the total education experienced within that sacred space, seemed to increase student determination to "hang in" with those difficult courses or the ones that might bore them into distraction. And, because of those chapel experiences, some students, who might have just barely slipped through the admissions door, seemed to get the extra boost they needed to study more diligently. It's what Delpit (1997) seems to intimate when she suggests that African American students learn best when they "connect to something greater than themselves."

Using music as ritual and as a collective everyday experience is deeply rooted in the African cultural experience. I was reminded of that when working in Alexandria, South Africa, one summer. I listened often as black South African workers, building homes in a Habitat for Humanities project, spontaneously burst into song when passing bricks to one another or when carrying food from one home to another; at the beginning and end of informal social gatherings; or in the middle of any mundane task such as washing dishes together. In that same tradition, during the Southern Freedom Movement, freedom fighters burst into song together in buses, churches, marches, and jails whenever fear became intense, struggle became burdensome, or short-term victory was working (Reagon, 1998). Regardless of the song, it seemed to invite the "spirit" into the human space. Music in the collective seems an integral part of African lives and struggle. How sterile our white institutions of learning must seem to such a musically sophisticated people!

Using Music in the Classroom

Though I have no training or talent in music, because of the powerful use of it in the King Chapel and my success in using music in high school classrooms, I began to play taped musical selections in my college literature and composition classes when students were writing. For many, their writing became more fluent while the music was playing. In literature classes, I brought songs whose lyrics and/or rhythms related to themes, metaphors, or forms being studied in specific genres. I often asked students to bring to class their choices of music to relate to what we were studying. On tests, I found that the students could demonstrate more effectively their conceptual understanding of those lessons that had been connected to their music. Many educational researchers have documented the use of music as a means of teaching a diverse range of skills from mathematics to poetry (e.g., Moffett & Wagner, 1983). The Algebra Project, initiated by Robert Moses, a mathematics educator and prominent civil rights activist, sometimes uses African drumming to teach algebraic concepts. Howard Gardner's research (Gardner, 2000) defines music as one of the distinct multiple human intelligences. To leave it outside the classroom door once students complete the third or fourth grade seems negligent on our part.

Nature versus Nurture

Hilliard (1999) has argued that in the United States there is a continuing "nature vs. nurture" educational debate about African American learners. Many Euro-centric scholars, represented by the likes of Murray and Hernnstein (1994) of the infamous *Bell Curve,* purport that the nature of the student defines his or her potential to learn and achieve. Because of these and similar educational theorists, the nature or capacity of African American learners to academically excel is more often than not questioned throughout our society, not just in our schools. Using his own educational experiences and research as well as the work of Shinichi Suzuki, "a teacher of world-class musicians who asserted that talent was not inborn but must be trained," Hilliard (1988) affirms that the nature of every human is to learn and that all students optimally learn when they are nurtured. It's rather, Hilliard explains, the "nature of the nurture" that promotes academic achievement, not the nature of the student. Delpit (1997), too, suggests that when teachers create "a sense of family and caring," students of color are more apt to excel.

That kind of nurturing exists at many of the HBCUs where I have taught or visited. The support system for excellence and the belief in the students' capacity to excel is so strong throughout these colleges that most of their students can survive "bad" instructional practices found within a few classrooms. Traditionally, the nurturing of African American students, especially in the segregated "colored" schools in the South, began with academic excellence as not just an expectation but a demand by their teachers (Siddle-Walker, 1996). Without that expectation and without taking the responsibility to ensure that students learn, questions of pedagogy seem irrelevant. Research suggests that we get what we expect, regardless of the methodology (Clark, 1989; Good, 1981, 1982; Rosenthal & Jacobson, 1968; Venter, 2000). Delpit (1997), who received the MacArthur genius award, admonished every teacher of African American students, including elementary teachers, that "Whatever methodology or instructional program is used, demand critical thinking." The demand for African American educators grows naturally from a place of nurture. In too many mainstream college classrooms (and in some HBCU classrooms) a nurturing spirit is sorely missing. Hilliard (2000) insists that education in the United States is characterized by its "pathological preoccupation with capacity."

Best Practices and Excellence

Nevertheless, if we are white professors teaching African Americans in a mainstream college where students' lives on the campus, outside the classroom walls, do not have this kind of nurture or support, then I believe we must diligently engage in "best practices" in our classrooms. Along with the indigenous African vision of a teacher, the framework for a discussion of best practices might include a definition found in Vincent Harding's (1999) *Hope and History*. In that text, Ronald Massanari says:

> Being a teacher refers less to one who gives answers and expects conformity . . . and more to one who is capable of providing contexts and stimuli so each learner can discover for him- or herself. Such teachers are skillful intermediaries and guides in the search for meaning and self-understanding. (p. 1)

That kind of skillful teaching within a cultural context is, in my experience, the basis for the academic success of many African American students in any classroom. And probably it is, as Massanari suggests, the basis for teaching students of any ethnicity. Many African American students can achieve academic excellence in spite of the absence of such a framework for teaching, even in majority white universities. However, those who fail to achieve at that level probably fail because of the other kind of teaching that caters to "giving information, answers, and demanding conformity," within a Euro-American cultural context—a practice that Dr. Alonzo Crim (1999), the first African American superintendent of the Atlanta Public School System, called the "Sage on Stage" model. To increase the rate of success for all African Americans in colleges, I believe, requires a shift away from that model. It requires an interactive, participant-centered approach to instruction.

Education for Liberation

Within that shift from conformity into a "search for meaning and self-understanding," I believe, is the demand for a pedagogy and a curriculum that is grounded in a philosophy of education for liberation. The Morehouse campus abounds in those conversations—in history classes, in African studies, in African American literature classes, in meetings in chapels, in campus-wide colloquia, etc. When taught outside a liberation context, knowledge learned in schools can become not only meaningless to African Americans and other students of color, but worse, a means to maintain an oppressive society. Culturally responsive pedagogy "prepares students to effect change in society, not merely fit into it" (Ladson-Billings, 1992, p. 382).

In the Americas in the twentieth century, great teachers like Ella Baker, Septima Clark, Paulo Friere, Fannie Lou Hamer, Vincent Harding, Myles Horton, Benjamin E. Mays, and others led the way in teaching how to educate to liberate. Indebted to their courage and intellectual integrity, many educators have learned how, as Hilliard (1997b, 1997c) suggests, to invite students, faculties, and communities to engage in conversations that question mainstream society's epistemologies as well as its assumptions about education, power, and social justice. Without those questions in mind, the disciplines of physics, literature, science, history, mathematics, and others often become intellectual scaffolds to sustain hegemony. For African Americans, living within a society that has for 400 years distorted past and present stories of history, economics, civilizations, and superiority, such a dialogue is imperative if these students are to assert themselves in an accurate historical context (Loewen, 1996). Moreover, if our society is to progress beyond materialism, militarism, domination, and greed, all students, regardless of ethnicity, need to explore knowledge in the context of liberation. So as a classroom strategy, what does that look like?

First, in any college classroom whether teaching business or humanities, a professor might begin each new semester with an exploration of the many facets of Education for Liberation. This can cause lively discussions of discovery of self and of the depth and breadth of human knowledge as professors and students try to examine just what liberation means. Who are we liberating? From what? And for what? What does liberation look like? Feel like? What does it have to do with studying physics, chemistry, mathematics, engineering, literature, history, art, etc.? Freire (1998) insists that there is "no such thing as a neutral educational process." It either sustains the status quo of the presently known, he suggests, or it uses what it knows to transform the world. If we choose transformation, then we must do as Hilliard (1997b) suggests: "change our intellectual structures, definitions and assumptions" that presume and foster white privilege and superiority. This means that in every discipline these conversations must be part of the strategy we use to engage our students in investigating the individual epistemologies of our particular content area. Can the laws of physics be seen only through a Eurocentric cultural lens, or is it possible that other cultures and other ancient traditions can offer new perspectives on those laws? In-service teachers (Perry, 2001) at Wheelock College in Boston have discovered methods of scientific inquiry different from the traditional Western model as they have immersed themselves in the Haitian culture.

The Common Good and Liberation

Many African American scholars argue that rooted deep in the culture of people of African descent are a curriculum, a pedagogy, and a practice that insist on the necessity to learn for the greater good of the community (Delpit, 1997; Hilliard, 1997a; Ladson-Billings 1994; Siddle-Walker, 1996; Wilson, 1998). When the purpose for learning any discipline is explicitly stated within a context larger than self-aggrandizement, these scholars indicate, the achievement level of African American students is favorably impacted. Benjamin E. Mays (1983), the President of Morehouse College for twenty-seven years, who saw his life's purpose as being "born to rebel," proclaimed that the purpose of education was not only "to train the mind to think" but also "the heart to feel . . . the injustices of mankind; and to strengthen the will to act in the interest of the common good" (p. 5). We know from such scholars' work that African American students take their studies more seriously when they assume that the purpose of exploring a discipline is to make a more just and equitable reality for the "whole" (Harding, 1999; Hilliard, 1997a; Moses & Cobb, 2001; Siddle-Walker, 1996). James Banks (1997) insists, "When the school fails to recognize, validate, and testify to the racism, poverty, and inequality that students experience in their daily lives, they are likely to view the school and the curriculum as contrived and 'sugar-coated' constructs that are out of touch with the real world and the struggles of their daily lives" (p. 16). The work of Herb Kohl (1994) indicates that when our curriculum and our pedagogy omit these realities, many students of color choose to resist learning. At Morehouse, many students come from economically privileged backgrounds, yet there was a concerted effort at the college to remind those students that their economic status demanded that they use their intellectual talents to battle against the poverty of their people. They were encouraged to understand what former SNCC member, Charles Cobb, once said of the students in Mississippi Freedom Schools, "What they must see is the link between a rotting shack and a rotting America" (Payne 1997, p. 5).

Strategies for Liberatory Education

Learning disciplinary content and exploring liberation are not mutually exclusive, as some professors might assume. Steeped in a tradition that honors a "pedagogy of the oppressed" (Freire 1998/1970), a science professor might, for example, encourage students to examine scientific content, laws, and theories, in a context of thwarting the use of science as a weapon against oppressed peoples. She might ask her students to ponder the probabilities that if they learned science well enough they might, indeed, together with their newly formed scientific community, be the instruments in discovering the end to world hunger, cancer, pollution, high infant mortality rates, and so on. Or the physics students might together discuss how to use the principles of physics, like those used to split the atom, to support life instead of death and destruction. For a people whose guiding principle of educational traditions for over 5000 years is spiritual transformation and liberation, studying to get a job or to make excessive amounts of money pales in the light of these grander purposes. For oppressed people, Ella Baker insisted that radical education "means facing a system that does not lend itself to your needs and devising means by which you change that system" (Grant, 1998). A first step in changing that system in education for African American students could mean facilitating open dialogue in the classroom to investigate the assumptions of oppression embedded in every discipline studied. For many professors, such discussions might unfold unconscious biases as well as wisdom.

In the humanities, raising questions of liberation is often more common than in the sciences. An English professor might ask students to connect the purposes of effective writing with countering the misconceptions in printed media about the disenfranchised. After ample student-driven discussion of larger contexts for learning to write than passing tests or better ways of competing in the job market, a professor might offer students opportunities to hone their skills by writing letters to editors, members of Congress, mayors, etc., about issues of social concern in their immediate college or home communities. They might also suggest ways to develop websites or chatrooms for students to discuss issues of social justice. In addition, that same professor when teaching literature might ask students to look at the literary canon not only for its aesthetic qualities, but also in the light of the unexamined racist, sexist, and other hegemonic notions that pervade Western literature as well as to question the choice of works admitted into that canon. In small groups, students might then debate the issues, thereby strengthening their oratorical and dialogic skills and then use what they are learning to educate students in K–12 institutions. In their exploration of racism and oppression, they might read to youngsters in surrounding schools of the story of an unschooled sharecropper named Fannie Lou Hamer (Harding, 1999; Moses & Cobb, 2001) who turned a national Democratic convention upside down by demanding to be seated. Some English professors, a history professor, and a few sociology and psychology professors at Morehouse used service-learning techniques like these to enhance their college students' acquisition and honing of skills in individual content areas.

Empowering students to use their skills as they learn them in a productive way to better their communities is a liberatory act. The "service-learning" literature prolifically chronicles the successes of such instruction in student acquisition of new skills as well as its positive impact on the communities these students serve. One of the characters in Barry Lopez's (1990) fables states that, "Sometimes people need a story more than food to stay alive" (p. 60). I believe that the stories of people of color, their histories, and their cultural legacies have been ignored or mutilated so often in the United States that their children need and deserve accurate cultural narratives told in schools and universities to "stay intellectually alive."

A compelling example of connecting education and liberation is the work of the Algebra Project (Moses & Cobb, 2001) in Mississippi, an effort that germinated from interrogating the implications of liberation pedagogy for the teaching of mathematical abstractions. Embedded in the project's process is the struggle of how to create a new sense of an educational "whole," where each piece of a student's life—her parents, her neighborhood, her community, her ancestors, her wisdom, as well as her ignorance—are all deeply respected and invited into the learning community—a process congruent with ancient African traditions. Such instruction excludes any suppositions about the capacity of a student to learn any given material, skill, or concept. Moses's success flies in the face of all our professorial complaints that the "admissions office needs to be more selective of the students it allows in the college"—a complaint any of us can slip into after a bad day in the classroom or too many student failures on a test. Are our complaints, I wonder, attempts to abdicate responsibility for using instruction that benefits the students who learn in nontraditional ways? Or could the complaints be symptoms of a desire to ignore the oppression that we think is about the "other," not ourselves?

Fundamental to Moses's (Moses & Cobb, 2001) purpose for teaching algebra to middle school, high school, and adult learners is his conviction that "math literacy—and algebra in particular—is the key to the future of disenfranchised communities" (p. 5). Moses contends that as voting rights in the 1960s gave Mississippi sharecroppers access to political power, mathematics and science literacy in our new technological age will give disenfranchised people control over their economic lives. Moses insists that without those necessary tools, many people of color and people living in poverty will be kept out of the loop of full citizenship (pp. 5–6). He suggests that teachers, students, and parents must understand those implications in order to make the sacrifices necessary to effectively learn and teach mathematical abstractions. The most significant part of his work, however, is grounded not only in the liberation struggle of the Southern Freedom Movement, but in the best tradition of indigenous African educational thought—that education is for the greater good. When discussing curriculum Moses states, ". . . a real breakthrough would not make us happy if it did not deeply and seriously empower the target population to demand access to literacy for everyone. That is what is driving the project" (p. 19). And that is what I think drives the educational efforts at many HBCUs: academic achievement for the benefit of the collective, not just for individual aggrandizement. And that component of African pedagogy, I believe, needs to be infused into every discipline's classroom discussions.

Moses's curriculum process can be extrapolated easily for use in the college classroom because it is so thoroughly grounded in research-based and experiential learning theory for the young and for adults. In my graduate courses at the university, urban teachers (the majority of whom were African American) have created curricula in different disciplines—literature, history, writing, government, etc.—using Moses's complete process from the experiential event to the symbolic representation. The concept to be mastered seems not to matter, primarily because the process works across disciplines because of its culturally responsive, research-based, and experiential pedagogy.

His pedagogy includes the following list that he explains as the "Five Crucial Steps in the Algebra Project curriculum process" (pp. 120–124):

1. **Physical Events:** A trip taken by the students and teacher is the central experience of the transition curriculum designed to illustrate the concept to be learned. [In mathematics, for example, Moses suggests, algebra students might take a trip on a metro transit system, bus tour, or walking tour; then come back to the classroom and moving through the next four steps, progress from a kinesthetic, very personal experience to learning the conceptual framework and symbolic representations underlying the mechanics of the event.]

2. **Pictorial Representation/Modeling:** In this and the next three steps, students move through a series of linked and progressively abstracted representations of the physical event, describing the event through pictures and everyday talk which the teacher builds on to introduce the language of the discipline and symbolic representation.

3. **Intuitive Language/"People Talk":** Students are asked to discuss and write about the physical event in their language.

4. **Structured Language/"Feature Talk":** This is not a language that anyone actually speaks. It is "regimented" language aimed at explicitly selecting and encoding those features of the event that are deemed important for further study. [Examples would be algebraic symbols and expressions, literary terms and abstractions, elements in chemistry, etc.]

5. **Symbolic Representation:** Once students have worked through the picture making, writing, and discussion of features, they construct symbols to represent these ideas. Through this activity, they begin to better understand the nature of symbol making, which moves them toward a fuller understanding and discussion of the symbols associated with the particular discipline being studied. Moses contends that many students have difficulty understanding the abstractions represented by the symbols of a specific discipline until they experiment with creating symbols for their own ideas.

Through the Algebra project, Moses and his colleagues have taught complicated conceptual material to unschooled adults, the children of those adults, and their teachers in poor, rural, and inner-city communities. Along with their new mathematical expertise and higher order thinking skills, these parents and students have become politically active in challenging the inadequacies of their schools, their teachers, and the systems that told them they couldn't learn algebra "because they are dysfunctional."

The work of Moses, Delpit, Freire, Hilliard, and others implies that rigorous intellectual growth is a possibility for every college student regardless of his or her

SAT scores, prior knowledge of content, or skill base—if the belief system is there at the college that we leave no student behind. Braced by that belief and willing to discover and employ new methods of instruction, every professor can teach any student. If we read Moses' successes with students (whom the larger society assumed could not and would not learn complicated abstract thinking), those of us who teach African American students in colleges (regardless of our ethnicity), should feel a new sense of hope for facilitating success for students who don't now excel in our discipline. Informed by Moses and other scholars' work, we can assume that anyone can be brought from a remedial position and encouraged to persist at the hard work of mastering a subject. As Hilliard says, it is the quality of the instruction, not the quality of the student that creates academic excellence.

There are a multitude of research studies that prove the efficacy of diverse teaching strategies in college classrooms. Yet, too many of us who teach in higher education institutions resist our reliance on the lecture as a means to engage students in the educational process. When that method doesn't work, we feel comfortable in blaming the student for "failing" the course. Although there are some gifted, lively, and dramatic lecturers whose lectures both entertain and inform, during my thirty or so years observing classrooms, the lecture format puts more students to sleep than it does engage them on a consistent level. The research of Howard Gardner (2000) on the multiple intelligences of the human brain indicates that our Euro-American educational systems typically attend to only one or two, linguistic and logical, of the seven intelligences thus far identified in the brain. In my observation in college classrooms where large numbers of students fail, the teachers typically use one method of instruction—lecture, take notes, regurgitate facts, theories, etc. Many research studies support the proposition that such pedagogy alone is a dinosaur that will accomplish little to facilitate the learning of many students in the twenty-first century. For many African American students, this myopic vision of teaching can be a hindrance to their content mastery and very often may bring on the end of their formal education. In all fairness, however, to college and university faculties, most of their institutions do not respect the art of teaching as much as research and reward publishing. Thus, many professors find little value or professional gain in time taken away from those efforts to learn how to expand their instructional repertoire.

Building a Community of Learners

To be able to explore the questions of justice and equity within a classroom (and for students to feel safe enough to risk exposing what they don't know in a specific discipline), a teacher must first build a community of learners. Most indigenous cultures are rooted in a strong sense of communal values. With the primary focus on individual rights in our U.S. culture, our sense of community is too often neglected. In many college classrooms, competition is the guiding principle, a principle that is outside the African worldview (Diop, 1989), a view described by Chibueze Udeani

(1989) as "the consciousness of a lively unity with community . . . where cooperation, collective responsibility, and interdependence are the key values" (p. 1). In
contrast to that, the predominant Eurocentric worldview is one that relies on competition, independence, separateness, and individual rights (Carruthers, 1999). Stark
differences exist between the two within the context of seeking knowledge. As educators, how do we create a sense of balance among both, where the individual and
the community are equally valued? How do we balance the creative tensions of the
dualities? Can we as educators in college classrooms continue to separate our work
from the community's work? These questions might make worthy discussion with
our students within classrooms as community is sought.

Taking the time to build a community within the classroom makes the most
sense, especially for African American students. Furthermore, if we have the integrity to honor the ancient traditions of the culture of the students we are teaching,
then we must pay close attention to the social nature of the African educational experience. Often on the Morehouse campus, I saw the reflection of Hilliard's research
(1997a), which found that "Education, to our [African] ancestors was regarded as a
social, rather than an individual process." Serious efforts were taken to establish the
social bonds necessary to create a cohort of learners who not only were students, but
who would be lifelong brothers and sisters in the most profound sense of those
words" (p. 25). Instinctively, Morehouse honored that ancestral wisdom and those
ancient practices. Though deliberate attempts to establish social bonds might not be
practiced in every classroom, the emphasis of brotherhood outside the classroom
walls sustained campus life and academic achievement.

Moreover, numerous scholars suggest that there is scientific data, from ancient Egypt to modern physics, that indicates the interdependence of all humanity,
all species, and all components of the universe from the subatomic level to the formation of the galaxies (Berry, 1990; Eisler, 1987; Swimme, 1992; Thomas, 1974).
Given those assumptions, why would we model in our classrooms a format of isolated thought and competition, a format incongruent with what we accept as true in
cosmic terms? Building a community of students in the classroom seems, then, not
just educationally sound, but also well-grounded in ancient and modern scientific
theories.

For those of us who teach where the campus life does not offer that sense of
community for African American students, or for those of us who have consistent
problems with student failure, I suggest that we, especially, spend some time building a community of learners. During course evaluations, my students have repeatedly
asserted that being part of such an experience assisted their performance in the classroom. Because I am convinced of the efficacy of this bonding, I utilize at least 30
minutes of the first class period of all my courses to begin establishing those bonds.
Thereafter, I establish small collaborative groups who will become peer editing
teams, literature discussion circles, speech critique groups, or textual analysis response groups in any discipline. Important to the construction of these groups is at
least one session dedicated to the simulation of just what makes good teams. Because

the mainstream culture of the United States primarily promotes competition, too few of us come to college with an adequate background in what it means to be an effective team player and little experience in group roles that lead to individual and group success. Nevertheless, we can find guides to facilitate such a process. Research literature and popular bookstores are replete with examples describing specific activities that create social bonding, team process, and group success (Campbell & Smith, 1997; Felder & Brent, 1994; Haller et al., 2000; Johnson & Johnson, 1989, 1995; Hrabowski & Maton, 1995; Starfield, Smith, & Bleloch, 1994). Such success with group process in college classrooms was recently validated by a group of African American graduate students. These teachers comprised three different graduating cohorts of an urban teacher leadership master's degree program. As a deliberately formed cohort, these students attended every course in their five-semester program. When asked during exit interviews to evaluate the program, all graduates remarked that the bonding of the cohort influenced their success more than any other component in the program. This type of peer support system is enormously important if we want to foster the intellectual growth of African American students in a mainstream college.

With the pressure on professors to cover material, raise standards, produce adequately prepared graduates ready either for a competitive market or for graduate school, many believe that bonding is a "nice idea," but too much "fluff" and too little substance. However, after many trials and errors, I have come to agree with Parker Palmer (1993), who states, "In the absence of the communal virtues, intellectual rigor too easily turns into intellectual rigor mortis" (p. xvii).

The Developing of Personal Relationships with Faculty

Professors at Morehouse spent many hours developing mentoring relationships with their students. Professors felt an obligation to know their students beyond the classroom. Many professors met students during late evenings to tutor or counsel them. One of the professors, a departmental chairperson, not only used his night hours to tutor college students, but also tutored high school students who showed promise in science but did not receive adequate instruction in the high school. He performed these uncompensated tasks in the midst of writing texts, grants, research, and teaching a full load. I used to tease him that he "needed to get a life." His practices, however, reminded me of the African vision of the teacher as "selfless." In the indigenous African context of education, serious learning occurs when teachers have established a personal bond with their students. In the Swahili tradition, this relationship of passing on knowledge through direct contact with people who are skilled craftsmen and instructors is referred to as fundi (Grant, 1998; Moses & Cobb, 2001). Unlike many white universities whose major focus is research, at Morehouse teaching is considered a serious and meaningful responsibility, the act of fundi.

It was not an uncommon practice for professors to invite their students in small groups to their homes. In my classroom, at the end of each semester, nearly 100 percent of the students on their evaluation cards commented on the benefit of meetings at my home in creating a harmony for struggling with difficult questions and concepts. In my experience with African American students in high school, college, and graduate school, this practice seemed to cement relationships that made room for a "mutual criticism of thought" (Palmer, 1993, p. 74). Many African American scholars insist that relationship building is a key value in African culture and, thus, African American students perform best for those teachers, whatever their ethnicity or racial background, who have authentically bonded with their students.

Other Issues of Culture

Intertwined within discussions of relationship building and other elements of African American culture are questions about culture in general. How do we respect each other's cultures, learn from all the variations, recognize the "hidden dimensions of unconscious culture" (Hall, 1989), and move as Edward T. Hall suggests in *Beyond Culture?* How do we grapple with the thoughts, feelings, communications, and behaviors that are molded by our separate cultures? How do we reckon with the good and bad in every culture? And, perhaps most importantly, through the investigation of culture, can we begin to break the chains of a hegemonic society where all citizens are held captive, not only the disenfranchised?

For most professors in the United States, issues of culture are deeply embedded in how we teach. Because most of us were educated in a Eurocentric (or a British) model of education—including those who have come to the university from previously colonized countries (Carruthers & Harris, 1997)—we seem obliged to consider the limits of teaching within one cultural framework. Connecting our classroom instruction to the culture of our students to help unfold their brilliance has been validated by a host of educational researchers (Delpit, 1995, 1997; Hilliard, 1997a; Irvine, 2002; Ladson-Billings, 1992; Wilson, 1998). Yet, in my numerous years of sitting in meetings with white university professors, I have been perplexed by our attempts to look outside the context of the African American culture—in fact, to look among ourselves—for answers to pedagogical problems in teaching students from another culture—a practice that seems not only arrogant, but also fruitless. We seem to assume that our wisdom, emanating from our one cultural perspective, is somehow universal—that our truths are not grounded in our particular cultural belief system, rather somehow gleaned from a cosmic logic. Delpit's research (1995) indicates that many mainstream teachers' confusion about culturally relevant instruction is common no matter where we teach—in African American communities, in indigenous communities in Alaska, Papua New Guinea, in elementary through college classrooms. Along with Delpit's, my experience, too, suggests that many of us in mainstream contexts seem confused as well about the significance of culture in the personal and the political lives of all people.

For example, when looking out my window from the predominantly white university where I once taught, I could take in a bustle of downtown activity. Just four blocks from the central office of the city's predominantly African American school system, I would observe as a multitude of young and old, mostly African Americans, rushed toward their destinations in banks, offices, and restaurants. Mothers dragged young children to subway entrances, making pit stops at the stalls of numerous street vendors hawking Kente cloth, leather goods, and "essential oils." Rap music and Caribbean melodies blasted from car radios and storefronts—all in all, a typical downtown city scene. Yet whenever I left my window gazing, I entered a college where the dean was a white male, and six out of six of the college's department chairs were white. At one of the college's faculty meetings of over 100 professors, I listened, astounded, as professors debated whether the college was an "urban institution." That same debate occurred again at a departmental faculty meeting when the vision of the college was discussed. I could only wonder if other professors had windows.

When the authority figures all wear the same face, we might all wonder if, in the twenty-first century, such colleges have a "sense of the whole," or at the very least, understand the physical space that they occupy. With such contradictions, might the 26 percent African American student population wonder if the university is serious about other peoples' cultures? On such campuses, culturally relevant instruction in classrooms would certainly be a breath of fresh air for students of color.

Because of institutional and societal failures to recognize diverse cultural realities and wisdom, can we who teach African American students in college assume that our content knowledge is enough to optimally support the intellectual growth of our students? Though expertise in a discipline is crucial, a culturally responsive context for teaching that discipline seems equally significant to the academic achievement of African American students as it is for all students. Too few students achieve at their highest potential when the instructional climate is alien to their cultural experience. White students are taught in the United States within their cultural context. But for African American students—and most students of color—whose culture and history have been denied or distorted in our schools, teaching within a cultural context becomes a mandate of intellectual integrity.

Sometimes when confronting the racist epistemology that dictates policies and practices of most of our institutions, especially education, I sink into disillusionment and hopelessness. In those moments I remind myself, however, that part of my hopelessness is driven by my own racism. Being white and a product of mainstream schooling, I have unconsciously absorbed many notions of supremacy. One of those is the assumption that if white people don't find a solution to the problems we have created in schools that supposedly serve African American youth, then those youth are all doomed. I now understand more clearly, however, that what we really need to do is get out of the way of those African American teachers, scholars, and researchers who already know the "way out of no way" (Young, 1994). For, the reality is that, with or without us—their teachers—as Richard Wright (1941) proclaimed in

12 Million Black Voices, "Hundreds of thousands [of African Americans] are moving into the sphere of conscious history" (p. 147), a history that includes Hilliard's assumption of intellectual and spiritual transformation.

Concluding Thoughts

All of the philosophical and instructional constructs for the classroom discussed in this chapter are valuable ingredients for creating an environment where African American college students achieve at high levels. Their cultural worldview clearly links music, liberation, relationship building, collaboration, and the spiritual to education and to life. Most of the scholars and teachers who successfully teach them typically vary their instructional practices to integrate these cultural links into the classroom. Two of those links, however, are fundamental for consistently delivering positive academic results and for grounding all of our classroom work in intellectual integrity. Without these two, expanding our use of creative instructional methodology becomes insignificant.

The first of these is discussed in the chapter under the section entitled "Nature versus Nurture." As Perry, Hilliard, and Steele (2003) indicate, the "nature" of the learner, his or her intellectual capacity to achieve in colleges and universities, is too often assumed to be a legitimate question. Professors many times doubt a student's ability to withstand the rigor of the college classroom if that student is admitted without a record of past high performance or high test scores. This chapter suggests that a belief in the capacity of all students to academically soar, regardless of SAT scores, previous skill-based competence in a discipline, or ethnic or socioeconomic history, is necessary for optimum academic performance of most students. This is especially important for African American students because myths in the mainstream culture assert that these students are intellectually inferior (Perry, Hilliard, & Steele, 2003). Not only does that myth have negative consequences for our students, but it also weakens the nation's capacity to benefit from all of its citizens' intellectual capital.

Research and many life stories overwhelmingly conclude that those who work hard to pursue excellence, regardless of previous manifestations of talent, can and do achieve at high levels when they know that their teachers expect and demand excellence. Within such a climate of respect and nurture, the students can perform well, regardless of the instructional strategies used (Delpit, 1995; Hilliard, 1997c; Steele, 2003). Septima Clark and others in the Southern Freedom Movement demonstrated this in the teaching of illiterate adults in the rural south. Moses continues that tradition in the Algebra Project. Hilliard creates that for graduate students in Atlanta. As professors, we might find it useful to school ourselves in those lessons.

The second imperative is discussed in the section entitled "Education for Liberation." Denying our students the opportunity to examine pervasive faulty notions of a history and epistemology rooted in oppression, which infects all disciplines, hinders honest intellectual discourse. Within such a discourse of liberation, African Americans like Vincent Harding seem to be asking educators the right questions. Harding (1999) wrote that, "Langston Hughes, our poet/teacher, said, 'We, the people, must redeem our land. . . . And make America again.' What does it mean to redeem a land, to remake a nation? Who are 'the people' who must do it? And who are the teachers, and what is the curriculum that will prepare us for such a task?" Along with Harding, many other African American scholars (Payne, 1995, 1997; Perry, 2001) suggest that a curriculum grounded in the old African American traditions of liberatory education is a first step in transforming our students, our schools and colleges, ourselves, and our nation.

Therefore, if we really want to call forth the intellectual dimension of African American students, we need to honor their histories within the perspective of liberation. Those histories demonstrate for students that struggles for liberation have been an ongoing movement in the United States since the days of slavery and that their ancestors for centuries have been pushing America to reach its dream. These stories can instruct and motivate. They privilege a narrative that counters society's diminishment of Black cultural power and intellectual traditions (Perry, 2003). At the same time, these more accurate American histories serve the larger society by forcing it to examine how such myths diminish the integrity of all of its institutions.

While inviting students to investigate science, mathematics, philosophy, and the humanities within the context of ancient Black civilizations, new ways emerge for thinking about each of our disciplines, about knowledge, and about the making of knowledge. As Linda Smith (1999, p. 1) argues in her work with graduate students, even "the term 'research' is inextricably linked to European imperialism and colonialism."

If we ignore the significance of examining cultural truths, our creative or cutting-edge strategies become meaningless and lead nowhere. Rather, they further buoy a spiritually and intellectually vacuous educational and societal "military-industrial complex" (Moffett, 1994). If our students are reading and writing historical and cultural distortions, yet ignoring the impact of those distortions on sustaining a hegemonic worldview, who cares what strategy we're using, or how well the students read and write? In such classrooms, the words of Maori writer Patricia Grace become particularly poignant. She said that "books are dangerous" because most books lie about indigenous people's values, actions, customs, culture, identity, and, ultimately, their existence (Smith, 1999, p. 35). When we do not confront the erroneous constructions of knowledge embedded in all of our disciplines, are not our classrooms dangerous as well? On the other hand, perhaps, books that do not lie about indigenous people are seen as "dangerous" by any society that wishes to privilege ideas of oppression and imperialism.

Martin Luther King, Jr., stated that "[t]he American Negro may be the vanguard of a prolonged struggle that may change the shape of the world, as billions of deprived shake and transform the earth in the quest for life, freedom and justice" (Harding, 1998, p. 108). From reading the stories of the long history of African people's resistance to oppression, I believe that the "American Negro" has been in the vanguard for over 400 years, struggling, changing, challenging the society to transform itself, and if we as teachers cannot bring those ancestors' children to higher levels of academic achievement, then we need to step aside and allow those who do know how to do it.

Essential Reading

- Carruthers, J. H. (1999). *Intellectual warfare.* Chicago: Third World Press.
- Carruthers, J. H., & Harris L. C. (Eds.). (1997). *African world history project: The preliminary challenge.* Los Angeles: Association for the Study of Classical African Civilizations.
- Delpit, L. (1995). *Other people's children.* New York: The New Press.
- Harding, V. (1999). *Hope and history: Why we must share the story of the movement.* New York: Orbis Books.
- Hilliard III, A. G. (1997). *SBA: The reawakening of the African mind.* Gainesville, FL: Makare Publishing Co.
- Perry, T., Hilliard, A., & Steele, C. (2003). *Young gifted and black: Promoting high achievement among African-American students.* Boston: Beacon Press.
- Smith, L. T. (1999). *Decolonizing methodologies: Research and indigenous peoples.* London: Zed Books.

REFERENCES

Banks, J. (1997). *Educating citizens in a multicultural society.* New York: Teachers College Press.

Berry, T. (1990). *The dream of the earth.* Berkeley: University of California Press.

Campbell W., & Smith, K. (1997). *New paradigms for college teaching.* Minneapolis: Burgess Publishing Co.

Carruthers, J. H. (1999). *Intellectual warfare.* Chicago: Third World Press.

Carruthers, J. H., & Harris, L. C. (Eds.). (1997). *African world history project: The preliminary challenge.* Los Angeles: Association for the Study of Classical African Civilizations.

Clark, D. (1989). High expectations. In *Effective schools: Critical issues in the education of black children.* Detroit: National Alliance of Black School Educators, p. 33.

Crim, A. A. (1999). *Psychological aspects of leadership.* A course taught at Georgia State University, Atlanta, GA.

Delpit, L. (1995). *Other people's children.* New York: The New Press.

Delpit, L. (1997, September). *Ten factors for teaching excellence in urban schools.* Speech at Urban Atlanta Coalition Compact Town Meeting, Atlanta, GA.

Diop, C. A. (1989). *The cultural unity of Black Africa: The domains of matriarchy and patriarchy in classical antiquity.* London: Karnak House.

Eisler, R. (1987). *The chalice and the blade: Our history, our future.* New York: Harper & Row.

Felder, R. M., & Brent, R. (1994). *Cooperative learning in technical courses: Procedures, pitfalls, and payoffs.* ERIC Document Reproduction Service, ED 377038.

Felder, R. M., & Brent, R. (2001). Effective strategies for cooperative learning. *Journal of Cooperation & Collaboration in College Teaching, 10*(2), 69–75.

Freire, P. (1998/1970). *Pedagogy of the oppressed* (trans. by Myra Bergman Ramos). New York: Continuum.

Freire, P., & Macedo, D. (1987). *Literacy*. New York: Bergin & Garvey

Gardner, H. (2000). *Intelligence reframed: Multiple intelligences for the twenty-first century*. New York: Basic Books.

Good, T. L. (1981, February). Teacher expectations and student perceptions: A decade of research. *Educational Leadership, 38,* 415–422.

Good, T. L. (1982, December). How teachers' expectations affect results. *American Education, 18,* 25–32.

Grant, J. (1998). *Ella Baker: Freedom bound*. New York: John Wiley & Sons.

Hall, E. (1989). *Beyond culture*. New York: Anchor Books/Doubleday Dell.

Haller, C. R., Gallagher, V. J., Weldon, T. L., & Felder, R. M. (2000). Dynamics of peer education in cooperative learning workgroups. *Journal of Engineering Education, 89*(3), 285–293.

Harding, V. (1998). *Martin Luther King: The inconvenient hero*. New York: Orbis Books.

Harding, V. (1999). *Hope and history: Why we must share the story of the movement*. New York: Orbis Books.

Hrabowski, III, F. A., & Maton, K. I. (1999). Enhancing the success of African American students in the sciences: Freshman year outcomes. *School Science and Mathematics, 95*(1), 19–27.

Hilliard, III, A. G. (1988). *Testing and misunderstanding intelligence*. Paper presented at Puget Sound Educational Consortium, Seattle, WA.

Hilliard, III, A. G. (1997a). *SBA: The reawakening of the African mind*. Gainesville, FL: Makare Publishing Co.

Hilliard, III, A. G. (1997b, Spring). The structure of valid staff development. *Journal of Staff Development, 18*(2).

Hilliard, III, A. G. (1997c, October). *Tapping the genius and touching the spirit: A human approach to the rescue of our children*. The Ninth Annual Benjamin E. Mays Lecture, Atlanta, GA.

Hilliard, III, A. G. (1999, February). *The spirit of the African child*. Unpublished speech at the Urban Atlanta Coalition Compact Town Meeting, Atlanta, GA.

Hilliard, III, A. G. (2000). *Awaken the geniuses of children: The nurture of nature*. Unpublished speech for Skylight 6th International Teaching for Intelligence Conference, (Cassette produced by Chesapeake Audio/Video Communications, Inc., 6330 Howard Lane, Elkridge, MD 21075 [00227-1160].)

Hrabowski, F., & Maton, K. (1995). Enhancing the success of African American students in the sciences: Freshman year outcomes. *School Science and Mathematics, 95*(1), 19–27.

Irvine, J. J. (2002). *In search of wholeness: African American teachers and their culturally specific classroom practices*. New York: St. Martin's Press.

Johnson, D., & Johnson, R. (1989). *Cooperation and competition: Theory and research*. Minneapolis: Burgess Publishing Co.

Johnson, D., & Johnson, R. (1995). *Creative controversy: Intellectual challenge in the classroom* (3rd ed.). Minneapolis: Burgess Publishing Co.

King, M. (1986). *Freedom song: A personal story of the 1960s civil rights movement*. New York: Morrow, Inc.

Kohl, H. (1994). *"I won't learn from you": And other thoughts on creative maladjustment*. New York: The New Press.

Ladson-Billings, G. (1992). Liberatory consequences of literacy: A case of culturally relevant instruction for African American students. *Journal of Negro Education, 61*(3), 378–391.

Ladson-Billings, G. (1994). *The dream keepers*. San Francisco: Jossey-Bass.

Loewen, J. W. (1996). *Lies my teacher told me: Everything your American history textbook got wrong*. New York: Simon & Schuster.

Lopez, B. (1990). *Crow and weasel*. North Point Press.

Mays, B. E. (1983). *Quotable quotes of Benjamin E. Mays*. New York: Vantage Press.

Moffett, J. (1994). *The universal schoolhouse: Spiritual awakening through education*. New York: Jossey-Bass.

Moffett, J., & Wagner, B. (1983). *Student centered language arts and reading, K–13: A handbook for teachers*. New York: Houghton Mifflin Co.

Moses, R., & Cobb, Jr., C. (2001). *Radical equations: Math literacy and civil rights.* Boston: Beacon Press.

Murray, C., & Hernnstein, R. (1994). *The bell curve.* New York: The Free Press.

Palmer, P. (1993). *To know as we are known: Education as a spiritual journey.* San Francisco: Harper.

Payne, C. (1995). *I've got the light of freedom: The organizing tradition and the Mississippi freedom struggle.* Berkeley: University of California Press.

Payne, C. (1997, March). *Education for activism: Mississippi freedom schools in the 1960s.* Paper presented at AERA conference, Chicago.

Perry, T. (2001, April). *Task Force on Black Education Report.* Panel for AERA conference, Seattle, WA.

Perry, T., Hilliard, A., & Steele, C. (2003). *Young gifted and black: Promoting high achievement among African-American students.* Boston: Beacon Press.

Reagon, B. J. (1998). "Oh freedom": Music of the movement. In G. Greenberg (Ed.), *A circle of trust: Remembering SNCC.* New Brunswick, NJ: Rutgers University Press.

Rosenthal, R., & Jacobson, L. (1968). *Pygmalion in the classroom: Teacher expectation and pupils' intellectual development.* New York: Holt, Rinehart & Winston.

Siddle-Walker, V. (1996). *Their highest potential: An African American school community in the segregated south.* Chapel Hill: The University of North Carolina Press.

Smith, L. T. (1999). *Decolonizing methodologies: Research and indigenous peoples.* London: Zed Books Ltd.

Starfield, T., Smith, K., & Bleloch, A. (1994). *How to model it: Problem solving for the computer age.* Edina, MN: Interaction Book Co.

Steele, C. (2003). Stereotype threat and African-American student achievement. In T. Perry, A. Hilliard, & C. Steele (Eds.), *Young gifted and black: Promoting high achievement among African-American students.* Boston: Beacon Press.

Swimme, B. (1992). *The universe story: From the primordial flaring forth to the ecozoic era—A celebration of the unfolding of the cosmos.* San Francisco: Harper.

Thomas, L. (1974). *The lives of a cell—notes of a biology watcher.* New York: Bantam Books.

Udeani, C. *The search for meaning in the traditional African worldview.* Upper Austria /Caritas Integration project. Kepler University Linz, Austria. Retrieved Oct. 5, 2001 from http://www.stfx.ca/people/wsweet/abstract-Udeani.html

Venter, E. (2000). Expectation of students versus expectation of lecturers of philosophy in a postgraduate course. *Philosophy of Education in the New Millennium: Conference Proceedings—International Network of Philosophers of Education* (Volume 3). Sydney, Australia: University of Sydney.

Wilson, A. (1998). *Blueprint for black power: A moral, political and economic imperative for the twenty-first century.* New York: Afrikan World InfoSystems.

Wright, R. (1941). *12 million black voices.* New York: Thunder's Mouth Press.

Young, A. (1994). *A way out of no way: The spiritual memoirs of Andrew Young.* Nashville: Thomas Nelson Publishing.

7 Cultivating the Education of African American College Students

A Learning Styles Approach

Angela Farris Watkins

Spelman College

To be successful, African American students must navigate between at least two cultures (Boykin, cited in Parham, White, & Ajamu, 1999, p. 89; Hale-Benson, 1986). I believe that the outstanding record of Historically Black Colleges and Universities (HBCUs) in preparing African American students for excellence and achievement is attributable to an unprecedented skill for training African Americans to function simultaneously amid mainstream culture and African American culture. HBCUs view their students within the context of culture and design their educational programs to meet their unique learning needs. Alternatively, the traditional educational process (typically found at predominately White institutions) requires students to assimilate to mainstream school standards derived exclusively from Western European philosophy and theory, without attention to relevant diverse cultural styles and practices. The resulting picture is bleak for black students, especially for those attending majority institutions.

The educational attainment for African Americans is nearly half of that of Whites. Of the total number of African American citizens in the United States age 15 and over, only 9.5 percent (compared to 16.5% of Whites) have acquired bachelor's degrees; only 3.2 percent (compared to 5% of Whites) have acquired master's degrees; and only 0.2 percent (compared to 1% of Whites) have acquired doctorate degrees (U.S. Census Bureau, 2000). The education of African Americans is deflated

Angela Farris Watkins is Associate Professor of Psychology at Spelman College, Atlanta, GA.

by school probation, high dropout rates, low standardized test scores, and poor academic performance, which lead to high unemployment rates and high rates of imprisonment.

As an alumna and college professor of an HBCU, I am especially appreciative of the academic programming established at HBCUs. I feel a personal sense of pedagogical responsibility to cultivate and promote the academic achievement levels of African American college students. In this chapter I share a practical and culturally responsive instructional method that I incorporate in my teaching—the use of Black Cultural Learning Styles (BCLS). This is an approach that allows me to blend the unique abilities and strengths of African American students with the skills that are necessary for survival in our present mainstream culture. In this chapter I also provide *Course Integration* stories and *Suggested Strategies.*

Learning Styles

Learning styles are central tendencies that students from different ethnic groups demonstrate in learning (Gay, 2000, p. 151). They are cultural guidelines that individuals use to interpret and attend to information (Durodye & Hildreth, 1995, p. 242). Scholars affirm a fundamental association between culture and learning (Cushner, McClelland, & Safford, 2000; Durodye & Hildreth, 1995; Gay, 2000; Hale-Benson, 1986; Ladson-Billings, 1994; Shade, 1989; White, 1984). According to White (1984), there is a cultural ethos, a set of guiding beliefs that particular groups of people use for teaching, learning, and interpreting the world. Shirley Brice Heath's (1983) revolutionary ethnographic research, *Ways with Words,* demonstrates that children acquire language and literary habits according to the norms of their cultures. Culture anchors learning during the very early stages of life and continues into adulthood. By 5 years of age, cultural socialization has determined individuals' rules and procedures for acquiring knowledge and demonstrating skills (Gay, 2000, p. 150).

After more than ten years of teaching experience, I am convinced that the use of learning styles is fundamental to academic success. The effectiveness of learning styles—based instruction in college courses is also documented in the literature (Appelhans & Schmeck, 2002; Berg & Poppenhagen, 1995; Boulmetis & Sabula, 1996; California Community Colleges, 1995; Dunn & Griggs, 2000; Hoofner, 1986; Lemire, 2001; Loo, 2002).

Black Cultural Learning Styles

For African Americans, learning styles, in part, express African American culture (Hale-Benson, 1986; Hilliard, 1976; Kwate, 2001; Nobles, 1985; Shade, 1982; Willis, 1992). More commonly referred to as Black Cultural Learning Styles

(BCLS), these unique practices reflect the influence of African American culture on students' preferred and persistent ways of learning.

In order to satisfy these cultural traditions of learning, I have looked to theory and research that note particular qualities of African American learners (e.g., Akbar, 1975; Boykin, 1983; Gardner, cited in Woolfolk, 2001; Hale, 1994; Hale-Benson, 1986; Hilliard, 1997; Houston, 1990; Jagers & Mock, 1993, 1995; Jones, 1980, 1991; Karenga, 1993; Nobles, 1972). This literature includes perceptual modality styles, African (Black) psychology, multiple intelligences, and African survivals.

More specifically, Boykin (1983) describes nine qualities that are rooted in African belief systems and that influence the behaviors of many African Americans:

1. Spirituality
2. Harmony
3. Movement
4. Verve
5. Affect
6. Communalism
7. Expressive individualism
8. Orality
9. Social time perspective

Because culture is expressed in students' learning styles, Boykin's descriptions are important to the teaching/learning process of African American students. I consistently accommodate them in my teaching.

Incorporating Black Cultural Learning Styles into Instruction

The rationale for integrating the unique qualities of African American learners is that learning styles provide functional directions for modifying instructional techniques to better meet the academic needs of ethnically diverse students. They illuminate values and behaviors that influence learning (Bennett, cited in Gay, 2000, p. 147). They add flavor to an otherwise unseasoned pedagogy. The goal is to broaden instructional strategies so that African American learning traditions are included. In this way, these strategies are applicable for classes that solely comprise African American students, as well as those that comprise students from various cultural groups that include African Americans.

What follows is a delineation of Boykin's (1983) descriptors infused with other relative theory that I have discovered to demonstrate how I have incorporated BCLS into my instruction. Each descriptor begins with an introductory statement (definition and explanation). I have also included *Course Integration* stories that are based on my successful experiences. Similarly, I provide a section of *Suggested Strategies* for those who are interested in incorporating these learning styles into their instruction.

Spirituality

Boykin's (1983) explanation of spirituality as a quality of African American behavior calls attention to the belief that there is a higher power at work in and around all mankind. According to Jagers and Smith (1996), spirituality is an essential part of culture for persons of African descent. Taylor and Mattis (1999) affirm that religion and religious institutions have contributed to the maintenance of political resistance; activism; social, emotional, and economic support; and intellectual, educational, and artistic development of African Americans. The National Survey of Black Americans (NSBA) reports that 62 percent of African Americans are church members, 63 percent consider worship important, 78 percent pray every day, and 34 percent consider themselves as "very religious" (Jackson & Gurin, 2000).

Moreover, the literature fully articulates the benefits of faith values for life management of college students, cross-culturally (Cook, 2000; Ellis & Smith, 1991; Epstein, 1998; Evans & Francis, 1996; Jeynes, 1999; Knox, Langehough, Walters, & Riley, 1998; Levin & Taylor, 1998; Maltby, 1998; Maton, 1989; Millet, Sullivan, Schwebel, & Myers, 1996; Regenerus, 2000; Wong-McDonald, 2000). Higher levels of religiosity have been associated with a variety of positive outcomes in the lives of college students. Walker and Dixon (2002) demonstrated a relationship between African American college students' spirituality and academic performance. Frankel and Hewitt (1994) discovered that students who were affiliated with campus faith groups had higher levels of physical and psychological health than students who were not affiliated with these groups. Knox and colleagues (1998) found higher levels of religiosity to be predictors of higher self-esteem and healthy growth among students. Researchers have also demonstrated a positive correlation between religion and grade point average (Trokel, Barnes, & Egget, 2000; Zern, 1987). Throughout my courses students and I frequently acknowledge spirituality.

Course Integration.

First Days of Class.   When I ask my students to introduce themselves on the first day of classes, I ask that they share their name, hometown, academic major, a positive personal quality, and a personal quality that needs to be improved. Invariably, there are students who express their relationship with God, with a range of religious beliefs expressed. However, I believe that God is universal. Religions are our separate pathways of travel toward seeking God. When I introduce myself, I share with my students that I am a Christian and that I am always seeking to strengthen my relationship with God. I have discovered that students appreciate the acknowledgment of spirituality from the very beginning days of class.

Advising.   A few years ago I was advising a student who was working on her thesis, when I became frustrated with the student because she seemed to have *senioritis.* She had not kept up with any of the thesis preparation deadlines. The time for final drafts was fast approaching and she had not identified an instrument to measure data, nor had she collected any data, analyzed it, or written it up. I was outdone! I told the student that I had done all that I would do at that point. I explained that until she identified an instrument, as she had been assigned some time ago, I could not help any further. The problem, as I viewed it, was that the student insisted on doing things her way. She wanted to investigate high school students' exposure to violence in the home, at school, and in the community. My advice was that she should search for instruments that would measure each variable separately. I was certain that she would not be able to find a single instrument that would measure all three variables, especially in such a short amount of time. I told the student that she would have to work things out before the deadline or she would face failure. I was concerned that she would fail. To my surprise the student found an instrument that measured all three variables. What's more, she had done it over the course of a weekend. She called first thing on the Monday morning after our conversation to explain that she had the instrument in hand. I asked her to bring it in so that I could see it. When she did, I discovered that it was a viable instrument, one that had been evaluated satisfactorily for reliability and validity. When I asked how she found it, she said that she prayed all night after our talk and that the next day she found inspiration to find the proper tools. Suffice it to say, this student went on to collect data and successfully finished the required project. For her, the time she spent gaining inspiration from a higher source meant eliminating her procrastinating tendencies.

Personal Engagement.   Prayer and meditation are an essential part of my preparing for teaching on a daily basis. This time allows me to gain inspiration and a "stillness of spirit" before a usually hectic day: I pray for innovative ideas and exercises. I confirm that my purpose for teaching is to fulfill a divine assignment. I pray for courage and I give thanks for daily strength and endurance. Marian Wright Edelman's (1995) book, *Guide My Feet: Prayers and Meditations on Loving and Working for Children* (teenagers and college students included), discusses the importance of a God presence in the learning environment. As an alumna of an HBCU, she specifically recalls her appreciation for a spiritually infused campus. I have selected some favorites from her book and I read them over and over again. I have committed some of them to memory. I also read the Bible at night; when I am able to gain some solitude, I meditate on my experiences from the day and I listen to the spirit within and search for answers to daily dilemmas.

Suggested Strategies for Integrating Spirituality.   Based upon my research and personal experiences regarding the historical emphasis on spirituality in most African American communities, I suggest the following strategies (Hill, 1999):

1. Allow students to acknowledge a spiritual presence during the beginning of the course. Discuss appropriate use and expression among classmates of diverse religious affiliations.
2. Encourage students to engage in spiritually based activities (meditation, prayer, reading scriptures or other spiritual texts, worship services) as a

way of increasing levels of concentration and relieving tension and frustration.

3. Do not allow differences in religious affiliations to create conflict so that any student is offended.
4. Engage in personal spiritually based activities as a teacher/leader to relieve stress and gain new insights.

Special Note: At state schools the separation of church and state law makes the integration of spirituality difficult. In these instances, parameters must be respected. However, creative and alternative strategies can meet the same goal. For example, scholarly and discipline-specific quotes that reference spirituality can be used.

Harmony

Boykin (1983) cites harmony as an African American cultural view that everything is interrelated or holistic—that is, there are connections between everything that exists. African Americans have a proclivity toward a search for balance in life. Other scholars describe this as *field dependence*. *Field dependent* learners rely on intuition, social context, and environmental cues. *Field independent* learners rely on analyses, self, objects, and tasks. It has been demonstrated that African Americans are more field dependent (Akbar, 1978; Anderson, 1988; Witkin, 1977). Hale-Benson (1986) attributes this to a need for material that has human and social relevance. For me, it suggests that I help students to see the connections between academic content and the real world.

Course Integration: Providing Real-World Examples.   Often, when I explain or demonstrate course content, my students ask for personal examples. Sometimes they supply the examples and look for my approval. Sometimes they share personal stories as a way of confirming those personal connections. In this way, students are determining how the information fits into their lives. I have learned to prepare myself for these situations by thinking through relevant examples in advance of my lessons. Also, during class I ask students to brainstorm about possible connections and meanings. An example of this is my General Psychology course. When I teach about hemispheric specialization (left brain/right brain emphasis), I allow students to take a brief survey that gives a sense of whether they are left-brain dominant, right-brain dominant, or neutral. Left-brain dominant qualities are more verbal, analytical, and spatial. Right-brain dominant qualities are more visual, creative, and intuitive. After students compute their scores and determine a match, we discuss whether their results are consistent with their preferences, selection of academic major, and special interests. I also ask them to reflect upon other disciplines and professional practices that could benefit from the concept of hemispheric specialization. These activities add meaning and value to the concept.

Suggested Strategies for Harmony.   Because African American students look for meaning:

1. Prepare adequate examples for each set of new information that will be presented.
2. Allow time for students to provide examples and personal stories that confirm their understanding of concepts and information.
3. Assign homework that will allow students to see human and social relevance
   a. Observation
   b. Mini experiments
   c. Data collection
4. Share current events from the news that relate to particular concepts and issues.
5. Ask students to write about the significance of concepts and issues.

Movement

Beginning in infancy, African American babies are kinesthetically precocious. The continuity of this energy is displayed in the disproportionate numbers of African American athletes in the general population (Hale-Benson, 1986). Boykin (1983) suggests that there is a "rhythm of life" displayed in the behavior of African Americans. Gardner (cited in Woolfolk, 2001, p. 109) delineates a *bodily-kinesthetic* type of intelligence. With every lesson I teach, I allow time and space for movement of some sort. I use movement as an alternative way of explaining concepts, theories, issues, or parts thereof. It may appear to some that movement is an elementary approach. Upon closer inspection, it may be understood as a creative and more complex quality of learning. I consider it as such.

Course Integation.

Class Exercises.   Sometimes I gather students into pairs for an activity. At other times I ask them to stand and face the front of the room to participate in a demonstration. Occasionally, I send some of them out of the room while I set up an experiment using the remaining students as assistants. Sometimes I ask students to sit and use their hands, fingers, eyes, and voices. Students always enjoy the movement. Because I have done this for so long, I now know the types of exercises that connect with my students.

One movement example is taken, again, from my General Psychology course. I use it to further explain the four lobes of the brain: frontal, parietal, occipital, and temporal. After I lecture about particular parts and functions of the brain, I follow up my lecture with this activity. I ask students to point to the area on the top of their head that corresponds with each lobe. First, I demonstrate. I touch the top front of my head and say "frontal." I touch the top middle of my head and say "parietal." I touch the back of my head and say "occipital." I touch the sides of my head and say "temporal." Then I quiz my students: I call out one of the four lobes and ask students to point to that area as quickly as they can. I also call for volunteers to come up to the front of the class to demonstrate their accuracy. Students enjoy this exercise—so much so that they don't want to stop. And, they usually correctly answer these items on exams! Later in the course, students are also able to refer to one or more lobes of the brain in our subsequent discussions and questions. This is one indication of comprehension.

Another effective example is taken from my Group Dynamics and Interpersonal Relations course. When students are working on the issue of intergroup conflict and cooperation I assign them to work in small groups. I give each group a set of materials. Some of the groups have the same materials and some of the materials, are given to only one group. For example, tape is given to one group. Scissors are given to one other group. White and blue paper is given to all groups. Red paper is given to only two groups. The task is to make a United States flag. In order to do this, students have to move around to other groups to negotiate for the materials that they need. In this way, they have a chance to see the emergence and resolution of conflict and the advantages of cooperation. The first group to finish is declared the winner. To make it really engaging, I offer extra credit points to each student of the winning group. Naturally, everyone wants to earn the extra points so everyone participates; everyone experiences the movement.

In my Educational Psychology course, which is taught in a computer lab and arranged in a WebCT (electronic course design) format, I use movement to demonstrate to prospective teachers how individualized instruction can work in a classroom. Students are assigned the task of an Internet search to locate information on standards for learning, according to city, state, regional, and federal mandates, one set of standards for each. As students are working at the computer, I require each student to move around the room for two to three minutes to observe particular classmates at work. Each student gets a chance to observe. The observer takes on the role of a teacher. She notes behaviors, makes suggestions, and writes about her experiences (e.g., similarities of student behavior, particular problems, and suggestions made). The movement creates an interest and level of engagement that I cannot achieve by lecturing.

Movement by the Professor.   I believe that many of my students attune themselves for movement and rhythm so another technique that I use in all of my courses is adjusting the intonation of my voice. Piestrup (in Hale-Benson, 1986, p. 71) says that among the strategies for establishing good rapport for teachers is the use of a rhythmic style of speech and distinctive intonation in speech patterns. Because I believe my students look for movement and rhythm, I walk and then I stand still. I turn and then I sit. I lean back and I lean forward. I use gestures for emphasis. I move my eyes and my jaws. I smile and I frown. I believe that any and all movement is helpful. These nonverbal gestures are important pedagogical tools for effective communication among many African American students.

Suggested Strategies for Movement.   To provide for the energy that African American students relate to:

1. Prepare exercises in advance of lessons. Become familiar with students' favorite movement exercises.
2. Make sure that the purpose for each exercise is explicit. Repeat if necessary.
3. Ask students for suggestions about future exercises—exercises they like and don't like.
4. Teachers should get involved in the exercises also. It adds credibility to the exercises.
5. Encourage students to stand when they are speaking.
6. Allow students stretch-and-move breaks. They can move to another seat, angle the seat, etc.

Verve

Verve is the psychological dimension of movement. It is a desire for a variety of stimuli (Boykin, 1983). The implication is that all students do not prefer the same mode of presentation. Research in perceptual mode and its relationship to learning performance occurred before the 1900s (Keefe, 1987, p. 6). A more widely used term for this is *perceptual modality.* Perceptual modality style provides an indication of a dominant personality quality. Perceptual modality dominance indicates that the degree of processing speed, accuracy, and retention that an individual is able to accomplish when encountering information depends upon the medium in which information is presented (Barbe & Milone, 1980, 1981; Buell, Pettigrew, & Langendorfer, 1987; Dunn, 1988; Ginter, Scalise, Brown, & Ripley, 1989; Ingham, 1991). Perceptual modality dominance emphasizes superior functioning in one or more perceptual channels (Barbe & Milone, 1981). Through the years, I have spent quite a bit of time researching this area.

Brain-based research suggests the power of modality differentiation and supports the idea that perceptual modality dominance is a by-product of the brain (Buzan, 1991; Springer & Deutsh, 1985; Stein, Wallace, & Stanford, 2001). A learner can be dominant in one modality (unimodal), two modalities (bimodal), or three or more modalities (multimodal). Perceptual modalities include visual, auditory, tactile, and kinesthetic.

Literature in psychology, education, and neurology documents the diversity among modality styles (Bandler & Grinder, 1979; California Community Colleges, 1995; Corina, Vaid, & Bellugi, 1992; Edwards, 1979; Gazzaniga, 1973; Sperry, 1973; Thomas, Cox, & Kojima, 2000). Barbe and Milone (1981) have conducted extensive research on perceptual modalities and reported that 30 percent of persons in the population have a visual dominance, 25 percent have an auditory dominance, 15 percent have a kinesthetic dominance, and the remaining 30 percent have a mixed dominance (i.e., bimodal, multimodal).

Data that I collected on 150 students of all classifications and majors at an HBCU also demonstrated a pattern of diversity among perceptual styles. Students completed the Self-Administered Inventory of Learning Strengths for College Students (SAILS) (Seigel & Lester, 1994) to assess their modality styles. The SAILS is a 25-item forced-choice learning styles scale that measures college students' preferences in one or more of three domains: visual, auditory, and tactile/kinesthetic. The SAILS also includes a handout of learning techniques that lists practical ideas for teachers and students, suited to particular learner types. The findings from the SAILS showed 37 percent as visual, 33 percent as tactile/kinesthetic, 14 percent as auditory, 13 percent as bimodal, and 3 percent as multimodal.

A most important point to note here is that researchers have demonstrated increases in learners' levels of understanding and confidence when the mode of presentation accommodates learners' dominant perceptual modality (Boulmetis & Sabula, 1996; Carnevale, Gainer, Meltzer, & Holland, 1988; Dunn, 1988; Hoofner, 1986; Ingham, 1991; Jiao & Onwuegbuzie, 1999; Miller, 2001; Warasila & Lomaga, 2000). I teach in a multimodal fashion.

Course Integration.

Identifying Learning Needs with Students.   During the first days of class, I discuss the concept of learning styles with my students and provide some relevant background. I also discuss the benefits and need for students and teachers to be aware of individual learning styles. As I am made aware of differential learning needs, I can better accommodate students. Additionally, I emphasize the point that as students are made aware of their own learning styles, they too can take responsibility for securing accommodations that will satisfy their particular needs. I tell students that several instruments assess varied dimensions of learning styles and explain my success with attention to perceptual modality styles. To better accommodate and assess those diverse needs, I give students the VARK (visual, aural, read/write, kinesthetic) questionnaire (Fleming & Mills, 1992). The VARK is a 13-item forced-choice questionnaire that indicates students' preferred mode(s) of learning. Like the SAILS, the VARK also offers teachers and students a variety of suggested learning approaches suited to individual types. Unlike the SAILS, and the reason I use VARK, is that VARK provides students with techniques for taking information in, techniques for studying the information, and techniques for testing well, each suited to particular perceptual styles. After I score the VARK questionnaires, I give students a written interpretation and VARK's suggested techniques for their particular types. For students who are bimodal or multimodal, I suggest that they use strategies for the modality that they have not used before. In other words, a student who is visual/aural (bimodal) and who has been paying attention to the aural need should begin to attend to the visual need.

I then devise a class profile from the students' VARK results. This profile informs my teaching strategies for the semester. I have found that this approach assures that students' perceptual needs are usually met. The student is made aware of and responsible for her learning needs and at the same time I acknowledge learning needs by varying the way that I deliver instruction.

Suggested Strategies for Using Perceptual Modality Styles.   The techniques suggested for teachers by VARK (Fleming & Mills, 1992) are ones that I use and suggest to others. Most, if not all, of these strategies can be easily managed with the use of educational technology.

Teaching/Learning Strategies

Visual
- Create concept maps
- Draw diagrams, models, flow charts, etc.
- Project computer animation
- Use videos, slides, photographs to explicate and to clarify or as discussion triggers

Aural
- Use audiotapes
- Have class debates
- Engage students in discussion
    Think-Pair-Share
    Small groups
    Large groups
- Brainstorming
- Guided lecture
- Responsive lecture
- Group presentations

Read/Write
- One-minute write
- Summaries
- Case studies
- Journals
- Create examination questions
- Formative quizzes
- Analytical lists
- Round table response
- Have students review each other's notes
    (pause procedure)

Kinesthetic
- Role play: Take character parts and act out a situation
    Represent parts of the body, government, etc.

- Create a physical representation
     Work problems on the board
     Use three-dimensional models
- Analyze a problem
- Have students plot information, create a histogram, develop a graph, etc.
- Create a value line based on an issue
- Thumbs-up/thumbs-down or stand up/sit down

The following practical recommendations for faculty might be helpful in preparing and planning for multimodal presentations more easily accommodated by the use of technology.

1. Engage in ongoing training in the use of educational technology (e.g., workshops, conferences) so that use of technological aids is familiar and comfortable.
2. Develop a personal library of relative materials on educational technology (e.g., books, training manuals, software) to extend personal knowledge of applicable resources.
3. Assess the perceptual modality styles that exist in each class (see James & Blank, 1993, for a review and critique of learning style instruments for adult learners):
   a. A class profile can be devised that lists the percentages of learners of each perceptual type.
   b. Students can be made aware of their own styles and can share in the responsibility of gathering appropriate resources.
4. Identify particular technological formats that will accommodate multiple modes (i.e., visual, auditory, tactile, kinesthetic).
5. Establish easy access to adequate and appropriate equipment.
6. Communicate issues of resource support to appropriate bodies (via faculty meetings, departmental and schoolwide evaluations, meetings with administrators, etc.).
7. Take advantage of opportunities to share and discuss dos and don'ts of educational technology among colleagues (formally and informally).

Affect

Shade (1991) demonstrated that African American students prefer affective materials and social interaction. Traditionally, intelligence has been defined as a measurable mental activity. It has also been said that intellect without feelings is incomplete (Hoskins & Butts, cited in Hale-Benson, 1986, p. 69). Howard Gardner (cited in Woolfolk, 2001, p. 109) redefined what it means to be smart with a theory of multiple intelligences. His theory is that individuals may have strengths or weaknesses in one or more of eight areas: logical-mathematical, linguistic, musical, spatial, bodily-kinesthetic, interpersonal, intrapersonal, and naturalist. According to

Gardner, there is no hierarchy among the eight types of intelligence. Salovey and Mayer (1990) honed the research on Gardner's interpersonal and intrapersonal types and determined an *emotional intelligence*. Emotional intelligence is a set of skills that allows accurate appraisals and expressions of emotion in oneself and others, effective regulation of emotion in oneself and others, and the use of feelings to motivate, plan, and achieve. It is the ability to process affective information.

Daniel Goleman's (1995) book, *Emotional Intelligence: Why It Can Matter More Than IQ,* describes the brain as comprised of three divisions: (1) the brainstem, which controls heart rate and breathing; (2) the limbic system, the center of emotions; and (3) the neocortex, processor for feelings and meaning. The result is two minds, a mind that thinks and a mind that feels. Emotional intelligence is the successful interaction of these two minds.

The heritage of African Americans bespeaks "I feel, therefore, I think, therefore, I am" (Dixon & Foster, cited in Hale-Benson, 1986, p. 69). In an investigation conducted by Gitter, Black, and Mostofsky (in Hale-Benson, 1986), Black and White students were asked to judge the emotions displayed on photographs of professional actors who depicted either anger, happiness, disgust, sadness, pain, fear, or surprise. Black students judged these emotions significantly more correctly than White students. To me, this emphasis on feelings impacts the academic performance of African American students.

Course Integration.

Name Recognition.   During the first days of class I memorize my students' first names. The way I do this is to make some sort of association with each student's face. It may be that a student has the same name as someone else that I know so I make an association between that recollection and the student's face. It may also be the case that a student's face matches my personal meaning of a name. For example, the student may look or act like "Cynthia" (according to my scheme of a "Cynthia"). Sometimes it's the way a student introduces herself that stands out, and I am able to make an association by remembering that particular behavior. As other students are introducing themselves, I practice the recall of these associations by quickly reviewing the names of students who have already introduced themselves. When all the students have finished introducing themselves, I go around the room and call every student by name. The level of amazement on the student's faces is something to behold! Students immediately ask how I achieved this recognition. I explain to them that although I do not take attendance, this suggests that I will know when anyone is absent. Later in the evening, I rehearse the names again by picturing their faces and recalling their names. When I return to class, I call the names again. Subsequently, when I call on students in class I am able to refer to them by name. I also encourage other students to refer to each other by name. Students catch on very quickly and communicate appropriately.

There is something meaningful about hearing one's name called by another person. In the classroom it is especially important for students to be acknowledged in such a meaningful way. This approach immediately closes any superficial distance between my students and me. It captures their attention. It stimulates their emotions. It assures them that they have a special place in my thoughts and that they have an important place in my life. I am reminded about how important this is when students watch me closely during class to see if I will remember their particular names.

Sometimes students pass by my office to say hello and ask if I remember their names. In other instances, when students come in for conferencing I greet them by calling their name. It is a guaranteed "icebreaker" for our conversation. Also, when I pass by former students in the hallways and around campus I greet them by name. I sense the empowerment when students say to me, "You still remember my name!"

Humor. I add humor whenever I can during the course of class because humor is a calming influence in folk's lives. It releases tension and confusion. It also helps students to relate to me. During the first day of class, while I am reviewing my syllabus with students, one of the things I mention is that students may not engage in "free-for-all" eating but that they may sip on something. Up to that point my tone is serious. Then out of nowhere I'll say, "Yes, you may sip on something NONALCOHOLIC, that is." Students always display a burst of laughter.

Another example is when I enter the classroom: I greet the entire class with a resounding "Good Morning!," "Good Afternoon," or "Good Evening!" On days when students do not respond so well, I'll say, "Oh, you all are not speaking to me today. Did I do something? Should I leave?" This gets a smile every time and students begin to relax.

Students often initiate humor in class, too. Sometimes students share personal stories with a funny ending. Sometimes they ask questions in a humorous way. They know that it's okay to laugh, so they laugh. Students enjoy the humor because it breaks the monotony. I must say that there is not a great deal of giggling in my classes. Quiet and serious engagement is not lacking. We engage in what I refer to as intellectual humor. It is a departure from traditional pedagogical deliveries and yet it can be intellectually stimulating.

Verbal and Nonverbal Expressions. Periodically, I inject class discussions with language that is particularly appealing to students. It's language that they use among their peers. For example, when a student repeats a correct answer, I say, "Go girl!" Or, when I make a mistake I'll say, "My bad!" When I want to acknowledge a student's level of improvement, I'll say, "You are blowin' up!" They love this vernacular level of interaction.

A lot of times when I respond to a student or to the class, I'll give a funny look, a look of extreme surprise, or a look of sassiness. At other times, when I am really proud of students' performance, I'll enact a shouting episode by stomping my feet and clapping my hands. When students are not engaging with me at a satisfactory level, I'll put my head in my hands and pretend to cry. Many times I put my hand on my hip and say, "Loooooooord, have mercy!"

I am a very passionate professor and I don't mind showing it. As I teach I display anger, excitement, and seriousness when and where each is appropriate. Integrating affect is emotionally rewarding for me as well.

Suggested Strategies for Affect.   Stimulate African Americans' emotional strength by:

1. For every lesson, planning design points where affect can be used.
2. Encouraging intellectual humor from students and allowing time for laughter when appropriate. Laugh time is okay.
3. Memorizing students' names. A seating chart is a useful tool.
4. Infusing lectures with a display of appropriate emotions.
5. As often as possible, allowing students to express their feelings.

Communalism

Boykin (1983) explains that African Americans are socially oriented. Of the several and similar dimensions of learning styles that describe the learning styles of African American children, communalism and cooperation have been delineated (Akbar, 1975; Bonner, 2000; Boykin, 1983; Diller, 1999; Hale-Benson, 1986; Slavin & Oickle, 1981; Willis, 1992). The suggestion that African American children learn effectively with others, around others, and in interaction with others, is consistent throughout this literature. During a formal investigation (Watkins, 2002) I discovered that the communal/cooperative learning style among many African Americans is present even at the preschool level.

I have noticed a consistent desire on the part of students to work together. I have also taken note of the quality of individual performance when students have had the opportunity to work with others. Students' comments on course evaluations and their face-to-face communication with me also reflect their appreciation for cooperative learning. As much as possible I allow students to work with classmates. When I was a student I enjoyed studying in a group: It afforded me the best of both worlds. There were times when I needed to study alone and there were times that I needed the reinforcement and clarification from the group. My students reflect the same sentiments.

Course Integration.

Cooperative Learning.   I assign students to study groups as a part of my course requirements. I encourage my students to gather at least twice a week for two or more hours. I have learned that students do not want to work together when the cooperative arrangement threatens poor performance. For example, when students know that they will suffer from another student's lack of concern and input, they resent grouping structures. To control for this, I assign a group leader to take attendance at group meetings, and I give unannounced evaluations of group meetings during class. If the responses of students in the same group do not corroborate, I call those groups in for a conference. Monitoring allows me to identify trouble spots and to correct them early in the semester. Students have the option of changing groups or dropping from the group structure, if there is a legitimate reason. I emphasize that the groups are meant to help and not hinder academic performance. If any student feels that she is placed at an academic disadvantage after having experienced the group structure, she may work alone.

I also use cooperative learning structures to meet specific course objectives. In my General Psychology course I require group presentations. The presentation is a supplement to course content. In my Educational Psychology course the group assignment is the design of a web page for student use. In my Psychology of the African American Experience course I assign group panel discussions. Occasionally, I assign in-class written work or homework and give students the option of working within a group or alone. Most students opt to work within groups.

In my courses I administer quizzes and exams. The quizzes are brief and serve as preparation for exams. They are assigned a lower percentage weighting than exams. In some of my courses groups of students take quizzes together. Students are told at the beginning of the course, and it is written in the syllabus, that they will take quizzes with their groups. The need for studying together then becomes clear. On quiz days students take the quiz twice, the first time alone and the second time with their groups. Students receive both an individual quiz grade and a group quiz grade. The real benefit is that since these students have been working together before the quiz and they are familiar with each other, the group quiz is another learning opportunity. As students are answering questions, they correct each other, clarifying and explaining information. This also preps students for the exam. My exam covers the same information as the quizzes but in much more detail. It may appear that the group quiz arrangement is nothing more than giving permission for students to cheat. However, when I observe closely, I can see that students are not simply getting answers and writing them down. Students are engaged in intellectual bantering.

Peer Tutoring.   On our campus, there is a Learning Resources Center. Among the services offered there is peer tutoring. Students from each department are hired and assigned as peer tutors for particular courses. Students may sign up and receive the help from a peer as often as the time slots permit. I encourage peer tutoring arrangements for students who desire other students to assist them.

Suggested Strategies for Cooperative Learning.   Capitalize on the communal learning styles of African American students by:

1. Using cooperative groups to vary instructional strategies.
2. Assigning peer tutors within particular courses.
3. Eliciting student feedback about group work.
4. Evaluating group performance in addition to individual performance.

5. Holding group office hours. Students with similar issues and concerns can meet with the instructor together (e.g., all students in General Psychology who want to discuss test performance/anxiety; all who want to make suggestions for the course; all who need to clarify particular concepts).

Expressive Individualism

Boykin (1983) points out that African Americans have a way of focusing and emphasizing individual uniqueness in their behavior (i.e., style of dress or hair, use of eyes, a certain walk or way of standing, a manner of greeting). One interpretation is that the preference for personal distinctiveness within the culture may be the alternative to oppressive conditions outside the culture (Hale-Benson, 1986; Hilliard, 1976).

The way that I capitalize on this quality is by taking note of students' particular ways of expressing: talking to others, writing, and questioning. Then, during class I point out these qualities and acknowledge that they are acceptable avenues for personal expression. For example, as I am making comments on an assignment I might say, "Now I know that Tonya does not follow my instructions without a fight. I told her that the word *provide* should be written in its plural form in this sentence. I had to suggest that she was wrong before she finally accepted my instructions. But that's okay (smile), she's an independent learner." Or, before an exam, I may say, "I must be in trouble. Jackie smiles all the time. She is not smiling today." In conferences I also make mention of students' particular styles. This strategy lets students' know that I have been paying close attention to them, that I acknowledge their uniqueness, and that I accept them. In turn, this builds students' trust in me and their level of confidence in the course.

Suggested Strategies for Expressive Individualism.   Watch for individual manners of African American students by:

1. Taking note of individual patterns in students' behavior.
2. Complimenting students' uniqueness in class and in individual conversations with students. Professors should call attention to their own individuality as well.
3. Being careful not to embarrass students. Watch for students' sensitivities.
4. Asking questions and assigning tasks and roles based on students' individuality (e.g., "Tony, I know that you will want to comment on this (smile)"; "June, will you get us started in our discussion?").

Orality

Nobles (1972) points out that there is an emphasis on oral-based communication within the African American community because of an African worldview. Boykin (1983) also stresses the importance for African Americans to transmit information in oral forms. Karenga (1993) notes orality as a vestige of African culture. McHenry and Heath (1994) provide historical evidence of the literary emphasis on orality among African Americans.

On our campus, the faculty is asked to demonstrate how students' oral skills are being developed. I can provide a number of techniques.

Course Integration.

Presentations.   I allow students to speak often. Because students like to talk among themselves, class discussions are fruitful. Oral presentations have always been an integral part of my courses. For every written assignment I require students to give a brief overview of their written work when they submit it. On group projects, members of the group must speak. By the end of the course each student has given at least three oral presentations.

Debates.   I organize debates around key issues in class. First, I present the issue. Then I ask my students to close their eyes, decide whether they will take the position of pro or con, and raise their hands accordingly. I write the names of students according to the side they choose. When students open their eyes I call their names and direct the "pros" to one side of the classroom and the "cons" to the other. Students rearrange their seats so that one side faces the other. Students complain about not having enough time. I give the rules ahead of time and make sure that they are followed. Students have a tendency to look at me the first time they experience the debate. I redirect their eye contact to their classmates. Suffice it to say, there is never a dull moment!

Panel Discussions.   I also arrange panel discussions. These are prearranged and required assignments. Students must sign up for at least one panel during the semester. Each panel addresses an identified issue by gathering information (as a group) about a different aspect of that issue. Students grade each other using a standard rubric/ rating form. The criteria include eye contact, clarity, substance, and insight. At the end of each panel, students may ask questions of any of the panelists. Panels are an alternative to lectures, they capitalize on peer interactions, and they advance public speaking skills.

Storytelling.   Frequently, I engage students in storytelling. It is an African tradition. After I introduce a topic, an issue, or some body of information, I ask students to share a story about their personal experiences. Sometimes I preface this activity with a question like, "Who knows someone with Alzheimer's disease?" or "Has anyone ever witnessed someone who is depressed?" I often relate personal stories in this regard.

Suggested Strategies for Orality.   Allow the flow of speech that is natural for African American students by:

1. Scheduling debates in course planning.
2. Using storytelling as an introduction or transition to new information. Teachers should also engage in storytelling.
3. Allowing group oral presentations.
4. Allowing students to discuss issues in small groups and report the consensus or forms of disagreement to the larger group.

Social Time Perspective

Houston (1990) describes the concept of time for African Americans as the perpetuation of African culture that is tied to religious ontology. Nobles (1972) identifies the notion of CPT (colored people's time) as an authentic cultural perception (communal potential time). The passing of events determines time, not mathematics. Further, time is understood as the beginning and ending of events and not as numbers on a clock (Boykin, 1983). Mbiti (cited in Houston, 1990) explains that African time consists of events: past, present, and immediate future.

> . . . an expectant mother counts the lunar months of her pregnancy: a traveler counts the number of days it takes him to walk (in former years) from one part of the country to the other. The day, the month, the year, one's life time or human history, are all divided up or reckoned according to their specific events, for it is these that make them meaningful. For example, the rising of the sun is an event which is recognized by the whole community. It does not matter, therefore, whether the sun rises at 5 A.M. or 7 A.M., so long as it rises. When a person asks that he will meet another at sunrise, it does not matter whether the meeting takes place at 5 A.M. or 7 A.M., so long as it is during the general period of sunrise. Likewise, it does not matter whether people go to bed at 9 P.M. or at 12 midnight; the important thing is the event of going to bed, and it is immaterial whether in one night this takes place at 10 P.M. while in another it is at midnight. For the people concerned, time is meaningful at the point of the event and not at the mathematical moment. (p. 21)

Because we live in a society that perceives time as a commodity, "time is money," I believe it is important to encourage students to respect that system of time but to also be mindful of the African tradition of time because it empowers them to view time on their terms.

The way that I acknowledge this alternative perception of time in my teaching is to be flexible, whenever possible, with parameters of time. For students who need it, I allow untimed tests. I also allow a ten-minute grace period for coming to class. I do not rush through course units for fear of running out of time. Rather, I consider whether adequate closure has been accomplished. Within reason, I am flexible with due dates and deadlines for assignments.

Suggested Strategies for Social Time Perspective.   Regard African American students' alternative perspectives of time by:

1. As much as possible, being flexible with time limits.
2. Discussing society's respect for time.
3. Discussing students' regard for time.
4. Asking for student input on deadlines and due dates, including their rationales.

Two questions have been raised with regard to BCLS:

Do Black Cultural Learning Styles establish stereotypes that result in unfavorable evaluations of African American students?

No, although BCLS are unique to African American culture, learning patterns of other cultures—Latino, Native, and Asian Americans—are described as well (Cushner, McClelland, & Safford, 2000; Gay, 2000; Heath, 1983). Stereotyping is not the intent of this discourse, rather workable solutions to maximize academic performance. The goal is for everyone to win. Also, just as various media forms—television, movies, and magazines—legitimize cultural influences in food, dress, music, and language, cultural influences on learning are recognized as well. Learning is another variable of culture, albeit one of the most important. It is appropriate for cultural influences on learning to be acknowledged in the classroom. With regard to the concern about resulting unfavorable evaluations, unfavorable evaluations already exist. The goal of BCLS is to eradicate unfavorable evaluations and stereotypes that already exist as a result of bias, discrimination, and misinformation.

Given the range of diversity within the African American culture, or any culture, do all African American students fit within the Black Cultural Learning Styles framework?

The implication for this question is that all African Americans have assimilated to mainstream culture to varying degrees and that those who have assimilated to higher degrees do not exhibit the purer ethnic learner type. Hale-Benson (1986) says that African Americans are sufficiently isolated in U.S. society to preserve and transmit cultural patterns because African Americans live and work together, go to the same schools, and socialize at the same places. Even in case of middle- and upper-class status, African American children are socialized by babysitters, grandparents, and other members of the extended family network who are less assimilated to mainstream standards. Hence, virtually all African American students are influenced by these cultural styles. Hilliard's (1997, p.iii) response to this is that although not all people of African descent reflect the core African culture, there is a deep cultural structure that remains for most. The vast majority of African Americans carry the core African cultural meanings because most live in the same communities, eat the same kinds of food, and use the same language (dialects and slang). Hence, there is a system for transmitting learning and behavioral patterns. Pedagogy must be sensitive to this fact.

Concluding Thoughts

More than anything else, experience has been my best teacher. I have experienced success with my students by capitalizing on their unique learning qualities. It has required a radical departure from traditional theories of learning and an understanding that African American behavior, in general, and learning, in particular, are influenced by deep cultural meanings that are rooted in African tradition. I have shared these strategies and suggestions with the hope of creating a better learning experience for African American college students and those who teach them. In summary, the techniques suggested for capitalizing on Black Cultural Learning Styles were:

- Acknowledge strong religious orientations
- Emphasize meaning in course topics, issues, and concepts
- Provide rhythm and energy
- Present information in a variety of modes
- Stimulate students' feelings
- Allow communal learning
- Watch for individual styles
- Utilize oral skills
- Regard the alternative social time perspective

REFERENCES

Akbar, N. (1975). The rhythm of Black personality. *Southern Exposure, 3,* 14–19.
Akbar, N. (1978). *Cultural expressions of the African American child.* (Eric Document Reproduction Service No. 179633).
Anderson, J. A. (1988). Cognitive styles and multicultural populations. *Journal of Teacher Education, 39,* 2–9.
Appelhans, B. M., & Schmeck, R. R. (2002). Learning styles and approach versus avoidant coping during academic exam preparation. *College Students Journal, 36,* 157–160.
Bandler, R., & Grinder, J. (1979). *Frogs into princes.* Moab, UT: Real People Press.
Barbe, W. B., & Milone, M. N. (1980, January). Modality. *Instructor, 89,* 44–47.
Barbe, W. B., & Milone, M. N. (1981, February). What we know about modality strengths. *Educational Leadership, 38,* 378–380.
Berg, K. J., & Poppenhagen, B. W. (1985). Adult learning styles and computer technology. *Studies in the Education of Adults, 17,* 75–82
Bonner, F. (2000). African American giftedness: Our nation's deferred dream. *Journal of Black Studies, 30*(5), 643–663.
Boulmetis, J., & Sabula, A. M. (1996, Fall). Achievement gains via instruction that matches learning style perceptual preferences. *The Journal of Continuing Higher Education, 44,* 15–24.
Boykin, A. W. (1983). On academic task performance and Afro-American children. In J. R. Spencer (Ed.), *Achievement and achievement motives.* Boston: Freeman.
Buell, C., Pettigrew, F., & Langendorfer, S. (1987). Effect of perceptual style strength on acquisition of a novel motor task. *Perceptual and Motor Skills, 65,* 743–747.

Buzan, T. (1991). *Use both sides of your brain.* New York: E. P. Dutton.

California Community Colleges. (1995). *An integrated approach to multicultural education.* Sacramento: Academic Senate for California Community Colleges. (ERIC Document Reproduction Service No. ED383365).

Carnevale, A. P., Gainer, L. J., Meltzer, A. S., & Holland, S. L. (1988, October). Skills employers want. *Training and Development Journal, 42,* 22–30.

Cook, S. W. (2000). College students' perceptions of spiritual people and religious people. *Journal of Psychology and Theology, 28,* 125–138.

Corina, D. P., & Vaid, J. (1992). The linguistic basis of left hemisphere specialization. *Science, 225,* 1258–1260.

Cushner, K., McClelland, A., & Safford, P. (2000). *Human diversity in education: An integrative approach.* Boston: McGraw Hill.

Diller, D. (1999). Opening the dialogue: Using culture as a tool in teaching young African American children. *The Reading Teacher, 52*(8), 820–828.

Dunn, R. (1988, January) Teaching students through their perceptual strengths or preferences. *Journal of Reading, 31,* 304–309.

Dunn, R., & Griggs, S. A. (Eds.). (2000). *Practical approaches to using learning styles in higher education.* London: Bergin & Garvey.

Durodye, B., & Hildreth, B. (1995). Learning styles and the African American student. *Education, 116,* 241–247.

Edelman, M. W. (1995). *Guide my feet. Prayers and meditations on loving and working for children.* Boston: Beacon Press.

Edwards, B. (1979). *Drawing on the right side of the brain.* London: Fontana.

Ellis, J. B., & Smith, P. C. (1991) Spiritual well-being, social desirability, and reasons for living: Is there a connection? *The International Journal of Psychiatry, 37,* 57–63.

Epstein, M. (1998). Therapy and meditation. *Psychology Today, 31,* 46–50.

Evans, T. E., & Francis, L. J. (1996). The relationship of personal prayer and purpose of life among church going and non-church going twelve to fifteen-year-olds in the U.K. *Religious Education, 91,* 9–13.

Fleming, N. D., & Mills, C. (1992). Not another inventory, rather a catalyst for reflection. *To Improve the Academy, 11,* 137–149.

Frankel, B. G., & Hewitt, W. E. (1994). Religion and well-being among Canadian university students: The role of faith groups on campus. *Journal for the Scientific Study of Religion, 33,* 62.

Gay, G. (2000). *Culturally responsive teaching. Theory, research, and practice.* New York: Teachers College Press.

Gazzaniga, M. C. (1973). The split brain in man. In R. E. Ornstein (Ed.), *The nature of human consciousness: A book of readings* (pp. 87–100). San Francisco: W. H. Freeman.

Ginter, E., Scalise, J., Brown, S., & Ripley, W. (1989). Perceptual learning styles: Their link to academic performance, sex, age, and academic standing. *Perceptual and Motor Skills, 68,* 1091–1094.

Goleman, D. (1995). *Emotional intelligence: Why it can matter more than IQ.* New York: Bantam Books.

Hale-Benson, J. E. (1986). *Black children: Their roots, culture, and learning styles* (rev. ed.). Baltimore: The Johns Hopkins University Press.

Hale, J. E. (1993). Rejoinder to "Myths of Black cultural learning styles" In defense of Afrocentric scholarship. *School Psychology Review, 22,* 558–561.

Hale, J. E. (1994). *Unbank the fire. Visions for the education of African American children.* Baltimore: Johns Hopkins University Press.

Heath, S. B. (1983). *Ways with words.* Cambridge: Cambridge University Press.

Hill, R. B. (1999). *The strengths of African American families. Twenty-five years later.* Lanham, MD: University Press of America.

Hilliard, III, A. G. (1976). *Alternatives to IQ testing: An approach to the identification of gifted minority children (Final report).* San Francisco: San Francisco State University. (ERIC Document Reproduction Service No. EC 103 067).

Hilliard, III, A. G. (1997). *Annotated selected bibliography and index for teaching African-American learners: Culturally responsive pedagogy project.* ERIC Document Reproduction Service No. ED 437 478).

Hoofner, S. M. (1986). *Adult learning styles: Auditory, visual, and tactile-kinesthetic sensory modalities* [Online]. (Doctoral Dissertation, Texas A &M University, 1986) Dissertation Abstracts: AAC 8625400.

Houston, L. N. (1990). *Psychological principles and the Black experience.* New York: University Press of America.

Ingham, J. M. (1991). Matching instruction with employee perceptual preference significantly increases training effectiveness. *Human Resource Quarterly, 2,* 53–64.

Jackson, J. S., & Gurin, G. (2000). *National Survey of Black Americans.* Retrieved March 6, 2002, from University of Georgia, Data Services Website: http://dadtaserve.libs.uga.edu/icpsr/6668/6668.html.

Jagers, R. J., & Mock, L. O. (1993). Cultural outcomes among inner-city African American children: An Afrographic exploration. *Journal of Black Psychology, 19,* 391–405.

Jagers, R. L., & Mock, L. O. (1995). The communalism scale and collectivistic-individualistic tendencies: Some preliminary findings. *Journal of Black Psychology, 21,* 153–167.

Jagers, R. L., & Smith, P. (1996, November). Further examination of the spirituality scale. *Journal of Black Psychology, 22.*

James, W. B., & Blank, W. E. (1993). Review and critique of available learning-style instruments for adults. *New Directions for Adult and Continuing Education, 59,* 47–57.

Jeynes, W. H. (1999, November). The effects of religious commitment of the academic achievement of Black and Hispanic children. *Urban Education, 34,* 478–479.

Jiao, Q. G., & Onwuegbuzie, A. J. (1999). Identifying library anxiety through students' learning-modality preferences. *Library Quarterly, 69,* 202–216.

Jones, R. L. (Ed.). (1980). *Black psychology* (2nd ed.). New York: Harper & Row.

Jones, R. L. (Ed.). (1991). *Black psychology* (3rd ed.). Berkeley, CA: Cobb & Henry.

Karenga, M. (1993). *Introduction to Black studies* (2nd ed.) Los Angeles: University of Sankore Press.

Keefe, J. W. (1987). *Learning style theory and practice.* Reston, VA: National Association of Secondary School Principals.

Knox, D., Langehough, S. O., Walters, C., & Riley, M. (1998). Religiosity and spirituality among college students. *College Student Journal, 32,* 430–433.

Kwate, N. (2001). Intelligence or misorientation? Eurocentrism in the WISC-III. *Journal of Black Psychology, 27*(2), 221–238.

Ladson-Billings, G. (1994). *The dreamkeepers.* San Francisco: Jossey-Bass.

Lemire, D. (2001). An introduction to learning styles for college teachers. *Journal of College Reading and Learning, 32,* 86–92.

Levin, J. S., & Taylor, R. J. (1998). Panel analyses of religious involvement and well-being in African Americans: Contemporaneous vs. longitudinal effects. *Journal for the Scientific Study of Religion, 37,* 695.

Loo, R. (2002). The distribution of learning styles and types for hard and soft business majors. *Educational Psychology, 22,* 349–360.

Maltby, J. (1998, August). Church attendance and anxiety change. *Journal of Social Psychology, 138,* 537–538.

Maton, K. I. (1989). The stress-buffering role of sprirtual support: Cross sectional and prospective investigations. *Journal for the Scientific Study of Religion, 28,* 310–323.

McHenry, E., & Heath, S. B. (1994). The literate and the literary: African Americans as writers and readers—1830–1940. *Written Communication, 11,* 419–444.

Miller, P. (2001). *Learning styles: The multimedia of the mind* (Research report). Michigan. (ERIC Document Reproduction Service No. ED451140).

Millet, P. E., Sullivan, B. F., Schwebel, A. I., & Myers, L. J. (1996). Black Americans' and Whites Americans' views of the etiology and treatment of mental health problems. *Community Mental Health Journal, 32,* 235–242.

Nobles, W. W. (1972). African philosophy: Foundations for Black psychology. In R. L. Jones (Ed.), *Black psychology* (pp. 18–32). New York: Harper & Row.

Nobles, W. W. (1985). *Africanity and the Black family: The development of a theoretical model.* Oakland, CA: The Institute for the Advanced Study of Black Family Life and Culture.

Parham, T. A., White, J. L., & Ajamu, A. (1999). *The psychology of blacks: An African centered perspective* (3rd ed.). Upper Saddle River, NJ: Prentice Hall.

Regenerus, M. D. (2000, September). Shaping schooling success: Religious socialization and educational outcomes in metropolitan public schools. *Journal for the Scientific Study of Religion, 39,* 363–370.

Salovey, P., & Mayer, J. D. (1990). Emotional intelligence. *Imagination, Cognition & Personality, 9,* 185–211.

Seigel, J., & Lester, S. (1994). *The self-administered inventory of learning strengths for college students.* New Mexico: Tests, Measurement, and Evaluation. (ERIC Document Reproduction Service No. ED372080).

Shade, B. J. (1982). Afro-American cognitive style: A variable in school success? *Review of Educational Research, 52,* 219–244.

Shade, B. (1989). Culture: The key to adaptation. In B. Shade (Ed.), *Culture, style, and the educative process* (pp. 9–15). Springfield, IL: Charles C. Thomas.

Shade, B. (1991). African American patterns of cognition. In R. L. Jones (Ed.), *Black psychology.* Berkeley, CA: Cobb & Henry.

Slavin, R. E., & Oickle, E. (1981). Effects of cooperative learning teams on student achievement and race realtions: Treatment by race interactions. *Sociology of Education, 54,* 174–180.

Sperry, R. (1973). Lateral specialization of cerebral function in the surgically separated hemisphere. In F. J. McGulgan & R. A. Schoonover (Eds.), *The psychophysiology of thinking* (pp. 209–229). New York: Academic Press.

Springer, S., & Deutsch, G. (1985). *Left brain, right brain.* New York: W. H. Freeman.

Stein, B., Wallace, E., & Stanford, T. R. (2001) Brain mechanisms for synthesizing information from different sensory modalities. In E. B. Goldstein (Ed.), *Blackwell handbook of perception* (pp. 709–736). Malden, MA: Blackwell.

Taylor, R. J., & Mattis, J. (1999, November). Subjective religiosity among African Americans: A synthesis of findings from five national samples. *Journal of Black Psychology, 25,* 524–544.

Thomas, H., Cox, R., & Kojima, T. (2000, March). *Relating preferred learning styles to student achievement.* Paper presented at the Annual Meeting of the Teachers of English to Speakers of Other Languages, Vancouver, BC.

Trokel, M. T., Barnes, M. D., & Egget, D. (2000). Health related variables and academic performance among first year college students: Implications for sleep and other behaviors. *Journal of American College Health, 49,* 125.

U.S. Census Bureau. (2000). *Educational attainment of the population 15 years and older, by age sex, race, and Hispanic origin: March, 2000.* [Data File]. Available from United States Bureau of the Census Web site, http://www.census.gov/population/www/socdemo/education/p20-536.html

Walker, K. L., & Dixon, V. (2002). Spirituality and academic performance among African American college students. *Journal of Black Psychology, 28,* 107–121.

Warasila, R. L., & Lomaga, G. S. (2000). Screening prospective telecourse students. *Journal of College Science Teaching, 30,* 202–205.

Watkins, A. F. (2002). Learning styles of African American children: A developmental consideration. *Journal of Black Psychology, 28,* 3–17.

White, J. L. (1984). *The psychology of blacks: An Afro-American perspective.* Englewood Cliffs, NJ: Prentice-Hall.

Willis, M. G. (1992). Learning styles of African Amercian children: A review of the literature and interventions. In A. K. Burlew, W. C. Banks, H. P. McAdoo, & D. A. Azibo (Eds.), *African American psychology: Theory, research, and practice.* (pp. 260–276). London: Sage.

Witkin, H. A. (1977). Educational implications of cognitive styles. *Review of Educational Research, 47,* 1–64.

Wong-McDonald, A. (2000). Surrender to God: An additional coping style. *Journal of Psychology & Theology, 28,* 149–516.

Woolfolk, A. (2001). *Educational psychology* (8th ed.). Boston: Allyn and Bacon.

Zern, D. S. (1987). The relationship of religious involvement to a variety of indicators of cognitive ability and achievement in college students. *Adolescence, 22,* 883–894.

8

Strategies to Improve Teaching "Feared" Courses to African American Students

Duane M. Jackson
Morehouse College

When I walk into my statistics class on the first day of the semester, I sense in my students apprehension, fear, and some despair. I have been teaching statistics for over twenty years and have found this to be the case when I was a Teaching Assistant at the University of Illinois at Champaign-Urbana, an Assistant Professor at Clark/Atlanta University, and an Associate Professor at Morehouse College in Atlanta. The students have entered one of the most difficult classes for a psychology major. Statistics is like no other class they have had in their major. It is a class that requires a different type of intellectual engagement. To be successful, one must think mathematically and logically. An understanding of statistics is crucial in navigating through such advanced courses as Experimental Psychology, Testing and Measurement, Learning and Memory, Animal Behavior, and Psychobiology. Statistics is the "gatekeeper" to graduate school. No matter what advanced degree one seeks in psychology, one will have to take a course (or courses) during the first year of graduate school in statistics. However, undergraduate students early in the major are unaware of this paradigm shift. They ask, "Why do I need statistics?" They wonder what this course has to do with psychology or with people or with behavior. Some students view statistics as entering the "The Class from Hell."

I not only teach statistics, but also courses in learning, memory, and animal behavior. Although there is the typical "first day apprehension" by my students in my animal behavior class, this is overshadowed by a feeling of excitement and curiosity by them. This is due in part by the proliferation of animal documentaries and cable channels dedicated in part or solely to animals and the fact that many students

Duane M. Jackson is Associate Professor of Psychology at Morehouse College, Atlanta, GA.

have had at some time in their lives a favored pet or pets. In addition, many students talk about how they enjoy going to zoos and aquariums. Animals are an integral part of their "real world." This makes it very easy for me to come up with a variety of examples, real and imaginary, in order to take a variety of paths to convey a single concept.

From my experience, the subject matter in learning and memory contains the most intricate and abstract material for undergraduates to conceptualize and, in my opinion, is their most difficult course in the major. Students enter apprehensively on the first day of learning and memory. Learning and memory is also an integral part of their "real world." For this course, I am also able to engineer many different approaches to convey a single concept.

As stated previously, many students view statistics as part and parcel of the abstract world. Minton (1983) went so far as to say, "Statistics has an identity problem. It is not visible as a discipline." Wild (1994) feels that ". . . statisticians have failed to communicate any coherent picture of the nature and scope of the discipline." Statistics can be seen as something very alien, and this notion can be reinforced if taught solely in the abstract. Also, the number of approaches one takes to explain a concept is far smaller than in my other courses. I have found, with the exception of probability, that teaching students more than three different ways to do the same type of problem can be confusing. Not only must students think differently than they have in previous courses, professors most also teach differently than they do in other courses. Hastings (1982), a psychology professor, discusses some of these challenges that professors face when teaching statistics. He states: "Statistics should be introduced to students as a means to an end, a tool to be used to answer questions rather than as a math course." Statistics is where there is an interface between algebra, logic, and the scientific method. When one teaches statistics, he or she must dispel the myth that statistics is some isolated entity. It must be taken out of the abstract world and become a part of students' everyday reality.

My approach to teaching statistics is due in part to my experiences as an undergraduate taking statistics and as a graduate student teaching statistics. My undergraduate statistics course was like a fast-moving basketball game in which both teams employed the tactic of "Run and Gun." We learned how to do a variety of statistical tests at a very rapid pace and took quizzes or tests every three to four class periods. Little emphasis was paid to the meaning of statistical concepts, the underlying logic for statistical techniques, or how statistics interfaces with the scientific process. All tests and quizzes were "closed book" and, therefore, we had to memorize statistical formulas. My strategy was to mentally repeat the formulas over and over again shortly before the test or quiz. When it was time to take the test, even before I wrote my name, I would immediately write the formulas down on my paper in the left-hand corner. Statistics was taught in a vacuum in the abstract and as separate entity from the real world. The fact that we would need statistics for other courses in our major was largely ignored. We were rarely taught how different statistical techniques were interrelated to one another. We did not see the utility of these tests until we were in advanced laboratory courses. This meant that many of us had to go back and relearn statistics on our own. At the end of the statistics course, we had learned how to do a variety of statistical tests but learned little in regard to the application of these tests. We had learned what to think but not how to think. While in graduate school, I quickly learned that many of my classmates had similar experiences with their undergraduate courses in statistics.

When I was a young child, I made the decision that I was going to be a scientist and study animals. When I entered graduate school at the University of Illinois, I prepared myself for a career in animal behavior. I majored in comparative psychology/behavior genetics and minored in zoology. I also made the decision to return and teach and research at a Historically Black Institution (HBCU). I was a graduate of Morehouse College and was very familiar with HBCUs. I knew that to make myself more marketable, I needed to be able to teach more than animal behavior. So I minored in experimental psychology and requested to be a Teaching Assistant (TA) for statistics. I knew that there was a need for experimental psychologists, many instructors could not teach statistics, and for those who could, few desired to teach it.

After being a Teaching Assistant in the lab sections of courses in my major and minor area of concentration, I decided in my fourth year of graduate school to be a TA for the lab section for statistics. I chose the undergraduate accelerated statistics course that combined two semesters of statistics into one semester. I felt at that time that working with the brightest students would be the most challenging. I know now that the brightest students are the easiest to work with and the real challenge is the students on the other end of the spectrum. For this course students had to attend a one-hour lecture three days a week, taught by a professor, and a two-hour lab one day a week, taught by a TA. As I prepared for the class, I thought of my own experiences as an undergraduate taking statistics. I also remembered a long group discussion I had during my first year of graduate school with other first-year students in regard to our first encounter with statistics. At the end of this conversation, we concluded the following:

1. We were not taught how to make decisions on choosing the appropriate tests to analyze data.
2. The data sets we analyzed in class were based on artificial textbook examples.
3. We learned very little about the underlying principles of statistical concepts. All of us knew how to compute a standard deviation, but most of us did not truly understand what a standard deviation was until our first statistics course in graduate school.
4. Many of us found our undergraduate courses in statistics boring and disconnected from our other courses.

Although as a Teaching Assistant I could not revamp the course, I did have some flexibility in my lab section. I decided to use real-life examples when ever possible and to spend some time showing how different concepts in statistics were interrelated. Also, through out the course, I would spend time on how to choose the appropriate statistical tests.

I also noticed that when I gave students a problem to work out in lab, and allowed them informally to work with each other, (relatively) permanent working groups began to emerge on an evolving basis. As I watched them work together, they were actually teaching each other. After the first major class test, I told the students in my section that I was competing with the other two Teaching Assistants in the statistics course and that I wanted students in my section to have the highest average test scores. I was somewhat surprised at their reaction. They were highly charged and informed me that they were "up to the challenge." In fact, they accomplished this goal. This was true not only for the lab section I taught in the fall, but also the section I taught in the spring. At the end of the year, I was evaluated as "excellent" by students in the Quantitative Methods course based on the Instructor and Course Evaluation System at the University of Illinois. The cooperation and competition I observed in the statistics lab was the genesis for my idea of the creation of Statistical Project Teams.

When I first started teaching as an Assistant Professor, I decided to formalize this group concept in my Statistics I and II courses. Over the years, it has evolved. During the first week of class, we talk about how statistics is all around us and how the application of statistics influences students' lives. I remind them how they cannot watch any sporting event without being "bombarded" by statistics. The news media, without fail, will have several reports that are based on some statistical finding, especially in the areas of health, crime, politics, finance, disasters, wars, and public opinion. The cost of their car insurance and the length of time for the warranties on their stereos, VCRs, and computers are based on probability theory. Even our weather reports are based on probability. During this first week and throughout the course, I attempt to interject relevant humor in lectures and discussion. Students are already uptight when they first enter the course, and the majority of statistical textbooks are dull, humorless, and sometimes even intimidating. Humor tends to relax the students and can be an effective tool in teaching. Friedman, Halpern, and Salb (1999) found that humorous vignettes stimulate classroom discussions. Richard Lomax and Seyed Moosavi (2002) have published a paper on humor and teaching statistics. They state, "Humor is a pedagogical method that can be used for engaging students in the exciting world of statistics and for fostering concept development." This paper also provides a series of examples that can be utilized in class.

We also discuss the abuses of statistics, which I sometimes call the "dark side" of statistics. One of my favorite examples is to draw a small circle on the board and call it 100% pure beef and then draw a large circle and call it donkey manure. I then say that I will take the donkey manure and flatten it out into the shape of a burger and stick the small piece of pure beef inside. Next, I will fry this burger and give to someone, stating that this burger contains 100% pure beef. I then ask the students, "Have I told this person a lie?" I then tell them that there was a big fast food chain that was advertising that its hamburgers contained 100% pure beef, which was true, but these burgers also contained fillers. Another favorite example that I like to use is a commercial that states that two out of three medical doctors stated that if they were on a deserted desert island, when it came to painkillers they would choose brand X over Y. However, this commercial does not state whether these results are based on 3 doctors or 3,000 doctors. The advertising world utilizes a lot of "smoke," "mirrors," and statistics. John Allen Paulos (1995), a mathematician at Temple University, stated: "As in magic, the problem with ads isn't so much what is said or demonstrated as what we infer from what is said or demonstrated, and the best way to induce false inferences is to sketch alluring pictures and leav[e] out crucial bits of information" (p. 86).

Making statements supported by statistical data, but leaving out crucial bits of information, is not just restricted to the world of advertisement. One example that I offer students is to think and question a statement that many have heard before.

"There are more black men of college age in prison than are in college."

There is an important piece of information that is left out of this statement—how many black men of college age are neither in prison nor in college. This missing information is vital in regards to the implications of the above statement.

I warn students that some statements based on statistical analysis can be very misleading. In fact, when I first started teaching, one of the books that was required reading was Huff's 1954 book *How to Lie with Statistics*. The students are told that when you read or hear statements in the popular press, supported by statistics, you should ask the following questions:

1. Who collected the data?
2. How was it collected?
3. What was the sample size?
4. Who was in the sample?
5. Is any pertinent information missing?

Also, in addition to the above questions, when students read scholarly publications, they should ask if the investigator(s) used the most appropriate statistical test for the analysis of their data and whether this data could be analyzed using a different statistical technique. There is usually more than one appropriate way to analyze data; the decision as to which statistical test to use is in part dependent on what the investigators examine.

During this first week of class, we also look at the role of statistics in the scientific method. When I make the statement that "All of the scientific principles and laws that you have learned are not absolute truths but probabilistic statements," many of the students have a look of total disbelief. I am a scientist and for me to make such a statement is viewed as blasphemous by some of my students. I then write on the board the most famous of all scientific equations, $E = MC^2$. I next tell them that there is no way we can test to see if this scientific fact was valid at the beginning of the universe during the "Big Bang," nor if it will hold up in a black hole, worm hole, other dimensions, throughout the universe for all time. In other words, it is impossible to test any scientific principle or law under all possible conditions throughout time. Therefore, we cannot be absolutely certain about any of these laws or principles. However, there is an extremely high probability that $E = MC^2$ will be valid, regardless of our time frame and location. This is true for all of the edicts of science.

Finally, during this first week they are told that they will be expected to use statistics in the lab components of their courses in Experimental Psychology, Learning and Memory, Psychobiology, and Animal Behavior. Also, in these courses, and others in their major, they will be reading journal articles and will be expected to understand and interpret the statistical results. Students are told that if they plan to get an advanced degree in psychology, there is no way that they will be able to avoid statistics, and statistics in many graduate programs is the gatekeeper for entry to the degree.

I also stress the importance of mastering statistics in regard to future career choices. The majority of our graduates who go on to pursue advanced degrees attend graduate school in the area of psychology, medical school, law school, or graduate school in public health or education. In all areas of psychology and public health, it is crucial to have strong foundations in statistics. Lawyers, doctors, and educators who have a mastery of statistics (especially lawyers) have an advantage over their peers who do not. The students are told that statistics is the most practical course they can take in their major. Students are surprised when I tell them how much I charge as a statistical consultant. They are even more surprised when I tell them that, on several occasions, students, while still undergraduates, have been paid to be statistics coaches for graduate students taking their first course who were never properly taught or simply forgot statistics. They are also told that the undergraduate student stat tutors for their course are paid by the department and, therefore, do not have to meet the same requirements as work-study students and, if an individual does exceptionally well in the class, he or she may be offered a permanent position. On two occasions, I have had the statistician for the Atlanta Braves baseball team come and talk to my class. He informed them that most of the sports statisticians have only had two courses in statistics at the undergraduate level. I stress the importance and benefits of mastery of statistics for the present and in the future.

The students are pleasantly surprised when I state, at the beginning of the course, that all of their tests are open book and open notes. I only have an open book policy in all my statistics courses. My rationale for this is that statistics is an applied course. I am far more concerned with students developing the ability to read and understand formulas and make logical decisions with regard to choosing the most appropriate statistical test. I am less concerned about students' committing statistical formulas to memory. In addition, the majority of researchers in the real world would find it difficult to regurgitate the formulas for the statistical tests they use on a daily basis.

Although I found early in my teaching career that this open book and notes policy does have its drawbacks, students tend to underestimate the difficulty of the test because they have access to their books and notes during the test. I also found that some students would spend an inordinate amount of time flipping through pages in their notes and book. I attempt to alleviate this problem by warning them initially of these pitfalls. Regarding the difficulty of the tests, if they do not believe me initially, they become true believers after the first test. To help students avoid spending unnecessary time and energy looking through their notes and the book during the test, I present them with a method of organizing their notes.

I introduce this method in all of my classes, but students find it extremely useful in the statistics courses. The method is simple: I tell the students to write their notes on a legal pad or notebook paper during class and then rewrite them in a spiral notebook. Although this is additional work, it assists students in several ways. First, by rewriting the notes students have the opportunity to regain information they may have missed. Second, by rewriting the notes, they are consciously (and to some extent subconsciously) reviewing the material again. Third, it is much easier reviewing notes that were written at one's own pace versus notes written at the pace of the instructor. I encourage students to number their pages and to have a table of contents so they know the location of the material. I also encourage students in the advanced statistics course to obtain a set of index cards that are connected by a spiral and to put a formula on each card. I tell them it is important to know where pertinent information can be found in their textbook. Not all of the students take my advice, but those who do tend to spend far less time searching for information during the test.

Throughout the course, whenever possible, examples are used from the real world or from a fantasy world that would interest traditional college-age students. Examples are also taken from material that will be covered in their advanced courses. Choosing the appropriate statistical test and how different statistical techniques are interrelated is constantly reinforced. Although I have found the formation of the Statistical Project Team (SPT) to be the most effective tool in teaching statistics, the SPT requires students to utilize a variety of skills, such as:

- Problem solving
- Oral and verbal communication
- Creativity
- Cooperation
- Organizational competency

When students receive their syllabus, it contains the following information about their Statistical Project Teams.

Statistical Project Team Introductory Information

You will either be randomly assigned or allowed to form your own Statistical Project Team (**SPT**). How teams are formed will be a class decision. Each **SPT** will

be approximately the same size and the number of students in each **SPT** will be dependent upon the size of the class. Normally, there are four to eight **SPTs** consisting
of three to six students in each team. Your team will do an oral presentation and turn
in one short paper for each project. Each member will receive the same grade; the
maximum that a team can earn is 12 points on the oral and 8 points on the paper.
Your team presentation and paper will be graded on the following: **statement of the
problem/purpose, hypothesis, description of method, results, graphics, and
conclusion.** For the oral, you will also be graded on overall delivery. You will only
have *five minutes* for your presentation. For the last team project, the class will vote
(you will not be able to vote for your own group), as to which group gave the best
presentation and which group had the best graphics. The winners in each category
will receive **5 extra credit points,** and the second place team will receive 3 extra
credit points added to their total points. Research projects (provided by your professor) will be randomly chosen by an elected member of your **SPT.**

Research/Design Paper

Each **SPT** will randomly choose a research topic (provided by your professor) that
will focus on a statistical test. The first section of your paper will deal with a description and background information on your topic; the second part of your paper
will consist of an experiment that your **SPT** has designed and tested that incorporates your topic. You will be given more detailed information on what is expected in
this paper during class time. Although everyone in your **SPT** has the same topic and
does the same experiment, to obtain the same results, each member must write his or
her *own unique paper.* However, you have the opportunity to pool your resources
for obtaining references and exchanging ideas. (Specific information on the
research/design paper is provided and discussed further on pp. 157–158.)

Formation of SPTs

During the second week of class, I have the students arrange their chairs in the shape
of a horseshoe. Then I have each student introduce him- or herself to the group, stating their class, hometown, and what they plan to accomplish after graduation. I then
tell the class that they can form their own groups. I state how many SPTs there will
be and how many individuals can be in each one. Depending on the size of the class,
the number of SPTs can range from three to seven and the number of individuals in
each SPT can range from three to six. The goal for each class is to have an equal
number of individuals in each SPT. No group can have more than one more member
than any other group. Before they form their SPTs, I stress the importance of teamwork and that teams that work as an efficient unit will find their tasks much easier
than those who do not. They are told that these projects have many components and,

therefore, many separate tasks must be accomplished. They can think of there projects as being akin to a mini-Broadway production. They will need to learn the strengths and weakness and likes and dislikes of the members of their SPT. By doing this, they will be able to better match individual members to particular tasks. I remind them that they will have to depend on one another and that part of their grade will be based on the performance of their group. I allow them five to ten minutes to form their SPTs. Once they have been formed, I assign each group a number. This is the same procedure I use for the creation of lab groups in the lab sections of my Learning and Memory and Animal Behavior courses. The only down side to allowing students the ability to create their own groups is that the "brightest" students tend to cluster in the same group and the "poorest" students (and those considered to be "outsiders") tend to aggregate into a group by default. Occasionally, I will have three to five females in the class (Morehouse College is a single-sex [male] college that allows cross-registration with other coed AUC institutions), who will tend to choose to be in the same group. Although there are some drawbacks in allowing students to form their own groups, I have found that it is crucial that they be allowed to engage in this manner. Several times I have experimented by randomly assigning students to groups both in my statistics course and the lab sections of my other two courses. However, whenever I have done this, students' performance drops. The group dynamics is not the same. Individuals within the groups take longer to merge into an efficient unit. When students are randomly placed into groups, infighting within groups increases, and competition between groups decreases. Whenever I have offered students the choice of creating their groups or having the groups randomly created, they have always voted against random group assignment.

The Rules

Each SPT has to complete three statistical projects and a research/design paper. These projects and paper constitute 14.5 percent of the students' final grade. I have created the research topics and designs for the first two statistical projects; for the third project, the students generate their own research topic and design. On the day the topics are assigned to the SPTs, I hand out four to eight sheets of paper. The number of sheets is usually one greater than the number of SPTs. Each sheet contains a question, method for collecting the data, statistical test to be used, and how the data should be graphically represented. I place the sheets face down and spread them across my desk. I then tell the class that each SPT is to choose one member to come up to the desk and take one of the sheets of paper. I also inform them that the degree of difficult varies among the topics and the topics range from dark and somber to light and whimsical. A representative from each team comes up to my desk one at a time to pick a topic and read it to the class. Although this technique may appear to be melodramatic, the students become animated and excited. A representative from a group will come up to the desk and reach for a sheet of paper, only to stop inches away from picking it up because someone in his SPT has risen out of his seat and shouted: "Don't pick up that one!" Students will give a sigh of relief if their SPT has chosen what they consider an easy topic, groan if it is difficult, laugh if it is whimsical, and usually remain silent if it is somber.

Students typically have one week to prepare for their presentations and complete their short papers. They have five minutes to make their presentations. They are given a signal when four minutes have passed. There is a reduction in points if a group goes over five minutes. Students in the class are given up to two minutes to ask the group questions after the presentation is finished. The only restrictions that I impose on the presentations are that they must not exceed five minutes and the graphic representation of their results must be visible to all of the students in the class. Other than these restrictions, students may decide the format for their presentation. The number of students who present the data before the class can be from one to the entire group. There are no dress requirements for the first two projects. There have been times when the students will appear in outfits that correspond with the theme of their project. Occasionally, I will require the students to dress in business attire for their third project. The visual aids used by the SPTs can be high- or low-tech. Their graphs can be on a large poster board, Power Point, overhead transparency, or handouts for class members. They may present their project in a "traditional" manner in which the presentation is similar to what one would experience at academic conferences, or they can also use nontraditional techniques such as skits, which may range from serious drama to light humorous parodies. Some SPTs have done their presentations in the form of a short video. I let the students know that these choices are theirs, and I encourage them to be creative and have fun.

Their third project, in which the students have to design and compete for extra credit, is the most challenging. The class is told that each SPT will have to design a project. The only information they are given is the minimum number of subjects and the statistical test they must utilize. In the Statistics II course, the students have to design a project utilizing a two-way analysis of variance that is a 2×3 factorial between-subjects design with at least five subjects in each cell. The SPT team that earns the best presentation will receive 5 extra credit points and the SPT that has the best visual aids will also earn 5 extra credit points. The SPTs earning second place in both of these categories obtain 3 extra credit points. The winners are decided by the students in the class and students in my upper-level courses. I offer students in my upper-level classes the opportunity to earn 5 extra credit points by attending this presentation and serving as judges.

On the day of the presentations, I place index cards with the number of each group face down. I have one of the students in my upper-level course randomly choose one card at a time. This dictates the order of presentation for each SPT. This is done to ensure that each SPT has an equal chance of presenting first, last, or somewhere in the middle. At the end of the presentations, each student is given a ballot in which he or she places his or her SPT number in order to ensure that individuals are not voting for their own SPT and that they vote for the best presentation and visual aids. The ballots are collected and tallied by upper-level students, and the winners are announced at the end of class. Normally, I ask SPTs questions at the end of their presentations, but on the day of theses presentations, I remain silent so as not to influence the vote. I have found that the interactions between the SPTs drastically change on this last project. Typically, members from different SPTs will talk freely with each other about their upcoming presentations. However, for this last presentation, where they compete against each other for extra credit points, the openness between groups ceases to exist and the SPTs become very clandestine about what they plan to do. The grading of the oral presentations is based on the following criteria:

- Clearly defining question/purpose and hypothesis.
- Clearly describing method used to collect data.
- Stating the results and graphical representation of the results.
- Demonstrating and understanding whether results support or do not support the initial hypothesis.
- Creativity.
- Overall organization and delivery of the presentation.

Each SPT, on the day of the presentation, is required to turn in a short paper (one to two pages, including a graph) summarizing its project. This summary must include question/purpose, method, results, conclusion, and a graph.

Students are also required to do a research/design paper. The majority of students are surprised when they learn that they are required to write a major paper in a statistics course. Each student must turn in an individual paper that is, in part, based upon a study collectively designed by his or her SPT. As a result, each student must work individually and also in a group. Each group randomly chooses a statistical test in the same manner as topics are chosen for oral presentations. This paper is divided into two major sections, a research section and a design section.

The research section has three major components. First, the student must find the individual who developed the test and provide the following information about that individual: place and year of birth, educational background, accomplishments, and when this test was first introduced into the literature. Second, the student must state the assumption(s) of the test, the type of data that can be used (nominal, ordinal, interval, or ratio), and how many samples can be studied at the same time. If more than one sample can be studied at a time, the student must state if the test can be used in or within design, between designs, or both. Finally, the student must review three journal articles that utilize this test. The review for these articles must contain question/purpose, hypothesis, method, results, and conclusion. Despite the fact that everyone in an SPT has the same topic, the research section must be written by the individual, although all the members in the SPT can review the same three articles.

The design section of the paper is based on a study designed by the SPT and uses the statistical test, which they have been assigned, to analyze their results. For this project, they must:

1. State the question/purpose and hypothesis, describe the method, report the results, and state the conclusions. The total number of subjects in the study must be equal to or greater than 50.
2. There should be one graph and one table based on the results; these will appear at the end of the paper.
3. The design section will be written in American Psychological Association (APA) format.

The entire paper should be, excluding graphs, tables, and references, 8 to 12 pages long. I also emphasize that everyone must do his or her own individually unique paper, but within an SPT the method and results section can be the same. This research/design paper serves several functions:

- Exposes students to some of the history of statistics.
- Introduces the APA format, which will be used extensively by the students in their advanced courses.
- Requires students to write a paper based on a study designed and conducted by a group in which the student was one of the investigators.
- Helps prepare students for working and writing in a group for their advanced laboratory courses.
- Helps bring statistics out of the abstract world and into the real world.

By making an association with a statistical test and a personality and using a statistical test to analyze a study, students bring statistics into their world.

Nature of the Projects

As I stated earlier, the first two projects that the SPTs randomly choose can range from dark and somber to light and whimsical. The students collect their data from college campuses, malls, neighborhoods, cemeteries, libraries, state and federal buildings, and at Zoo Atlanta. In addition to being a college professor, I am also Curator of Invertebrates/Research Scientist at Zoo Atlanta. Usually, during the spring semester and occasionally during the fall semester, one of the projects is conducted at the zoo. The majority of projects for my statistical course deal with human visitor behavior. The projects deal with such questions as:

- Are some directional or informational signs for visitors read more than others?
- What is the effect of an animal's behavior on the time a visitor will spend at an exhibit?
- What effect does the visitor's group size and the number of children in the group have on how long a visitor stays at an exhibit?
- Does the sex of the visitor influence his or her interest in certain animals?

■ When visitors have a choice of going in two or more different directions, which way are they more likely to go?

Using Zoo Atlanta as a place for students to conduct research has not been restricted to college students in my statistics and animal behavior courses, but is also open to high school students in summer programs at Morehouse (Jackson, 1994). The zoo has provided my students the opportunity to work in a unique lab, a lab that is somewhere between the traditional laboratory—in which the investigator has control, but must contend with a degree of artificiality—and the field, where there is reality, but no control.

So that the reader can obtain an idea of the nature of the projects, listed below are five actual projects that the students randomly choose.

Project 1: Is the preference of choosing one path over another random in entering the reptile house? Record the number of individuals entering each path. From these results, construct a bar graph with "Path" as your x-axis and "Number of Individuals" as your y-axis. Construct a second graph, but this time base it on what you would predict if each path had equal probability of individuals' entering. Do these graphs look similar or different? What can you conclude?

Project 2: Your group will go to the "Dead Zone." Go to the graves of 100 men and 100 women and compute the life span. Next, construct a frequency polygon with two lines, one for males and one for females. Next, do an independent t-test. Your question: Is there a difference in life span between males and females?

Project 3: Is there a difference between African American males and females regarding which leader they think did the most for our race? Ask 100 males and 100 females, "Which of the following leaders did the most for our race—Malcolm X, Martin Luther King, or Jessie Jackson?" From these results, construct a bar graph with "Leader" as your x-axis and "Frequency" as your y-axis. Analyze your results using a chi-square of independence.

Project 4: Go to a police station downtown and find out how many murders were committed in Atlanta over the past twenty years. Predict how many murders will be committed in 2010. Present a scattergram, draw the least squared regression line, and state your error.

Project 5: Ask 100 males and 100 females, "If the following creatures existed—Dracula, Frankenstein, the Mummy, Freddie Kruger, Predator, or Jason—which one would you least likely want to face alone in a dark alley?" From these results, construct a bar graph with "Creature" as your x-axis and "Frequency" as your y-axis. Analyze your results using a chi-square of independence. Is one creature feared significantly more than the others? Are fear of the creature and sex of the individual independent or dependent?

The Downside of SPTs

Although I have found the use of SPTs to be one of the most effective techniques in teaching undergraduate statistics, it does have some inherent problems. First, some students have a difficult time working in a group and are frustrated by the fact that a part of their grade is dependent on the actions of others. I find this to be more of a problem with very bright students.

Second, when there are more than three to four members in a group, there is the potential to have one or two individuals in the group who contribute very little or nothing at all to projects. To deal with this problem, I provide the SPTs two strategies. The first is to inform me of the problem; I will then talk to the student one-on-one and have a meeting with all of the members of the SPT, including the individual in question. I also tell the students that if there is an individual or individuals in the group who are not contributing, leave their names off the short paper summarizing your project. When I receive these papers and see a name missing, I check with the group to make sure that it is not an oversight. If it is not, the missing students receive a grade of zero for that assignment. I have found that students tend to be reluctant, on the first project, to turn in another student or leave names off the paper. If there is no change in behavior, the students in the SPT will either come to me and/or leave the student's name off the second project.

Third, as I have stated earlier, the brightest students tend to cluster in the same group, and the poorest students and those considered the outsiders tend to end up in the same group by default.

Finally, about every two to three years there is a SPT that is totally dysfunctional. When I detect a group having major problems, I talk to them as a group and also with each member of the SPT personally. If this does not work, I disband the group and have them move into existing SPTs. This is accomplished in one of two ways. First, I tell the members of this SPT that their group has been dissolved. They can go to another SPT and ask if they can join that SPT, or I will randomly assign them to other SPTs. The only restriction is that no two members of the disbanded SPT can join the same SPT.

The Upside of SPTs

Incorporating SPTs into a course can have some negative outcomes, but this is far outweighed by positive outcomes. The use of SPTs enhances organizational competence, problem solving, oral and verbal communication, cooperation, and creativity. Also, using SPTs provides students with the opportunity to bring the notion of "team concept" out of the playing field and into the classroom. Alexander Austin (1987) commented, ". . . the capacity to be a good team member and to work cooperatively with coworkers should be one of the basic skills we try to develop in our general education programs" (p. 4). Getting the students to work as a team is enhanced by the fact that everyone in an SPT gets the same grade. Jay Mathews (2002), in an article entitled "The Powerful Force of Cooperative Learning," reviews how faculty members at Brigham Young University use a technique that is reminiscent of my days in the Army, where it was instilled in us, "if one fails you all fail," and "we never leave anyone behind." At BYU, faculty members were concerned by the fact that students were having a difficult time with a section of a sequential biology course. They decided to put students in work groups, and no individual in a work group would receive a grade higher on the exam for that section of the course than the lowest grade for anyone in his or her working group. This forced the students to work together or suffer the consequences. The faculty found this to be very effective in increasing exam scores. I have also found that for many students it is just as important (and in some cases more important) to impress their peers as it is their professor.

The classroom projects require the following tasks:

1. Data collection
2. Organizing the data
3. Statistical analysis of the data
4. Graphical representation of the results
5. Oral presentation of the project
6. Written summary of the project

The projects are designed so that it would be extremely difficult and time consuming for one to two individuals to complete all of these tasks within the given time frame. The students quickly learn that to be an effective group they must work as a team and match individuals within the group to certain tasks. Normally, there is one person who does the graphics; one to two people emerge as being responsible for the statistical analysis. I encourage SPTs to have two people responsible for the statistical analysis so that one person does the initial analysis and second person double-checks it. The best writers in the group tend to do the paper. Data collection tends to be partitioned and done by all or the majority of the members in the SPT. The number of members involved in oral presentation tends to vary between SPTs and from project to project within SPTs. I have been impressed by the fact that the majority of SPTs have quickly transformed from a set of three to six separate individuals going in different directions to an effective single unit focused on one goal. It does not take long for the students to figure out who is good at what.

The students have also demonstrated an ability to deal with adversity, especially when it comes to data collection. One example that comes to mind, before the Internet, one SPT was having difficulty obtaining information from the police about a specific type of crime that had been committed over the past twenty years in the Atlanta area. I told the students to go to the main police headquarters downtown to get this information. The police department had always been very helpful in providing crime statistics to my students. Nevertheless, for this particular SPT, this was not the case. Rather than be dissuaded, my students boldly walked several blocks from the police station to the Federal Building and asked for the regional headquarters for the Federal Bureau of Investigation. When the students stated during their presentation that they went to the FBI and that they were very helpful, many students were surprised that the group had the nerve to walk into FBI headquarters. When students asked the presenters if they were at all nervous when they went to FBI, their response was "No, we had to get the information so that we could start our analysis."

I have constantly been amazed and pleased by the creativity in some groups. Many of the presentations have been in a traditional format. One student will discuss the problem/purpose and describe the method; a second student will talk about the method, results, and present a graph; and a third student will present the conclusions. However, there have been SPTs that have presented their results in the form of skits; some have mimicked mystery shows, game shows, talk shows, the nightly news, popular television series, and movies. Some have done a presentation in which they mimic the class, including the instructor. Some groups have even used costumes in their presentation. One SPT,when doing the project about "which of the following creatures you would least likely want to meet," actually dressed up like these creatures.

Regarding graphics: On several occasions, SPTs have decided to use three-dimensional rather than two-dimensional graphs. One SPT had an individual who was extremely talented in creating different shapes out of Styrofoam, and a second member in the group was very good with electronics. This SPT's graphs were always made out of Styrofoam in a shape that corresponded to some theme in their presentation and contained a series of little electrical lights. My most vivid memory of this group was of a project in which they had to go to the cemetery and record life spans. During their presentation, students presented their graph in the shape and color of a tombstone. It was a histogram that would light up with different colored lights for males and females. The graph would gradually light up and then the lights would slowly fade out. It was most impressive.

Normally, students do their projects after they have had a homework assignment on the material and usually before a quiz, but definitely before an exam. I have found that students tend to have better quiz scores when they do a project before the quiz versus doing the project after the quiz. This could be due in part to the fact that students are learning how to apply statistical techniques on data that was collected by their SPT. Cralley and Ruscher (2001) found that in an experiment looking at the relationship between students analyzing unique data sets versus a common data set analyzed by the entire class, ". . . analyzing unique data sets appeared to promote learning of statistical principles and procedures" (p. 501). Also, Salih A. Hakeem (2001) found that students in his business statistics course engaged in a semester-long activity/project performed better on the average than students not exposed to this activity.

In spite of all of these positives, I feel that the most important outcome is that the students begin to relate to statistics. It is no longer some abstract alien entity. It is no longer something viewed as being unrelated to their major. It becomes a part of their reality. The statistics course is still viewed as a tough class, but no longer a class from hell. This is because statistics has become real.

Concluding Thoughts

One of the most difficult courses psychology majors must take is statistics. When I enter my statistics class on the first day of the semester, I sense apprehension, fear, and despair. Some students view that first day as entering "The Class from Hell." It is a course like no other in their major, and it requires a different type of thinking. To be successful the student must think mathematically and logically. Not only must the students think differently, professors much teach differently. Many students view statistics as something alien and not part of their real world, and this notion can be reinforced if statistics is taught as an abstraction. All too often statistics is taught in a vacuum, disconnected from other courses in the major, by analyzing data sets based on artificial textbook examples. Statistics must be taken out of the world of abstractions and brought into the students' world. Statistics is not a math course. It is a course in which students learn how to use a tool to answer questions.

I have found the creation of Statistical Project Teams (SPTs) to be the most effective tool in teaching statistics. For students to work in teams collecting their own data, analyzing and presenting their results, requires problem solving, oral and verbal communication, creativity, cooperation, and organizational competency. The most important outcome of working in SPTs is that the students begin to relate to statistics, thus it is no longer viewed as an abstract alien entity.

REFERENCES

Austin, A. (1987, September/October). Competition or cooperation?: Teaching teamwork as a basic skill. *Change.*

Cralley, E., & Ruscher, J. B. (2001, December). To share or not to share: Unique data sets facilitate performance in a psychology statistics course. *College Student Journal, 35*(4), 498–503.

Friedman, H., Halpern, N., & Salb, D. (1999). Teaching statistics using humorous anecdotes. *The Mathematics Teacher, 92*(4), 305–308.

Hakeem, S. A. (2001, November/December). Effect of experiential learning in business statistics. *Journal of Education for Business, 77,* 95–98.

Hastings, M. (1982). Statistics: Challenge for students and the professor. *Teaching Psychology, 9*(4), 221–222.

Huff, D. (1954). *How to lie with statistics.* New York: W. W. Norton.

Jackson, D. M. (1994). Zoos—An undergraduate research experience. *Council on Undergraduate Research Quarterly, 4,* 188–189.

Lomax, R., & Moosavi, S. (2002). Using humor to teach statistics: Must they be orthogonal? *Understanding Statistics, 1*(2), 113–130.

Mathews, J. (2002, October 22). The powerful force of cooperative learning. *Washington Post.* To view the entire article, go to http://www.washingtonpost.com/wp-dyn/articles/A64580-2002Oct22.html

Minton, P. D. (1983). The visibility of statistics as a discipline. *American Statistician, 37,* 284–289.

Paulos, J. (1995). *A mathematician reads the newspaper.* New York: Basic Books, p. 86.

Wild, C. J. (1994). Embracing the "wider view" of statistics. *American Statistician, 48,* 163–171.

9 Mentoring Lifelong Learners

Living and Learning Programs at Historically Black Colleges and Universities

Fleda Mask Jackson
Emory University

As a graduate student, I was confronted with the widespread view that the poor academic performance among black children was attributable to their lack of exposure to the cultural knowledge promulgated in schools. While I acknowledged, to some extent, the adverse consequences of limited material and cultural resources on classroom performance, I nonetheless challenged this deficit model. I rejected the view that there was an inherent dissonance between what children experienced in their home and community environments and the expectations of them in school. Moreover, the underlying assumptions that black families, by comparison to others, placed less value on education was incongruent with my encounters (and those of my peers) as a child growing up in the 1950s and 1960s in a midsized southern city. Deeply troubled by assertions that were disconnected from my realities, I sought to delve beyond the surface for explanations for disparities in the educational outcome among African American children. My quest for answers was motivated by the desire to uncover the complexities of the learning experiences of children that impacted their performance in school. I wanted to elevate the competencies of black girls and boys and their families, rather than dwell on their shortcomings.

With academic training in the fields of psychology, anthropology, and education, I was intrigued by the impact of cultural and social conditions on educational

Fleda Mask Jackson is Visiting Professor in the Rollins School of Public Health, Emory University, Atlanta, GA.

processes. From my courses in anthropology (Anthropology of Education), I embraced a broad conceptualization of education that permitted me to explore the dynamics of teaching and learning taking place beyond the confines of the classroom (Leichter, 1974). What emerged from a liberated understanding of "education" (coupled with my lived experiences) was an exploration of the impact of the black church on the education and socialization experiences of African American children. I embarked upon this research as a way to uncover the matrix of expectations for performance that children experience across educational settings. As anticipated, I witnessed discontinuity in the skills and behaviors children displayed in the settings of their schools and churches (Sunday schools). At the same time, however, I documented points of convergence between what was expected of children in church and in school; there were instances where children could apply what they absorbed in Sunday school and the larger church environment to negotiate the school setting (Jackson, 1989).

If what children learn in a nonschool setting could potentially have a positive impact on performance in the classroom, then what factors contribute to the transference of skills from one setting to another? Conversely, I asked, how are the learning experiences from the classroom translated to the skills needed in churches and other "educational settings"? Those questions guided my research pursuits and consequently have stimulated inquiry about teaching and learning within college settings.

In 1987, I assumed the position of the Director of Spelman's Living and Learning Program, while teaching a course on multicultural education. In that position I had the opportunity to observe first hand out-of-classroom educational experiences in a college setting and explore their connection to students' experiences in the classroom. This chapter provides a description of that living and learning program operating out of the context of a historically black college for women. Accounts of the activities of Spelman's Living and Learning program are intended to illuminate the structure and content of cooperative learning among students, faculty, staff, and administrators. Correspondingly, this chapter offers a glimpse of the infusion of conceptions of race and gender in the living and learning program. This examination of the recent history of a living and learning program is aimed at providing context for the development of existing co-curricular and experiential activities taking place at Spelman and other HBCUs.

Developing the Whole Person

The question of what distinguishes a liberal arts education from other types of instruction is a core concern informing the design of the curriculum and co-curricular experiences for students. Implicit in the notion of "education" in a liberal arts context is the perception that it embraces all components of the learning experiences—what takes place within the classroom and the structured activities that occur elsewhere (Dewey, 1938). This all-encompassing view of education with its aim of developing the "well-rounded person" is fostered before students actually enroll in college. Specifically, the college application process, with its emphasis on both academic performance and participation in out-of-classroom activities, is indicative of the educational repertoire students are expected to exhibit and to some extent projects their (or at least their parents') expectations for what they anticipate experiencing during college as well. Thus, families invest considerable personal and financial resources in an array of extracurricular programs and out-of-school activities with the belief that doing so will ensure that their progeny are competitive.

Sustaining, during college, the preexisting "balance" between schooling and out-of-classroom educational activities experienced during high school may be desirable but is impeded by the demands of classroom work and the social and cultural activities of college students. That is, the volume and intensity of course work at the college level (particularly within a selected major course of study) may limit engagement in nonclassroom activities. Correspondingly, college students are likely to devote nonclassroom time to social activities. Despite competing commitments, however, the aim of providing a holistic educational experience persists. Therefore, colleges and universities continue to promote and construct activities complementary to the classroom that are aimed at developing autonomous lifelong learners.

The significance of out-of-classroom experiences for career and personal development over the life course has stimulated a number of curricular/programmatic initiatives. For instance, experiential approaches have gained momentum as educators recognize the benefits of promoting self-efficacy among students through hands-on learning activities such as service learning, internships, and so on (Jackson, 1993; Lin & Scott, 1999; Smith, 1994). At the same time, collaborations between faculty and students have been assailed as effective approaches for professors to gain insights into the learning styles employed by students. An example of an activity that endorses collaboration and promotes agency among students is the residentially based, co-curricular living and learning program.

Living and Learning Concept

Residential learning programs have long been endorsed by colleges and universities (Ryan, 1995). Theme houses where students are immersed in a subject area, including language studies, have been touted as an effective format for merging the classroom with learning experiences in the residence halls and other nonclassroom settings (Stevens, 2000). Under the current rubric of the living and learning concept, residential learning persists in the form of a plethora of activities ranging from classroom instruction in residential facilities to regularized thematic programming organized in multiple residential sites.

Living and learning programs are unique in their ability to provide opportunities for students to integrate the intellectual skills honed in the classroom into residential learning activities. The experience offers a forum where students can apply their learning in the classroom to analysis of local, national, and international issues affecting their lives, thus demanding that students be active rather the passive agents in the acquisition of knowledge and skills.

The living and learning concept is not novel to HBCUs, yet the aims and content of living and learning programs at HBCUs are reflective of the intellectual, social, and cultural milieu at those institutions. Over the past decade, HBCUs have increasingly adapted the living and learning concept, shaping their programs in ways that reflect the mission of the institutions.

Living and Learning at Spelman.   In 1983, Spelman College, a historically black college for women, established its living and learning program. The program was the presidential initiative of Dr. Donald M. Steward, the sixth president of Spelman College. A graduate of Yale University and formally an administrator at the University of Pennsylvania, he sought to adapt the college house concept to the learning environment at Spelman (Ryan, 1995). As a holistic approach to liberal education, the program's main goal was to "promote a love of learning" as students engaged in critical analysis of selected topics. Furthermore, the intent was to increase self-motivation for learning among the participants by demonstrating the empowering nature and personal satisfaction of knowledge acquisition. Students participating in small discussion groups, seminars, convocations, weekend trips, and other activities formed a community of independent scholars with significant input for the content and form of their learning experiences. Their participation became an avenue for leadership development as students collaborated with faculty and residential staff to implement activities involving the entire Spelman College community as well as neighboring institutions.

Beyond the development of organizational skills, an aim of the program was to encourage the students to see themselves as change agents. This promotion of activist scholarship was framed in the identities of participants as African Americans and as women.

Convocations: President, Faculty, Staff, and Students in Partnership

From its inception, the living and learning program at Spelman assumed a multi-tiered approach for providing learning experiences. One component of the program was the weekly convocation: lectures or performances that first-year and sophomore students were required to attend. Dreaded by many students, convocation is nonetheless the activity that convenes students from all of the major areas of study. With the exception of commencement and the Founders' Day program, convocation is perhaps that one experience shared by students across the generations of women who have attended Spelman College (Edelman, 2000).

In the past, convocations, chapel, vespers, and other similar programs were inextricably linked to the educational offerings of colleges and universities nationwide, but over time their significance has faded. Throughout the 1980s, for Spelman College and other HBCUs, however, this "ritual" gathering of students continued to be viewed as a critical component of the teaching and learning at those institutions.

But tradition alone was insufficient to sustain this weekly gathering; it needed to be infused with vitality to boost interest among the students. Linking it with the living and learning program was an attempt to "renovate" convocations through a more systematic coordination of its programming with other activities taking place on the campus. Specifically, the thematic dormitory groups assumed the sponsorship of selected programs, providing input on the speakers and participating in post-convocation activities, for example, luncheons, small discussion groups, and book signings with convocation participants.

During its pilot phase, only four convocations were sponsored by the living and learning program. But by 1987, all of them were coordinated through the living and learning program office. Although this was a seemingly logical placement of the convocations, as the new director I was admittedly daunted by the prospect of arranging weekly programs throughout the fall and spring semesters (on average fourteen programs per semester). This task was made palatable by the work of a convocation committee comprised of a masterful college chaplain, Dr. Norman Rates; the Vice President for Student Affairs, Dr. Freddye Hill; and the Assistant Academic Dean, Dr. Cynthia Spence, along with faculty and student representatives who not only made recommendations for speakers but offered insights on audience development.

Implicit in our decisions about the convocation programs was the desire to have speakers who would reinforce a core mission of the college: the development of leaders who serve. The service agenda of the institution, embedded in the goal of developing well-prepared leaders, was shaped by the historical and contemporary realities of the lives of African American women. The college's tradition of regular convocations had seen luminaries from all professions stand before the students delivering messages that challenged them to make important contributions. While both men and women had been presenters, by the 1980s there was a shift with more women than men—particularly African American women—coming before the students to recount experiences in their professional and personal lives. That change was undoubtedly tied to the increased educational and career opportunities for African American women and the subsequent leadership roles they assumed.

The convocation committee continued to consider and include diverse speakers, men and women from different racial and ethnic groups. Nonetheless, our core mission was to provide African American women with role models who looked liked them as a way to demonstrate the possibilities for their futures. Students were now exposed to African American women leaders in the fields of medicine, government, science, higher education, and religion. Alongside the focus on the advancing careers of African American women was a reexamination of the "traditional" professions and roles of African American women as teachers, nurses, social workers, caretakers, and nurturers. The contributions of African American women from all walks of life were routinely celebrated at convocation through poetry, prose, song, and dance.

Convocation was a time of explicit articulation of racial history and the promotion of social responsibility and activism. During the late 1980s, the messages were transformed by more explicit focus on gender (contextualized by racial history). With an emphasis on community service, coupled with the focus on history and culture, the speeches and performances emphasized the intersection of "race, gender, and calling" (Taylor, 1996).

In addition to the work of the committee, the success of the convocations was attributable to three key factors: the involvement of key faculty members, the impassioned participation of students, and the significant contributions of the President. Presidential approval of the convocation schedule was required before the programs could be implemented. The role of the president, though, extended far beyond "rubberstamping"; her involvement signaled the importance of convocations as an integral component of the learning experience.

In 1987, convocations at Spelman College received a boost with the appointment of Dr. Johnnetta Cole as its president. A combination of curiosity and anticipation surrounding her presidency led to a dramatic increase in the attendance by faculty, staff, and upper-class students. Eventually attendance decreased, but not as soon nor to the extent anticipated. What sustained the interest in this gathering was the actual physical presence of Dr. Cole at all of the convocations during the first year or so of her presidency. Seeing her on the stage, an African American women president for the first time in the college's history, provided the students a mirror image that projected back to them the possibility of their assuming the leadership of an institution of higher education, or other leadership positions for that matter. Spelman students had always been exposed to individuals who excelled, but this presidency became a magnet for the increased visibility an array of African American women and men. Her consistent appearance on the chapel stage (the place of convocation), whether functioning as the presider, delivering the key address, or merely being a platform participant, reenergized convocation. That transformation set the stage for the revitalization of other similar gatherings such as the town hall meetings where the college community converged to strategize during times of crisis that were often linked to gender issues.

The role of the president was significant but equally important were the contributions of faculty, particularly senior level faculty members. Their input on the planning of convocation was the initial step for ensuring continuity between the classroom and the convocation programs. To the extent that faculty participated in the implementation of the programs—deploying their intellectual and pedagological skills—convocations became a way of illuminating the lessons taught in classrooms. Being attuned to the lived experiences of students, their world, and their perspectives on that world was essential for convocation programming. Faculty skilled at incorporating the sensitivities of the students into intellectual aims employed a number of strategies for enhancing convocations. Foremost in those efforts were attempts to advance from a unidirectional process to a more didactic approach, involving students in the planning and presentation of convocation activities. The yearly program celebrating Kwanza, an African American holiday, offers an example of the collaborative process operating in the production of a convocation program.

With her distinct abilities for stimulating critical analysis and activism among students, Dr. Gloria Wade Gayles was one of the faculty participants guiding students in the planning of an annual Kwanza program. An English professor, prolific author, and civil rights veteran, Gloria Wade Gayles provided "spaces" within the parameters of her classroom and elsewhere for student's self-expression and intellectual exploration. It was those opportunities coupled with Dr. Gayles's promotion of communication skills (written and oral) among the students that contributed to the production of programs that were simultaneously provocative and inspirational.

At the Kwanza programs, the rhythms of female drummers were prelude for a symphony of prose, singing, dancing, and poetry orchestrated to detail the history and the contemporary aspirations of African Americans. Without fail, thunderous applause was the response from audiences who had intensely observed every frame of the program. The audience resonated with the performers as they gave expression to their lived experiences and aspirations.

Faculty-guided convocation programs offered a template for student-led activities in the chapel. When given the opportunity to direct the convocations programs, students employed many of the organizational skills they had gained from involvement in other events. But they also exerted their own perspectives on how to craft a convocation activity. The students' planning for one particular Kwanza program resulted in a decision to invite a group of elderly African American women to sing during the program. The recommendation came from a living and learning program participant who had been volunteering with a weekly Bible study group that met at a community center not far from campus. She had provided assistance for members of the group who had difficulty reading their Bibles either because of impaired vision or illiteracy. In making her appeal for the elders, she described the singing that was part of their weekly gathering. She asserted that their "lining of the hymns" (call and response singing) during the Kwanza program would both enrich the experience for the audience and become a treasured moment for the women. Her prediction was exceeded by the actual responses from the audience witnessing the performance of twenty-five women, ranging in ages from late sixties to mid-eighties. Reverent silence was interrupted by thunderous handclapping and cheers as the mostly student audience rose to their feet once the elders completed their performance.

Comments and inquiries that I received after the program from faculty confirmed what I suspected and desired. The students who had participated in the program, and many who had been in the audience, shared that experience in their classrooms. Faculty indicated that students had excitedly described the performance while drawing comparisons with what they observed during convocation and the discussions in the classroom.

The Gathering of Scholars: Theme Groups

Convocation activities were an important component of the living and learning experience, but core to those activities were the programs conceived by members of theme groups affiliated with designated resident halls. Students competed to become members by submitting an application, essay, and proof of a GPA that was 2.8 or higher, thus they were unlikely to be in academic jeopardy. On the application, students were requested to select a theme group for the year. From small-group discussion to panel presentations, program participants coalesced around a variety of topics. Over the course of several years, the themes for the living and learning program included (1) women in technology, (2) international studies/African studies, (3) black contributions to American higher education and philanthropy, (4) liberal arts and the life sciences, and (5) self-discovery through the arts.

Students were encouraged to participate in theme groups that departed from the subject of their academic majors. Individuals who were pre-med majors, for instance, were recruited for the programs that emphasized the liberal arts, history, or the fine arts. One of the chemistry majors enrolled in the theme group on history and philanthropy revealed: "Since I am in the sciences, I don't have to take courses in other areas. In the Living and Learning program I learned about a lot of things that we don't talk about in class."

At Spelman, only a few classes were scheduled after 6:00 P.M., yet most evenings a number of educational programs were scheduled. While many of the activities occurring in the evening were organized by faculty and staff, students likewise assumed leadership for numerous events that took place during that time. I would assert that after 6:00, the campus was invigorated by a "curriculum" and standards for performance that were different from but complementary to what happened during daytime classes. In the evenings, students assumed sole responsibility for the construction of learning activities for their peers. Alongside forums and at times major addresses sponsored by sororities and clubs, living and learning program participants exerted a major influence on the types of activities taking place in the afternoons.

The activities of the living and learning program were intended to be intellectually stimulating. At the same time, they were designed to foster student efficacy as the result of the interactions and discourse among students, faculty, and residential staff (Zeller, 1994). As expected, I did not witness significant discontinuity between the classroom performance of the students and their participation in the program, comparable to my research findings. But what I did observe was that for students with diminished status (as a consequence of any shortcomings in their classroom performance), participation in the living and learning program permitted them the opportunity to demonstrate unexpressed competencies or develop new ones.

The expanded parameters of the living and learning program challenged the hierarchical interactions between students and faculty that is typical of the classroom. In other words, students and faculty were encouraged to become collaborators in their intellectual quest. For this to be accomplished, it was imperative that the students be given opportunities for their authoritative voices to be heard. Recognition of the agency that students have in their lives was the foundation for collaboration. Thus, programming attempted to allow full expression among all of the participants. For example, four of the living and learning programs examined the genesis and development of hip-hop music, particularly rap. The programs, which took place during the 1988 and 1989 academic years and included two major addresses by the highly respected music critic and author Nelson George, were my first exposure (and I suspect for my faculty colleagues as well) to the world of this form of popular music.

It was intriguing to hear about the history of rap and to learn about it roots going back to music heard in the 1920s. But equally fascinating for me were the students' perspectives on the value and impact of rap music for their lives. During one of the evening sessions, the students debated over the negative images of women put forth in rap music, particularly gangsta rap. Comparisons were made between that form of rap music and the soul music of the 1960s. It was argued by a female student that there were no appreciable differences between the two forms of popular music in terms of their derogatory depictions of women. The speaker then posed a question to her about the distinctions between rape and seduction. The response from that student was they were essentially the same. Others in the audience of students dissented from that response (Cole, 2003).

From that discourse I gained entry into the tensions and tangles accompanying popular culture and music for teens and college-aged individuals. How females negotiated their culture was fraught with the desire for acceptance in the face of considerable risk from acts of misogyny and violence. While the speaker and I were troubled by the reaction of that Spelman student, the event became the catalyst for dialogue between residential staff and students. This controversial event provided the impetus for "teachable moments" in the intimate surroundings of the residential halls.

During another living and learning program, students reviewed the movie *Fundi,* an autobiographical account of the life of Ella Baker, a civil rights champion. A panel presentation preceded the commentaries offered by the students. The panel was comprised of veterans of the civil rights movement, most notably Bob Moses, the coordinator for SNCC. Emerging from the discussion was the articulation of the struggles women encountered in their efforts to assume and maintain leadership roles during the civil rights era. That dialogue underscored the nexus of race, class, and the social status of women participating in the struggles against oppression.

Essential for the "shared learning" in a living and learning program is strategic planning of activities where the process, the content, or the analysis is in some way novel or at least stimulating for all program participants. The diversity in expertise and experiences among program participants was simultaneously a challenge and opportunity for reaching that objective. Professors brought to the process extensive, specialized knowledge and a cornucopia of lived experiences that informed their intellectual expertise. By comparison, residential staff that included young adults enrolled in graduate school was less likely to have the academic skills of the professors but might have experiential advantages over the students. Students, on the other hand, contributed their lived experiences that were embedded in the social and political contexts of their era. It was their desire for discovery that became the catalyst for innovation—the prerequisite for intellectual stimulation.

The promotion of living and learning programs by residential staff was required for the success of the program. Their knowledge of the students, understanding their motivations, and the demands on their schedule were essential for effective programming. Furthermore, residential staff was positioned to facilitate sustained dialogue among the students well after an activity ended.

Creating a Space for Collaborative Learning: The Learning Weekend

Theoretically, the physical spaces where the living and learning programs take place—resident halls and other non-classroom locations—are an important component for stimulating and maintaining discourse among diverse program participants. Two residential living and learning centers were constructed at Spelman during the 1980s. Those facilities included gathering rooms, an auditorium, and guest suites for visiting faculty. Despite the accommodations, the status and identities of members may nonetheless impede the progress toward nonhierarchical interaction among participants. To address this concern, a new component of the program was added. In 1989, the Learning Weekend, where participants traveled to locations away from campus, was developed as a core activity for program members.

Because of limited time and resources at HBCUs, there may be few opportunities for faculty, students, and staff to explore settings outside of the college campus. That is, "field trips" away from the campus are warranted to enhance learning but may nonetheless be prohibited. With the resources provided for the living and learning program, coupled with the aim of enhancing the learning experiences of students, a series of trips in Georgia, Alabama, and South Carolina were planned. The rationale for those trips was informed by my observation that the students seldom visited historical sites in the region. Specifically, despite the close proximity of several major sites of civil rights campaigns or other places associated with events in African American history, students read about them, but rarely, if ever, actually saw them. It was especially disconcerting when I realized that after four years attending college in Atlanta, some students would graduate and leave the city having not visited the Martin Luther King Center Complex.

Several of the faculty and the staff affiliated with the program had recently relocated to Atlanta after working at other colleges and universities. Therefore, a majority of them also had not visited historical sites outside of the metropolitan Atlanta area. Our travels became that space of "shared learning experiences" transcending age, gender, class, and to some extent, education. Those experiences were intended to equalize, to whatever extent possible, the expertise among the program's membership. Of course, all individuals brought to those experiences insights drawn from their personal histories. But during the trips, faculty, staff, and students established a group culture and history that permitted less hierarchical discourse on what they had encountered. The responses after a trip to Macon, Georgia, underscore the learning and, most important, the reflection that took place during these journeys.

A group of students, faculty, and residential staff traveled to Macon, Georgia, to see a yeoman plantation that had operated during the antebellum period. During the tour, they were shown how the typical plantation before the Civil War was virtually a simple farm rather than the white-columned, vast acreage site that is commonly associated with the pre–Civil War South. That reality of how the majority of the slave owners and slaves coexisted was the topic of considerable conversation during the lunch that followed the tour. Our reflection on the historical depiction of the pre–Civil War era was interrupted by the high-pitched voice of another guest dining in the restaurant. To our surprise and delight, the voice we heard was that of Butterfly McQueen, the actress who had played the role of the befuddled slave in the movie *Gone with the Wind.* I greeted her and asked if she would briefly speak to the students. Without hesitation, she stood near our tables and provided her perspective on the significance of the movie and the role that she had played in it. She reflected on her decision to accept the role she portrayed and the controversy surrounding the movie's negative stereotypical depiction of African American women. Her presentation stimulated further reflection on the realties and myths about slavery and the Civil War as they had been presented in textbooks and movies.

During the discussion that took place as we traveled on the bus back to campus, one of the professors confirmed my perception of the impact of this type of activity for all of the program participants. A history professor, who lived and taught in the Northeast and had not been in the South for any appreciable period of time, revealed the significance of the trip for him. He shared that while he had taught about the antebellum period during most of his teaching career, this was his first visit to a plantation. He went on inform me that, no doubt, this experience would transform his teaching.

What that history professor said about the trip, its importance for his scholarship and teaching, was connected to another aspect of the living and learning program: student mentoring and role modeling. The learning partnerships encouraged by the program fostered interaction among program participants that permitted students to observe first-hand how faculty absorbed new information. Unlike the modeling and guidance faculty can provide for future careers, within a living and learning context, the focus on learning is underscored. Students can observe, participate in, and adopt processes of inquiry employed by their professors in ways that are not possible or perhaps even desirable in the classroom.

The Learning Weekend was comprised of several phases intended to maximize its impact on program members that included preparation, engagement, and reflection. More than a bus ride to a tour destination, the weekend began well before the actual trip took place. In preparation for the journey, students were prompted with reading materials, shown films, and heard lectures about the locations they were to visit. The first Learning Weekend was a two-day trip to the Georgia Sea Islands and Savannah. These locations were selected because of their reputations as sites with evidence of the retention of African culture and language among the African American residents. Faculty members, including myself, who had studied the cultural traditions on the islands and Savannah had never actually visited those places. I had purchased crafts from the island, but this would be my first time seeing the fish nets constructed in the place where they were tossed out into the ocean.

But the goal of this trip was not only to expose the students to African American history but to also promote the preservation of that history. To accomplish these objectives required locating individuals who were activists for the protection of African American history and culture. We solicited the support and guidance of a Spelman alumna living on the island. Tina McElroy Ansa, a noted author, led us on a tour of the island, pointing out sites of particular significance for African American history. But the trip was not confined to explanations of ruins throughout the island: It included contact with lifelong residents of Jekyll and St. Simon Islands who were devoted to retaining what had been passed on to them. Among the memorable moments on the islands was a performance by a local singing group. Students were likewise intrigued as they observed one of the elders—also a lifetime resident—construct a fishing net that he would use for his catch.

In contrast to the islands, Savannah offered our group a view of city life before 1865. The expert for this tour was the highly regarded historian W. W. Law. Formerly a mailman, Mr. Law was widely regarded as the undisputed authority of African American history because of his intimate knowledge of the terrain of the city, its architecture, the people, and the history behind it all. A master storyteller, his words transported us to the past when Savannah was a major slave port. His accounts carried us through the decades of the 1800s, including the day when in a local church, slaves were read the Emancipation Proclamation. And he provided a cogent explanation for why Savannah was spared destruction from Sherman's fiery campaign that destroyed the city of Atlanta.

As predicted, the experiences promoted thoughtful interactions as the students reflected on what they had seen and heard over the course of the weekend. The experience stimulated further inquiry. I observed individuals who had not read the assignments before the trip now examining the reading materials, searching intensely for answers to questions that had arisen in the aftermath of the tours. Some of the students who pursued their questions organized their answers in papers and theses generated from the trip. Students demonstrated agency in their learning and seemed to gain a better understanding of an inclusive group process for learning.

Concluding Thoughts

The living and learning program at Spelman provided a forum where students could integrate their learning across multiple settings. It attempted to erase the boundaries between the lessons in class and what students experienced elsewhere on campus. Furthermore, the process sought to diminish the borders separating the intellectual lives of students, faculty, and staff. The activities of the living and learning program at Spelman were never purely exercises in learning for the sake of learning. Rather, in some respects they were the initial phase for informed activism by African American women. From my observations of living and learning programs at other HBCUs, in some instances those programs were synonymous with the service agenda for the college. Students participated in community service and service learning as part of the living and learning program. Spelman's program did not include an actual service component, but I would assert that it set the stage for the subsequent establishment of a community service department at the institution.

As it succeeded in improving residential life, the program also stimulated changes in the curriculum. In the early 1990s, Spelman faculty (many of whom participated in the Living and Learning Program) inaugurated the course Africans in the Diaspora and the World (ADW). This multidisciplinary course included a series of out-of-classroom activities patterned after the activities of Spelman's Living and Learning Program.

As new iterations of experiential and cooperative learning emerge, it is crucial that they embrace strategies for sustaining the interest and involvement of faculty, staff, and students. Faculty participants in Spelman's program received a very modest stipend, but their involvement resided in genuine interest in the focus of the topics and the opportunities to interact with students outside of the classroom. The program also provided other avenues for discourse among the faculty participants, offering a time and place for interdisciplinary discussions. To the extent that faculty viewed their participation as an investment in their careers (with support from the administration), and if they desired opportunities for interaction with students away from the classroom, the living and learning experience was value-added. Key to the enhancing the benefits of the program is the development of processes encouraging input from all of the constituents, faculty, staff, and students.

Regardless of the content of living and learning programs at HBCUs, the requirements for their effectiveness remains constant. They must embrace strategic programming, emphasize student efficacy and participation, promote collaborative learning, and affirm gender and race specific sensitivity. These elements are essential for the development of lifelong learners.

REFERENCES

Cole, J., & Guy-Sheftall, B. (2003). *Gender talk.* New York: Ballantine Books.

Dewey, J. (1938). *Experience and education.* New York: Collier.

Edelman, M. (2000). *Lanterns: A memoir of mentors* (pp. 26–28). Boston: Beacon Press.

Jackson, F. (1989). Educational experiences of black children: The case of the black church. In J. Allen (Ed.), *Teaching and learning qualitative traditions* (pp. 37–43). Athens: University of Georgia Press.

Jackson, F. (1993). Evaluating service learning. In T. Kupiec (Ed.), *Rethinking tradition: Integrating service with academic study on college campuses* (pp. 129–136). Denver, CO: Educational Commission of the States.

Leichter, H. J. (1974). *The family as educator.* New York: Teachers College Press.

Lin, W., & Scott, L. (1999). Adapting internships in changing times. *National Society of Experiential Education Quarterly, 24*(3), 23–27.

Ryan, M. (1995). The collegiate way: Historical purposes of residential colleges. *ACUHO-Talking Stick, 12*(7), 8–16.

Smith, T. B. (1994). Integrating living and learning in residential colleges. In C. C. Schroeder & P. Mable (Eds.), *Realizing the educational potential of residence halls.* San Francisco: Jossey-Bass.

Stevens, R. (2000). Welcoming commuter students into living-learning programs. In B. Jacoby (Ed.), *Involving commuter students in learning* (pp. 71–79). San Francisco: Jossey-Bass.

Taylor, E. (1996). Race, gender, and calling: Perspectives on African American women Educators, 1861–1870. In J. A. Banks (Ed.), *Multicultural education: Transformative knowledge and action.* New York: Teachers College Press.

Zeller, W. J. (1994). Residential learning communities: Creating connections between students, faculty, and student affairs departments. *Journal of College and University Housing, 24*(2), 37–43.

Louis B. Gallien, Jr.

Regent University

Marshalita Sims Peterson

Spelman College

This book is intended to assist professors and administrators in higher educational institutions in planning and promoting strategies that will improve the retention, promotion, mentoring, and academic achievement levels of African American college students at their institutions. It offers successful strategies from the perspective of professionals who work at historically black colleges and universities, because (as documented in this and other research) HBCUs successfully graduate more alumni who are pioneers in careers, professions, and vocations that have historically been closed to black Americans in the past century. As a result of HBCUs successes in the areas of pedagogical innovation, retention, and mentoring, we believe that we possess unique perspectives and proven strategies worth offering to majority institutions on this subject.

Synopsis

In Chapter 1, Louis B. Gallien, Jr. (from his perspective of fifteen years of teaching and administration at both an historically black institution and four majority institutions), posited seven persistently problematic areas that impede the overall success rates of African American college students at many majority institutions:

1. A campus environment or long-held sagas that are contrary to the lives and culture of many African American students.
2. Classroom environments of professors who are unwilling to examine their pedagogical patterns for the advancement of African American students.
3. Curricular dissonance.
4. Consistent and persistent patterns of miscommunication between majority students and professors and African American students that result in greater campus segregation patterns.
5. The refusal by professors and students to recognize the importance of African American history, tradition, and culture with regard to campus organizations, events, and classroom discussions.

Louis B. Gallien, Jr., and Marshalita Peterson are co-editors of this book.

6. Lack of administrative support for mentoring programs that would increase the retention and graduation rates of African American students.
7. The pejorative perceptions of affirmative action by majority students and professors on the perceived academic abilities of African American students.

In Chapter 2, Zenobia Hikes presents an Afrocentric approach to student recruitment and retention that addresses the particular issues, culture, and social concerns of black students. In this context, it is defined as an approach whereby enrollment efforts on and off campus are developed collaboratively to openly acknowledge the black experience and accentuate institutions' African-centered cultural advantages and academic opportunities. She then describes how HBCU Spelman College—one of the most successful colleges in recruiting, retaining, and graduating African American female students—implements its programs that advance this Afrocentric philosophy.

In Chapter 3, Cynthia Neal Spence explains how successful mentoring occurs at Spelman College and offers the following suggestions to other institutions on the topic:

1. The most effective initiatives in higher education are those that can be traced to the mission and goals of an institution.
2. Recognition and appreciation for the diversity that exists within African American student populations inhabit all institutions, especially HBCUs.
3. Intellectual engagement and exchange between faculty mentors and students should be fostered and supported.
4. Student development and growth is promoted by encouraging supporting activities that provide firm foundations for successful mentoring—speaker series, special seminars, collaborative efforts between faculty and students.
5. The use of external sources of support should be developed to sustain mentorship activities.
6. The value of peer mentoring also cannot be understated.

In Chapter 4, Marshalita Sims Peterson provides an overview and theoretical framework relating to communication, highlighting "curriculum as conversation," communication competence, models of communication, speech and language components, nonverbal communication, ethos and communication, and stereotype threat. She also discusses the significant role of professors as effective communicators. She outlines components of African American culture and communication and provides specific strategies/elements relative to effectively communicating with African American students in higher education including:

1. Contextualization
2. Interactive/participatory approach
3. Communal approach
4. Paraphrasing/repetition

5. Phrasing/pausing/pacing
6. Listening skills
7. Topic discourse variance
8. Nonverbal communication/body language
9. General descriptors for self-assessment

Peterson asserts that presentation and communication of content for African American students in higher education provide the foundation from which students are engaged and intellectually stimulated.

In Chapter 5, Louis Castenell and Joya Carter provide strategies (taken from professors at HBCUs) that can accurately assess what African American students learn.

1. Examine your sociocultural views and pedagogical philosophies based on students' reference points and course context.
2. Provide relevant assessment that reflects students' lived experiences, interests, and learning styles.
3. Engage students in authentic assessment by providing practical and collaborative learning opportunities.
4. Create opportunities to self-evaluate teaching while utilizing various sources of information to improve course design.

In Chapter 6, Joan Wynne promotes the following pedagogical methods and epistemologies for African American college students:

1. The assumption of spiritual connections to educational pursuits.
2. The infusion of music into the total educational experience rather than just as an elective course(s).
3. The explicit premise of challenging an oppressive and racist society.
4. The expectation and demand for excellence in a holistic sense (mind, body, spirit) in the midst of a nurturing environment.
5. The development of familial relationships between faculty and students with the expectation that faculty members are also responsible for the success of all of their students with accompanying high expectations.
6. A belief in the collaborative nature of the educational journey from teaching to research.

In Chapter 7, Angela Farris Watkins documents the literature that supports the idea that all African American students must be bicultural in order to succeed in their various chosen careers and lives. As a result, it is incumbent upon professors of African American students to be cognizant of teaching from a bicultural perspective. Echoing Boykin's research in this area, she demonstrates how professors can utilize the strength of African American culture, history, and tradition in the classrooms by paying particular attention to the following dominant characteristics of African Americans:

1. Spirituality
2. Harmony
3. Movement
4. Verve
5. Affect
6. Communalism
7. Expressive individualism
8. Orality
9. Social time perspective

Additionally, she places Boykin's research within her research on learning styles (or VARK inventory), which she gives to all her students. VARK is a thirteen-item, forced-choice questionnaire that indicates students' preferred mode(s) of learning. Finally, she echoes Wynne's call for attention to the spiritual backgrounds of African American students and chronicles some suggestions from her teaching experiences on avenues to promote spirituality in the classroom without proselytizing or alienating students from faiths outside the dominant Christian tradition.

In Chapter 8, Duane M. Jackson chronicles his efforts at teaching one of the "most feared courses" at Morehouse College. He offers several pedagogical techniques, based on cooperative learning, on how to effectively teach statistics courses to African American males. Based on several decades of successful teaching and mentoring in the field of psychology, his efforts have proven successful, as shown by the number of students who have left his classroom to go on to successful careers in psychology.

In Chapter 9, Fleda Mask Jackson chronicles her experiences in directing the Living and Learning Program at Spelman College in the last decade. The program provided a forum where students could integrate their learning across multiple settings. It erased boundaries between the classroom and what students experience in the real world. Furthermore, the program diminished the borders separating the intellectual lives of students, faculty, and staff. And, finally, it stimulated changes in the curriculum with the inauguration of the highly acclaimed Africans in the Diaspora and the World requirement for all Spelman undergraduates.

Implications for Further Study and Reflection

As we have outlined previously, there is a need for further research on the barriers, limitations, and solutions for advancing achievement patterns of African Americans in higher education. Specifically, we believe the following themes, issues, and subjects need to be examined and considered in a more thorough manner.

Campus Environment

Administrators at many majority campuses need to become more intentional and personally responsible for providing culturally responsive campus environments for all students of color, but especially for African American students who have had minimal culture contact with majority students before arriving at their institutions. Becoming more responsive means hiring administrators, staff, and faculty members who have a personal and professional commitment to seeing to it that *all* students in their respective programs (academic, student affairs, athletics, etc.) can and will achieve at their highest levels. When administrators are placed in charge with this type of commitment, they will produce and direct programs, workshops, seminars, and so on that will inform and inspire all members of their respective communities to achieve at their highest potential. Without correlated personnel hirings, accompanied by specific commitments to equity and advancement, campuses will typically be no better than the leadership they provide and exemplify. Therefore, there needs to be more emphasis placed on programs that have been successful on majority campuses (as highlighted by Zenobia Hikes in this book) and those at historically black institutions, as researched by Jacqueline Fleming in those environments (Fleming, 1984). Also, administrators need to offer their staff examples of success stories on campus to both inspire and relate how their programs work to others.

Additionally, those universities that have resources to begin new research centers on their campuses need to consider founding centers that will positively impact nationwide educational policy decision making in the areas of black student achievement. One of the more underutilized sources of scholarship and research on university campuses are Schools of Education. Typically, Schools of Education generate great amounts of tuition revenue from their vast array of programs for the entire university, yet they are not able to keep those revenues for their current internal priorities. Presidents and chancellors should allow Schools of Education to retain their tuition dollars in exchange for continuing research and best practice policies on achieving academic excellence among African American students.

Classroom Environments

Higher educational institutions need to do more in preparing novice professors for multicultural classrooms. *One size does not fit all* when it comes to the different ways that students digest and make sense of new information. Those campuses that have teaching and learning centers need to sponsor year-long programs for new professors (and for others who voluntarily seek their aid) focusing on the academic success of African American students. Also, administrators who are serious about faculty development should utilize those centers and/or bring to campus outside consultants and speakers who have gained pedagogical success with African American students. As a result of the growing research on this subject that has been seriously conducted since the end of the last century, there is a good deal of information on successful pedagogical practices that align with black student achievement (see chapter references). These practices need to be disseminated, shared, and systematically delivered to the teaching faculty of all institutions. In her recent book on promoting high achievement among African American students, entitled *Young, Gifted and Black*, Theresa Perry (and her co-authors Claude Steele and Asa Hilliard) pointed out again and again the relationship between exposure to dedicated and outstanding instructors from Kindergarten through college with heightened levels of achievement among black students. Their message was clear: Without concerned and committed teachers at all levels of instruction, black students will continue to "fall through the cracks" on the ladder toward equity and achievement (Perry, Steele, & Hilliard, 2003).

Curricular Dissonance

There needs to be more thoughtful reflection and serious consideration on faculty curriculum committees regarding the inclusion of works and topics that are focused on Africa and the Diaspora and Africans in America as they examine both their general education requirements and additional prerequisite courses in their majors and minors. Much research has been conducted and discovered that explores, in new and more nuanced ways, the contributions Africans have made to diverse societies and to the United States, specifically, before and after slavery. Since most of these works and discoveries have not made their way into "mainstream" texts and thus rarely make it to the K–12 levels, they should be widely known on collegiate levels in order for everyone to possess a more balanced and heightened sense of African American contributions to world and national history. Since universities and colleges provide teacher certification preparation for teachers, it becomes even more paramount to offer these courses for their pre-teaching undergraduates. Replacing Black History Month with serious course offerings in these diverse fields of study will signal to the black community that the campus is serious about the contributions and efforts of African Americans through the Diaspora and not just for a month or an enslaved period of African American history.

Communication Patterns

As outlined in the first chapter, there are several miscommunication patterns that can be anticipated and avoided if administrators are aware that they exist. First, administrators/faculty can educate staff and faculty about the type of patterns that exist and then concentrate their efforts on establishing a campus environment that acknowledges and accepts differences among varied cultures. Second, academic affairs administrators can encourage their faculties to acknowledge and digest the multitude of research that suggests that African American students respond positively both personally and academically to professors who (1) express a genuine interest in their personal lives outside academe, (2) apply a skillful combination of challenging students to greater heights while assuring them that they will do all that they can to help them achieve, (3) respect differences without accentuating them, (4) demonstrate knowledge of their history and culture, and (5) demonstrate mastery of their academic content.

Additionally, there are two major stereotypical and perceptual hurdles for many collegiate African Americans: Either a professor or group of students believes that black students must possess "superhuman" tendencies to gain admission into a selective majority university or college and are, therefore, a distinct racial anomaly, or they are on campus because of affirmative action or because teachers "passed them along" in high school. Accordingly, the worst classroom scenario for these students is to have professors and their classmates treat them superhumanly *("They must be better than their race and, therefore, deserve every benefit of a doubt.")* or patronizingly: *("I guess that's the best they can do so I will just give them Bs.")* Either perception is perniciously racist because it leaves "them" on the margins of their environments with racist assumptions about their intelligence.

Assessment

Since standardized tests remain the gatekeepers to many post-graduate institutions and professional schools, we must "teach the test," or we must give African American students the same testing strategies that we afford upper-middle white students since middle school as taken from the highly successful Princeton and Kaplan agencies. So, it is appropriate to give the same multiple-choice examinations in the classroom. However, that is the least favored assessment strategy among professors who want to ascertain what students learned "beyond the facts." Therefore, we recommend a variety of assessment procedures, but particularly those that will call upon their analytical skills in reading, writing, and speaking.

Historically, black communities via the church have placed a lot of emphasis on rhetorical speaking skills. Therefore, there are many African American students who carry this tradition of oratory excellence into the classroom. We must learn to capitalize and refine those historic strengths. We must also refine their analytical skills. In our experience, we have found black students much more willing to debate with their peers and professors once a safe environment for debate has been established by the professor. As a result, we have found that black students are not afraid to stretch boundaries and look for new and different paradigms for envisioning situations, problems, and policies.

A critical next step accompanying encouragement of those skills is the ability to turn those arguments into well-written prose. We have found that take-home examinations that focus on actual contemporary events can inspire and evoke great writing because they have struck an emotional cord. As a result, we have many writing assignments that are based on texts and classroom discussions. Indeed, in our Urban Advocacy Class at Spelman College we require four papers (ten pages minimum in length) based on three texts and a final synthesizing paper that places all the texts into a larger cultural context.) Taken together, students will have written four papers of at least forty pages in length that have been extensively reviewed and revised, if necessary. Given time and the ability to edit their work, we have found that their analytical and writing skills climb to higher levels.

We have also found that clinically based field experiences motivate students to improve their writing skills. Typically, when they have returned from actual experiences, they have more than they can write about in a day. We get them to focus on one student and a single topic and develop a theme such as: How can we develop and encourage the innate abilities of children in a particular community? As they see local children's artistic skills develop outside the classroom or notice their interest in other endeavors that can translate or transfer into academic achievement, they become excited about this potential connection and turn that excitement into a meaningful thematic piece of writing. We believe there are a multitude of avenues available for creative professors to authentically assess what their students have learned and know in their respective subjects. Multiple-choice testing is an easy and timeless avenue, but for those of us who need to know more, we should assess students on the same levels that we ask them to reflect and write.

Service Learning

As a successful corollary to differential assessment, service learning has remained a central activity of many HBCUs and women's colleges. In her recent book entitled *Educating Citizens,* Anne Colby suggests that those institutions placing a high emphasis on service to the community produce students who have a heightened sense of moral and civic responsibility that they transfer into the world after graduation (Colby, Ehrlich, Beaumont, & Stephens, 2003). Indeed, women's colleges and HBCUs have produced an extraordinary array of civic and political leaders (disproportionate to majority institutions), but they also graduate students who have high levels of commitment to civic engagement. Therefore, majority institutions need to take advantage of these historic trends among black Americans and incorporate service learning, as appropriate, into their courses and allow students to express what they have learned through assessment measures that take advantage of their enthusiasm for community service.

Mentoring and Retention

We believe that one of the hidden secrets to higher retention efforts is dedicated faculty members who take a personal interest in their students, especially those who are endangered due to cultural and racial disconnections to majority campuses. As mentioned in Chapter 1, successful mentoring and concern for students does not have to be of a same-race relationship. However, a great deal of harm can be done by well-meaning mentors who do not understand and examine the other's real world. Stories abound of professors throughout this country who have changed the lives forever of minority students by their expressed concern with follow-up telephone calls, visits to their extracurricular activities, or invitations to lunch. Successful mentoring relationships are also about the intangibles of personal chemistry and charisma, but what they all share is a genuine concern and commitment by the older adult. And, in regard to retention, your institution will normally retain those you mentor.

Spirituality

As Parker Palmer, Jane Tompkins, Robert Coles, and bell hooks have noted in their books on teaching, the spiritual element to a student's life is a major aspect of his or her intellectual development. Because professors typically do not feel comfortable (especially at public institutions) delving into the spiritual dimensions of an individual's life, this fruitful arena remains largely ignored. As you have read, we recommend that professors explore issues of spirituality with sensitive and open-minded attitudes, especially toward religious traditions outside the Judeo-Christian mainstream. We have consistently found that students appreciate professors who are unafraid to discuss those areas of their lives as a way to make distinct connections between specific areas of study and possible causal connections to behavior, attitudes, or beliefs. For example, we often raise the issue of the (so-called) biblical justification for slavery in the United States (Haynes, 2002). We examine, in depth, the textual readings of the Old Testament that were used for slavery's justification (Genesis 9–11) and examine them through multiple lenses of race, class, and gender. Also, we examine the ways that churches used this doctrine to justify war and class struggle. Finally, we examined the issue from the emotional and spiritual levels of both white and black congregations. We find that, in the hands of knowledgeable professors, there are multiple avenues for exploring issues of faith and spirituality that actually complement the academic environment along with students' and professors' personal spiritual beliefs without proselytizing or marginalizing other belief systems.

Concluding Thoughts

To summarize our research and findings based on our classroom experiences, we would list the following traits of a successful administrator who is committed to the advancement of African American college students:

1. Maintains a personal and professional commitment to equity and advancement of African American students.
2. Hires personnel who have the same commitment and vision.
3. Promotes programs and policies that will address systemic barriers on campus for black students.
4. Is a recognized leader on campus in promoting the interests of black students and translating plans into action.

We believe, as stated earlier, that professors are the hidden (and least often recognized) advocates for black students on majority campuses. If administrators and professors work together to assist black students in their efforts toward achievement, there will be a marked difference in achievement patterns. To this end, professors who maintain a personal and professional commitment will possess the following traits:

1. They will demonstrate an attitude of care and concern for the personal lives of black students.
2. They will feel personally responsible for the success of these students. This is not meant to imply without students' work and effort.
3. They will contextualize their lessons, when applicable and relevant, to their history and cultural backgrounds.
4. They will maintain passion, enthusiasm, and mastery of their academic content that are contagious and infectious for all students.

As Ronald Edmonds (1986) noted long ago, we know what it takes for black students to succeed in academic environments. The real question is: *Do we have the will to see them succeed?* This hope is the motivating factor behind this book, and we encourage professionals in our respective fields to make a personal, professional, spiritual, and political commitment to narrowing the achievement gap on their campuses.

REFERENCES

Colby, A., Ehrlich, T., Beaumont, E., & Stephens, J. (2003). *Educating citizens: Preparing America's undergraduates for lives of moral and civic responsibility.* San Francisco: Jossey-Bass.

Edmonds, R. (1986). Characteristics of effective schools. In U. Neisser (Ed.), *The school achievement of minority children.* Hillsdale, NJ: Lawrence Erlbaum.

Fleming, J. (1984). *Blacks in college: A comparative study of students' success in black and white institutions.* San Francisco: Jossey-Bass.

Haynes, S. (2002). *Noah's curse: The biblical justification of American slavery.* New York: Oxford University Press.

Perry, T., Steele, C., & Hilliard, A. (2003). *Young, gifted and black: Promoting high achievement among African American students.* Boston: Beacon Press.

INDEX

189